Virginia Piedmont Blues

Virginia Piedmont Blues

The Lives and Art of Two Virginia Bluesmen

Barry Lee Pearson

ułł UNIVERSITY OF PENNSYLVANIA PRESS • Philadelphia

Publications of the American Folklore Society
New Series

General Editor, Patrick Mullen

Copyright © 1990 by the University of Pennsylvania Press
All rights reserved
Printed in the United States of America

Library of Congress Cataloging-in-Publication Data

Pearson, Barry Lee.
   Virginia Piedmont blues: the lives and art of two Virginia
bluesmen / Barry Lee Pearson.
       p.   cm. — (Publications of the American Folklore Society. New Series)
   Includes bibliographical references.
   Discography: p.
   ISBN 0-8122-8209-4 — ISBN 0-8122-1300-9 (pbk.)
       1. Edwards, Archie, 1918–   . 2. Cephas, John. 3. Blues musicians—Virginia—Biog-
raphy. I. Title. II. Series: Publications of the American Folklore Society. New series
(Unnumbered)
ML385.P4 1990
782.42164'3'0922755—dc20
[B]   89-28014
                                                                                                  CIP
                                                                                                  MN

Contents

Acknowledgments

First and foremost, I would like to thank my family, Elizabeth and Segrid Pearson, for all their contributions, including manuscript preparation, photographs, editorial assistance, and overall tolerance and support. This book is dedicated to them. Secondly, I would like to thank Archie Edwards and John Cephas for their willingness to share their tradition and for giving so freely of their time and friendship. By extension, I would also like to acknowledge their teachers and partners: Roy Edwards, Boyd Maddox, John Hurt, Lillian Dixon, David Talliaferro, Big Chief Ellis, and Harmonica Phil Wiggins.

Over the years I've counted on the help of so many people it's difficult to assemble an accurate listing of everyone involved. However, a partial listing of contributors would include Charles Camp and the Maryland Arts Council for a 1977 research grant which effectively launched this project, and the University of Maryland General Research Board for a 1987 grant which allowed me to finish my research. Along the way various scholars, friends, and colleagues have offered comments, suggestions, and corrections. I especially want to thank Richard K. Spottswood, Kip Lornell, David Evans, Patrick B. Mullen, and Bill Ferris, and hereby release them from any blame if I failed to follow their advice. I would also like to thank Henry Glassie, Bill Lightfoot, and Joe Wilson for everything they have taught me and for their continuing direction and support.

More specifically, I wish to thank and acknowledge: Wynwood Music for allowing me to use John Hurt's "Candy Man" © 1963 and "Coffee Blues" © 1963, as well as Skip James's "Sick Bed Blues" © 1965, "Cherry Ball Blues" © 1965, "Cypress Grove Blues" © 1965, and "Special Rider Blues" © 1969; Otis Williams for allowing me to use his poems "Hoodoo Woman" and "Sweet Bitter Blues"; Harmonica Phil

Wiggins for permitting me to use "Dog Days of August" and "Guitar Man"; as well as Flying Fish, Blue Ridge Institute, and Lippmann and Rau records.

Photo credits are due to Cheryl Brauner, Lewis Campbell, Archie Edwards, Lisa Falk, The Folklife Center of the Library of Congress, Dexter Hodges, Mike Joyce, Axel Küstner, The National Council for the Traditional Arts, Segrid Pearson, Robert Saunders, Nick Spitzer, Joyce Tennyson, The United States Information Agency, Otis Williams, Jesse Winch, and Irene Young.

I would also like to acknowledge several audio and videotapes that supplemented my own interviews and recordings. These include Greg Drust's "Blues Like Showers of Rain," Jim Haynes's "Blue Monday," and The Folklore Society of Greater Washington's "Houseparty," produced by Eleanor Ellis. David Goren, Kip Lornell, Richard K. Spottswood, Joe Wilson, and Larry McBride provided supplemental recordings.

Furthermore, I wish to acknowledge the help of Bob Attardi, Patricia Smith, and Ruth Veleta. Finally, I want to call the names of Steve Abbott, Bill McCulloch, Craig Jones, and Rob Riley for their indirect contributions which have shaped the way I think about music.

1
Introduction

Union Hall lies nestled in what Archie Edwards calls the flatlands of the Blue Ridge, five miles outside Rocky Mount, the county seat of Franklin County, Virginia. Traveling east on Route 5 from Rocky Mount, I could have easily missed Union Hall if I hadn't noticed a weather-beaten sign, almost lost among the weeds, advertising Clayton's Service Station. The station itself was long gone, but I remembered Archie telling me that fifty years ago he saw two of the Piedmont's greatest blues musicians, Blind Boy Fuller and Sonny Terry, stop and play a song at Clayton's in exchange for a pint of white whiskey. I stopped at the nearby country store and asked about the Edwards family. Sure, the shopkeeper knew them. Archie's father, Roy Edwards, used to own a farm a half mile up the dirt road in back of the store, and Willie Edwards, Archie's brother, lives up the hill past the Union Hall grocery. Archie himself, they told me, had been down to visit just a week ago.

Following their directions, I drove out to Willie Edwards's house and found him working on a tractor mower. We talked for a while, and he told me that the old family home had burned down some years back and that he used to be quite a musician himself when he was younger. I asked if I could get a picture of his old log barn, but he preferred a shot of himself in front of his nice brick home.

As I started back to Washington, D.C., I remembered a verse from one of Archie's autobiographical blues compositions:

> I walked to my automobile
> Man, I headed back to town
> I had two hundred and fifty miles to drive
> I told my baby I'd make it home before the sun went down.[1]

Archie Edwards in barbershop.
Photo by Lisa Falk.

John Cephas. *Photo by Lewis Campbell.*

Bowling Green lies some ninety miles southwest of Washington on Highway 301. It is the county seat of Caroline County over in the tidewater region of Virginia. "Bowling Green" John Cephas actually lives in the small community of Woodford, five miles outside Bowling Green, in a house he built. With few exceptions, his life has been divided between Bowling Green, where he chooses to live, and Washington, D.C., where he was born and where he later found work. The citizens of Woodford and Bowling Green, along with his co-workers at the National Guard Armory in Washington, know that he is a musician of some reputation. Just this year the city of Washington, D.C., honored John and his partner, "Harmonica" Phil Wiggins, with the Mayor's Arts Award for Excellence in an Artistic Discipline.

Archie Edwards's and John Cephas's lives are linked by the music they play. Both men are recognized masters of a regional folk music style known as Piedmont blues. To a certain degree their experiences are similar to those of other black Americans in Washington, D.C., whose families traded the relative security of country life in Virginia and the Carolinas for the promise of the city. What sets them apart and makes them the subject of this book is the music they play and the recognition it has brought them.

They are, of course, two very different individuals whose lives have taken different twists and turns along the road to being recognized as masters of their idiom. But they share a regional and ethnic heritage, and an art form which more than anything else connects their lives and their voices. This book focuses on their lives and art. Both men touch on such diverse topics as religion, folklore, African-American life, blues, and musicians. It is their book in the sense that it is a forum for their words and experiences. It also provides them with an opportunity to teach us about the Piedmont blues from their perspective and about how it affects their lives. Their words offer us the opportunity to learn about a lesser-known regional blues style and what it meant to the rural black communities in Virginia.

In the next few pages I will discuss my relationship with these two musicians, provide a brief survey of the Piedmont blues tradition as general background for their commentary, and explain the format of the book.

I met Archie Edwards in 1976, our country's bicentennial and my first year in the Washington, D.C., area. He was a participant at the Maryland Folklife Festival and a resident of Seat Pleasant, Maryland. I was a rookie stage manager and a visiting lecturer at George Washington University. Archie backed up Mother Scott, another local traditional artist, but toward the end of the set he played several blues songs on his own and the quality of his work impressed me. Having grown up in

Chicago, I was familiar with Chicago blues and its Mississippi roots. As a newcomer to the area, I was unfamiliar with the local style and had met only one other Piedmont artist, John Jackson, before hearing Archie. After the set we spoke at some length, shared a few beers, and agreed to keep in touch. In 1977 we met again and began to talk about the local blues tradition. Now, a dozen years later, we put this book together.

Folksong scholar and radio personality Richard Spottswood introduced me to Bowling Green John Cephas at yet another folk festival at Glen Echo, Maryland, in 1978. Both of us were performing so we had little time to talk. Later, however, I moderated a blues workshop which included both John Cephas and Archie Edwards. We worked together at many similar events and in 1982 Cephas called, asking if I wanted to go on a tour with him and Harmonica Phil Wiggins. I agreed, and over the years I have worked with them as rhythm guitar player, workshop leader, road manager, and biographer.[2]

Archie Edwards and John Cephas have been friends for years, working together first with the Travelling Blues Workshop and later with the Living Blues U.S.A. Tour in Europe. Most recently they formed the D.C. Blues Society together. Needless to say, we all know each other well, and our long-standing friendship no doubt affects this collaborative biography. It should be obvious that I admire both men greatly and they, in turn, trust me to present their stories, comments, and songs in a manner in which they can take pride.

Any bias on my part is hopefully offset by my familiarity with their songs and background. As our shared frame of reference has grown larger, I have found myself able to understand more of what their words mean. I am also familiar with most, but by no means all, of the songs they know and have watched them add, delete, and reshape material over a ten-year span. I began to interview Archie Edwards in a formal sense in 1977 and John Cephas in 1981, but over the years we have worked together so often that I can't keep track of the countless conversations that supplement the dozens of more structured interviews. On the road John Cephas and I literally spent hundreds of hours talking trash in distant hotel rooms, suffering airports together, telling jokes on too many airplanes, or discussing the human condition as we watched the sun rise in Caracas or Nairobi.

Like their song repertoires, which never seem to end, their stories and philosophical commentary could go on forever. During all the years I have taped them—in concert or on the road, in their homes and workplaces—I have grown to appreciate them as artists and friends and complex human beings. After all the time and tape, there is always something new to add or clarify.

Piedmont Blues

Archie Edwards and John Cephas refer to themselves as bluesmen, although both play a variety of styles including religious songs, ballads, ragtime, country, pre-blues dance music, and even marginal rock and roll. Yet if you ask them what they do, they will quickly tell you they play Piedmont country blues. Personally, I feel that rigid musical categories often distort our perceptions of the interplay between musical styles that usually overlap or draw from the same wellspring.

Still, the emphasis is theirs. They stress the regional roots of the style and repertoire they learned growing up in rural Virginia. Although they have heard other kinds of music and have dabbled and even seriously worked with other styles, they have consistently returned, or as Archie puts it "come back home," to the Piedmont blues. And there is a consistency to what they play deriving from region, ethnicity, rural experience, shared musical influences from recordings, and personal preference. They know when a song is a spiritual or a ballad, a Delta blues or a "sawmill" song, but overall they see a unity to their music which they relate to the Piedmont tradition. This unity stems in part from the acoustic guitar accompaniment to their songs and the local finger-picking style they emphasize. It also comes from the rural background and the traditional blues themes of their songs. From their perspective, there may be other forms of blues, perhaps equally valid. But the Piedmont blues is what they have inherited and choose to keep alive.

The term "blues," meaning a type of African-American folksong, first appeared around the turn of the century.[3] Although rooted in earlier forms of black musical expression including spirituals, ballads, reels, hollers, and work songs, blues music is a twentieth-century form that quickly achieved popularity in the black community and shortly after in mainstream popular culture. Although musically connected to a cross section of black life, the church and the house party, leisure and work, blues was never accepted by all black Americans. Nevertheless, it became a major vehicle for expressing social concerns and ethnic identity while providing the sound track for Saturday-night dances. Since its arrival, blues has been the twentieth century's most influential musical form serving black and white, rural and urban musicians. By the 1950s, it provided the backbone and heart for the then-emerging rock and roll and can be heard today through the world's popular music.

As a form of poetry, blues has developed its own particular idiom, employing strikingly visual imagery to describe common problems of interpersonal relationships in a highly stylized and personalized manner.[4] Structurally, blues comes in a wide variety of packages including the common twelve-bar, three-chord, three-line format. However, we will notice that Archie Edwards and John Cephas are equally at ease with eight-bar blues and other more unusual song lengths as well as a wide variety of chord progressions and rhyme schemes.

Their songs correspond to Michael Taft's rather expansive description in which blues is defined as "a secular song composed of rhyming couplets in which one or both lines of the couplet may be repeated one or more times and in which the couplet itself might be embellished with refrains."[5]

Many other definitions abound, describing the blues musically, poetically, or in regard to content. Paul Oliver's definition in *The New Grove Gospel, Blues and Jazz*, and David Evans's definition in *Big Road Blues*, are the most comprehensive and easiest to digest.[6] Blues musicians may also have their own definitions which may or may not share the technical concerns of the scholar. As I noted in my earlier book, *"Sounds So Good to Me": The Bluesman's Story*,[7] musicians tend to define the blues in the poetry of the blues, stressing that it is a poetic system, a way of talking about life; blues is the truth, representing common concerns of everyday people; blues is a sound, a particular approach to vocal and instrumental expression; and blues is a feeling, an emotional dimension shared by the singer and the audience. Simply put, John Cephas states, "You have to be able to feel the blues to play the blues."[8]

On this point blues scholar Paul Oliver concurs: "To many it is the essence of the art; a singer or performer who cannot, or does not express blues feeling through his performance is not a bluesman."[9]

Piedmont blues refers to a regional substyle characteristic of musicians from the Piedmont region. Geographically, the Piedmont means the foothills of the Appalachian Mountains, west of the tidewater region and Atlantic coastal plain, stretching from Richmond to Atlanta. Musically, the Piedmont describes musicians from Georgia, the Carolinas, and Virginia, and ranges from as far afield as Florida, West Virginia, Maryland, and Delaware.

Technically, Archie Edwards and John Cephas come from the edges of the geographic Piedmont, but musically they both play in the Piedmont style. This style, like other regional categories, refers to a wide assortment of aesthetic values, performance techniques, and shared repertoire rooted in common geographical, historical, and sociological circumstances. To put it another way, Piedmont blues refers to a constellation of shared musical preferences, or a sound that seems typical of a region.

Although scholars perhaps abuse regional breakdowns in their attempt to organize and, ideally, better understand the diversity of the musical approaches they encounter, regional categories, like genres, can be useful tools if they correspond to the categories used by the musicians being studied. Like genres such as blues, ballads, or spirituals, which categorize songs by subject matter, function, or typical audience, regional divisions, like their generic counterparts, are not always clear-cut in the real world of living musicians. Archie Edwards and John Cephas tend to speak of two broad regions, the Piedmont and the Delta, and two broad styles, electric urban blues and acoustic country blues.

Scholars, for the most part, include a third region, Texas and the Southwest, which Archie and John acknowledge but tend to dismiss as less important. Scholars also track other pockets of tradition working from the three common regions: the Mississippi Delta, Texas and the Southwest, and the Piedmont, or even more broadly, the East Coast blues tradition. Delta people carried their traditions north to Chicago and the Midwest. Texas folk moved out to the West Coast and Piedmont folk moved to Washington, D.C., Philadelphia, New Jersey, and New York.

Archie Edwards and John Cephas exemplify the connection between rural Virginia and Washington, D.C. Unlike the blues of Chicago or the West Coast, their regional style did not adapt significantly to its new urban surrounding. Although both men own electric guitars, they play acoustic instruments, which they associate with the country roots of their tradition. As stated earlier, they are quick to acknowledge that they are Piedmont bluesmen, noting the similarities between what they play and the music of other North Carolina and Virginia artists.

Within the Piedmont, however, we also find tighter local traditions that are generally shared by a network of artists who work, perform, and live together in the same community and who influence each other's style and repertoire. Spartanburg, South Carolina, was a major musical center for many years and attracted artists such as Willie Walker, Simmie Dooley, Gary Davis, Josh White, and Pink Anderson, and their reputations drew musicians from throughout the region. Nevertheless, Spartanburg's importance was eclipsed as musicians hit the road for Raleigh, Durham, or Richmond.[10] These cities, in their turn, served as magnets by drawing other aspiring musicians anxious to develop their craft under the tutelage of recognized masters. Durham was an especially active blues town, attracting major Piedmont musicians including Sonny Terry, Gary Davis, and Blind Boy Fuller, the Piedmont's most popular recording artist and most influential performer. Local traditions often appear to focus around artists like Fuller, who had access to the recording industry. Fuller was a hero and musical model for both Archie Edwards and John Cephas, and both include a significant number of his songs in their repertoires.

The importance of regional centers like Atlanta, Greenville, or Durham depended in part on economic conditions, which determined whether or not a musician could make a living. Historically, however, blues scholars have tended to evaluate a location's importance by the extent of recording activity by local musicians in the area. Until recently, documentation of the Piedmont tradition was thin in comparison to the Delta or Chicago. One reason for this imbalance was the limited recording of Piedmont artists.

Phonograph Recordings

The historian's tendency to use phonograph recordings as primary documents reflected especially badly on Virginia blues. Several writers—Kip Lornell, Bruce Bastin, Paul Oliver, and Sam Charters—have surveyed the history of blues recordings in Virginia.[11] Another such survey would be redundant, but let's take a moment to consider recorded artists in relation to our two subjects. Archie's major influences from recordings were Mississippi John Hurt, Blind Lemon Jefferson, and Blind Boy Fuller. Fuller was a Piedmont artist and John Hurt played in a style compatible with the Piedmont style. Cephas lists Fuller and Gary Davis, both Piedmont artists, as his two major inspirations. Looking to Virginia musicians, or musicians with ties to Virginia, the connections, if any, become more difficult to trace.

During the 1920s and 1930s, only two Virginia residents produced a significant body of recordings. William Moore, a barber from Tappahannock, recorded for Paramount in 1928. Half of his eight issued songs were ragtime or country dance instrumentals reflective of the pre-blues string-band tradition. According to Bruce Bastin, Moore could play the fiddle and was an excellent guitarist as well, which is typical of the region. Moore's best-known piece, "Old Country Rock," may be the source of Cephas's instrumental "Chicken, You Can't Roos [*sic*] Too High for Me."[12] Since Tappahannock is not too far from Bowling Green, a shared tradition is also possible.

Lynchburg's Luke Jordan also recorded a number of sides for Victor in 1927 and 1929. Archie Edwards's wife, Frances, used to see Jordan performing for tips on the streets of Lynchburg. Although Archie never saw Jordan, Lynchburg is relatively close to Union Hall, and both men may have worked with a shared tradition even if there is no evidence of a more direct influence.

Carl Martin, another native Virginian, moved out of the state as a youngster, but his 1930 recordings show his Piedmont roots. During the blues revival of the 1960s, he teamed up with his old string-band partners, Howard Armstrong and Ted Bogan, and worked the festival circuit. John Cephas met him at several festivals and credits Martin with teaching him the Piedmont classic "Crow Jane."

Stephen Tarter and Harry Gay made a single recording for Victor in 1928, but until field-worker Kip Lornell rescued them from obscurity,[13] almost nothing was known of their lives. During the 1940s and 1950s, Alec Seward of Newport News made some records in New York City. Another Virginia artist, Silas Pendleton from Rappahannock, Virginia, was field-recorded by folklorist Horace Beck in Newport, Rhode Island. His repertoire of pre-blues songs included several songs performed by both Archie Edwards and John Cephas, demonstrating a shared musical background. Franklin County resident John Tinsley made a single recording for a local label at the end of the 1940s. Archie Edwards knew Tinsley in his youth and recently met him at several festivals. Tinsley's initial recording, "Keep Your Hands Off Her," is also in John Cephas's repertoire.

Spurred by the folk revival of the 1960s, other artists with Virginia ties were located, including Bill Williams, who was discovered living in Kentucky. A brilliant guitarist who claimed he toured with Blind Blake, Williams was born near Richmond, not far from Bowling Green. Pete Lowry recorded Pernell Charity of Sussex County for his Trix label, and Richard Spottswood recorded Delaware guitarist Frank Hovington. Hovington learned his guitar technique from a Virginia musician named William Walker, and Cephas and Hovington played together on several occasions. Kip Lornell recorded a number of musicians for the Blue Ridge Institute, most notably the Foddrell family: Marvin, Turner, and Posey Foddrell. Cephas worked with the Foddrells on several occasions and learned at least one song from them.[14]

Finally John Jackson of Fairfax, Virginia, has been the most extensively recorded Virginia artist. Discovered in the 1960s, Jackson has recorded for Arhoolie, Rounder, and the Blue Ridge Institute labels. Today, he and his son James continue to perform in and around Washington, D.C., and are close friends with Archie Edwards and John Cephas. Other more obscure artists recorded a few songs from the 1920s on, and many white country musicians also recorded blues songs. However, it should be apparent that this list, and it is little more than a list, is quite short.

If phonograph recordings were the only source of information, it would appear that Virginia blues was hardly a vital tradition. More recent research, however, suggests otherwise. Field-workers Kip Lornell, Bruce Bastin, Pete Lowry, and Vaughan Webb[15] have located and interviewed other blues musicians and former musicians who in turn recall still other musicians and musical events. The majority of these musicians never came close to recording but nevertheless actively performed at informal local community events and for their own amusement. Their recollections and collective voices—to which we now add Archie Edwards's and John Cephas's—provide a clearer picture of a vital blues tradition that has persisted to the present day.

Piedmont Style

Before moving on to the more detailed accounts of Archie Edwards's and John Cephas's experiences in Virginia and in Washington, D.C., let us consider the characteristics of the tradition they represent, keeping in mind that generalizations about a broad regional style tend to be riddled with exceptions. Music is kept alive by individuals who have personal styles influenced by an enormous number of variables, for example whether or not they are left-handed, what prior experience with musical instruments they have had, and who, if anyone, they emulate. However, we can still observe the musical elements shared by Virginia blues artists.

Over the years scholars such as Kip Lornell, Bruce Bastin, and Sam Charters have listed what they perceive as the characteristics of the Piedmont tradition and the factors that seem to have shaped the regional style. These range from strictly musical considerations—musical models, the dominance of the guitar, the impact of the string-band tradition, and the input of other musical forms such as ragtime—to sociological considerations such as the harshness of living conditions, patterns of segregation, and the institutions or contexts which supported musical performances in a specific community.

Shared musical models, especially such recording stars as Blind Blake, Blind Boy Fuller, Blind Lemon Jefferson, Buddy Moss, or Lightning Hopkins, partially account for similarities in the repertoire and style of local musicians. Certainly most of these artists influenced the music of Archie Edwards and John Cephas. These musicians happen to be guitarists, as are most of the Piedmont blues musicians who managed to be recorded. The guitar, in fact, is the dominant instrument of the blues tradition in general. Nevertheless, acoustic guitar playing and specific guitar-playing techniques dominate critiques of the Piedmont style. Indeed, even the supposition that a regional style exists has been largely predicated on a guitar frame of reference.

Although fiddle, banjo, harmonica, piano, and even accordion were common folk instruments, the majority of Piedmont artists—Blind Blake, Blind Willie McTell, Buddy Moss, Willie Walker, Josh White, Julius Daniels, Gary Davis, Blind Boy Fuller, Brownie McGhee, William Moore, Luke Jordan, and John Jackson—were, or are, exceptional guitarists. Sam Charters's typical assessment of the region illustrates the tendency to focus on guitar style and the chronological and geographical distance separating regional recordings: "Except for the Piedmont guitar school that centered around Buddy Moss, Gary Davis and Blind Boy Fuller, the recordings of the coastal blues are scattered and inconclusive."[16]

The southeastern emphasis on acoustic string instruments and instrumental dexterity connects Virginia blues with a vital and persistent string-band tradition shared equally among black and white musicians. The fiddle and banjo string-band tradition, the result of years of musical interplay between blacks and whites, served as a staple at country parties common to both segments of the rural population and musically, at least, illustrates mutual respect between black and white musicians. As Kip Lornell has noted, it is difficult to discern separate racial or ethnic repertoires in rural Virginia.[17] This earlier shared tradition survived through Archie Edwards's father's generation, and is still evident in the music of Archie, John Cephas, John Jackson, and other Virginia musicians.

Among whites the string-band tradition shaped the evolution of bluegrass. Among blacks it resulted in a highly instrumental acoustic guitar–dominated blues style, with strong links to earlier banjo and fiddle music. Because the pre-blues string-band tradition was a shared tradition, Piedmont blues is often described as heavily influenced by white or European folk-music values. Unwittingly perhaps, scholars suggest that the persistence of pre-blues traditions in Virginia detracted from or diluted the ethnicity or "soul" of the Piedmont sound. Writing in 1965, Pete Welding connected the minstrel show to the string-band repertoire and eventually southeastern blues:

> The style drew together a number of strains in Negro music. At the root was the minstrel tradition (basically a white burlesque of Negro musical style) that had, in turn, gone back into and nourished Negro tradition itself. This was brought to bear on blues forms and, as a result of their more extensive grounding in European music, attained to a higher degree of musical sophistication in the areas of melody and harmony at any rate, than did the more "African or Primitive" styles to the west, in Texas, and the Delta.[18]

The existence of a long-standing string-band tradition does not necessarily translate to an emphasis on the European side of this interactive process. One could as easily characterize the Virginia string-band tradition from an Africanist perspective, focusing on African values, African-American adjustments, and white responses to this constant pressure. In this light, the pre-blues string-band tradition indirectly connects Piedmont blues to African roots. The banjo and bowed stringed instruments akin to the violin, for example, are traceable to African antecedents. African people who came to or were brought to Virginia carried with them, if not the instruments, the instrument-making and instrument-playing techniques.

Blues historian Sam Charters, who did fieldwork in West Africa, was among the first blues researchers to comment on the African roots of black music in Virginia:

> The blues of Virginia and Carolina areas seem, in some respects, to reflect an earlier musical tradition than the blues that emerged from the Mississippi Delta. The earliest importation of slaves had been to these colonies, and the roots of Afro-American culture had been shaped here among the Mandingo and Wolof peoples who found themselves in the New World. The Wolofs brought the banjo with them—a small wooden instrument with a skin head called the halam—and the Mandingos brought the playing techniques of their stringed instrument, the kora. The kora is played with an alternating thumb technique, the other strings plucked with the first finger, much as Gary Davis played the guitar.[19]

While it may be difficult to prove the connection between techniques used on the *kora* or the smaller *donzongoni*, a much better case can be made for the banjo. While the guitar became the primary instrument for blues accompaniment in the Southeast, as it did throughout the country, evidence suggests that the transition from banjo to guitar occurred more slowly. Over the years scholars such as David Evans, Paul Oliver, Kip Lornell, Robert Cantwell, and Bruce Bastin have demonstrated this point.[20] Bastin, for example, makes a strong case connecting the tunings and frailing picking styles of several of the Atlanta twelve-string guitar players with banjo techniques.[21] After his fieldwork in Archie Edwards's home county, Lornell commented on the connection between guitar techniques and banjo practices. Describing the local guitar style, he noted, "The style in which it was played, though, owed much to the traditional techniques of the dance instruments, particularly banjo. Some researchers suggest that the open tunings used by some blues guitarists . . . originated as typical banjo tunings."[22]

Archie Edwards's father, Roy Edwards, was a noted banjo player who could only play the guitar in open tuning. He played blues, as well as pre-blues, banjo songs, and ballads, several of which Archie still plays, corroborating Lornell's contention that "Even musicians who grew up in the 1930's and 1940's when blues was popular learned tunes from older fiddle, guitar and banjo players of the community who were steeped in music that predated blues, and songs from both traditions coexisted."[23]

Banjo and fiddle eventually fell out of fashion, but they colored the texture of Archie Edwards's and John Cephas's music. *New York Times* critic Robert Palmer brought up the same point in a review of John Cephas and Phil Wiggins: "Early black guitarists in the Piedmont tended to play with banjos and fiddlers in string bands ... and they learned from both. They imitated the complex tune and finger picking patterns that the banjoists employed and they imitated the sliding voice-like inflections of the fiddlers."[24]

The tenacity of black string bands in the Southeast and of the string-band repertoire is only unusual in contrast to other parts of the South where the evolving blues form quickly superseded and largely eradicated pre-blues styles. In the Southeast, the transition was slower and never complete and the conditions that kept the string-band tradition alive may have also impeded the initial proliferation of the blues. Scholars generally agree that blues became popular roughly ten years later in the Piedmont than in the Deep South, but they don't know exactly why. Perhaps the simplest answer is that the older styles continued to suit the recreational needs of rural black Virginians.

Nevertheless, the transition did occur eventually, connecting the Piedmont guitar style to its African roots. As Paul Oliver asserted: "The point is that a continuity of string playing traditions can be clearly and unarguably demonstrated: from 'Khalam' to 'bania' to banjo to, ultimately, guitar, the European instrument being adapted and used as it became available to blacks."[25] The persistence of the string-band tradition does not translate to evidence of white or European influence. In fact, the shared tradition of the Southeast may be more "African" than later developments further south or west. Piedmont blues may be cooler and more rhythmically regular than Delta stylings, but these characteristics also have African parallels. For example, contemporary Ghanian social music, as performed by guitarist Ko Nimo, is also dominated by an aesthetic of cool that mandates restrained, well-articulated vocals and the role of the guitar, one of several rhythm instruments, tends to be melodic and rhythmically steady.[26] While vocal styles influenced by Islam may be hard-edged, overt emotionalism by no means characterizes a style as more African. Moreover, it should be noted that early Mississippi artists Papa Harvey Hull and Long Cleve Reed, as well as Mississippi John Hurt, also performed in a more restrained style, implying that Mississippi passion may reflect later, and not necessarily more African, developments.

Technically, the characteristic Piedmont guitar style involves variations on a thumb and finger picking technique. Generally a regular, perhaps alternating, thumb bass pattern supports a melody line played with one or more fingers on the treble strings. Depending on the skill of the performer, the overall sound is rich and full and solid as a rock. Artists like Archie Edwards and John Cephas are proud to have mastered this style and believe it is more difficult than other guitar styles.[27] Masters like Blind Blake and Gary Davis achieved an unmatched technical brilliance, applying their three- and four-finger picking techniques to ragtime, string-band, and blues songs.

Ragtime, another pre-blues, Afro-American musical style, affected the blues tradition throughout the country but seems to have had its greatest stylistic impact and to have persisted longest in the Southeast. Ragtime moved from folk roots to popular culture and back to folk tradition. Recording stars like Blind Blake, or hometown heroes like Willie Walker or Gary Davis, adapted piano figures for the guitar and, along with other anonymous guitarists, integrated ragtime into the string-band and then the blues tradition. With its melodic orientation, stately syncopated rhythms, and greater harmonic complexity, ragtime easily dovetailed with a centuries-old string-band tradition. More important, it was eminently suited to the dance functions of house-party music.

As evidenced in the narratives of Archie Edwards and John Cephas, their version of the blues was keyed to the country house party. Describing Piedmont blues, Pete Lowry noted, "It was truly the music of the houseparty, a rural and urban southern music for Saturday nights."[28] Although a few artists made records or were professional performers who worked as street singers or in taverns, the majority of Virginia blues artists were amateurs or part-time performers who played house parties and similar events which have left little historical record beyond the warm memories of the participants.

Mention the words "Saturday night party" and you evoke images of music and dance, good food, and good friends gathered together at country house parties and other community-based social events. Frolics, suppers, selling parties, hoedowns, breakdowns, and seasonal collective work parties all served as homegrown recreation and as a secular counterpart to Sunday church meetings. These affairs rotated from one location to the next in a reciprocal round of weekend affairs—house to house, Saturday to Saturday, Christmas to Christmas. Different households took the responsibility for accumulating the necessary refreshments and, in return, earned both social esteem and the opportunity to pocket any profit once expenses were met.

While some musicians could earn as much playing on a weekend as a laborer could in a week, most played for fun, recognition, and a chance to test their skills against other performers. As the dance music for Saturday night parties, blues took its place alongside other types of pre-blues or non-blues dance music, co-existing with, rather than displacing, string-band tunes, ballads, and ragtime. The house-party context affected Piedmont blues historically and stylistically, blurring the distinctions between these related musical forms.

It is harder to characterize a general Piedmont vocal style because, once again, critics tend to describe it in what I feel is a negative light. Because blues instrumental values are largely centered around emulating the expressiveness of the human voice, the voice should be considered the primary blues instrument. Within the blues tradition, other instruments—the guitar or the harmonica—follow the lead of the voice in establishing the emotional tone color which musicians refer to as "feeling." If the Piedmont vocal style is characterized as emotionally weak, a point I strongly disagree with,[29] then by extension instrumental techniques keyed to the voice should be correspondingly colorless. But Piedmont vocal and instrumental style can be as deep as Delta or Texas blues, depending on the artist, the song, and the context in which it is played. Piedmont artists do seem to value vocal clarity and control, but such values are not unique to the Piedmont. All blues is stylized, and careful or controlled emotionalism characterizes the work of the best blues artists from B. B. King to Robert Cray. Although a shared string-band tradition, the persistence of dance instrumentals, and the house-party tradition do influence Piedmont style, they do not negate its emotional power.

Critics tend to generalize when they compare and contrast regional blues styles, and their generalizations are often based on personal preference. Further exposure to any blues tradition shows a wide range of vocal approaches, and Piedmont bluesmen, including Gary Davis, Sonny Terry, and Barbecue Bob, sing with as much feeling as their Delta or Texas counterparts. Archie Edwards and John Cephas have two very different vocal styles. Cephas, for example, sings hard with a great deal of soul because of his exposure to church music, torch songs, and rhythm and blues and because his major heroes, Fuller and Davis, sang hard. Archie Edwards, on the other hand, is more restrained, as was his hero, Mississippi John Hurt.

The implication that the Piedmont blues sold its soul for instrumental technique or was emotionally diluted through white contact does not hold up under close scrutiny. The perpetuation of instrumental dance songs amenable to group participation and the house-party institution also affected the music of the Delta. Furthermore, Piedmont audiences appreciated deeper blues in contexts ranging from work camps to house parties. As we shall see, Archie Edwards and John Cephas play a mix of songs: fast, slow, some traditional, some based on personal experience, but all played and sung with feeling. They are, after all, blues musicians, and while they play other styles of music, they apply blues values to their blues songs.

Format

Both Archie Edwards and John Cephas contributed to my earlier book, *"Sounds So Good to Me": The Bluesman's Story*, and I envisioned this book as a sequel to that work. *"Sounds So Good to Me"* treated the blues artists' life story in general, comparing many life stories collected from dozens of musicians.[30] Focusing on the bluesmen's stories as a form of oral literature and as their occupational résumés, I looked for the common motifs shared from one musician's story to the next. I was interested in how these selected images shape and reflect our understanding of the blues tradition and serve as bridges connecting the blues artists' world to our own. Since my concern was with the common topics musicians usually offer interviewers, or, conversely, that interviewers generally request, I simply asked musicians to tell me their story, content with whatever they chose to represent their musical lives.

In retrospect, they provided and I worked with the short version of their story. Although the length and quality of the narratives varied, their accounts were relatively brief and tightly focused on subjects connected with their traditional bluesman role. In that book I spoke of their public persona as a type of traditional mask commonly shared by the majority of the contributing artists. Now, however, focusing on only two artists who share a regional tradition, I want to consider the long versions of their stories and illuminate the men behind the mask.

Different goals call for different methods, and Archie's and John's extensive narratives, along with musical commentaries and repertoires, called for multiple interviews conducted over a ten-year span, more direct questioning on my part, and eventually more ordering or editing of the materials they provided.

John Cephas's partner, harmonica ace Phil Wiggins, once told me he enjoyed reading *"Sounds So Good to Me"* because I let the musicians tell their own story, and I remain committed to the ideal of letting Archie Edwards and John Cephas speak for themselves. In fact, I see this book primarily as a forum for their words. At the same time, I am aware of the needs of the reader. Perhaps more important, I understand Archie's and John's wish to reach and hold an audience who can appreciate what they have to teach us. So it fell to me to weave the dozens of interviews together, shaping their spoken words and performed songs into sentences, paragraphs, and verses suited to the conventions of print. Translating their ongoing narrative to the cold face of print is a tricky business which has generated its fair share of scholarly debate among folklorists. In the past I have published exact transcriptions of interviews with musicians, including Archie Edwards and John Cephas.[31] In this case, however, working with materials from so many sources, I was forced to make adjustments to the transcriptions for clarity's sake or, most often, simply to avoid deadening repetition. All told, I have attempted to balance my commitment to accurate transcription with what I perceive as the reader's need and the subjects' wishes to achieve the book's major purpose: to allow the subjects to explain their lives and art. Hopefully, I have presented their words in a manner that does justice to their story-telling skills.

I also acknowledge my role regarding the book's overall format. Working with three sets of connected data—autobiography, artistic commentary, and song texts—I present what I consider a more balanced picture of the traditional artists, their products, and the context and values that shape their creativity. Initially, I considered putting both life stories together for comparative purposes but, after careful consideration, I decided to present each artist's life story, artistic commentary, and repertoire together as a connected whole. Following this introduction I begin with Archie Edwards because he is the elder statesman of the pair.[32] Edwards's story is preceded by a brief anecdote representative of his musical life. After his story, I supply a brief introduction to his music, followed by his discussion of his music and his songs with his comments and my notes. I then follow the same format with John Cephas, ending with a brief conclusion comparing and contrasting their lives and art.

I have included eighty-three of their songs drawn from their more extensive repertoires.[33] These are the songs they commonly perform or consider significant to their musical development. I have not included notation, which some readers may consider old-fashioned, but well over half of their songs are currently available on phonograph recordings. Blues songs, even with notation, remain skeletal outlines, and listening to a song, even on record, is a far better way of approaching a blues song than simply reading it. Simple vocal melody does not significantly add to a song and total vocal and instrumental transcription is overly complex. In any event, I do not project a substantial readership capable of using full transcription, but I accept the responsibility for the absence of notation and pass along the artists' suggestion to buy the records. To that end, I have included a discography as well as notes leading to other versions, transcriptions, and related recordings.

Finally, before we move on to Archie Edwards's story, I would like to call attention to two important documents which have influenced and, to some degree, set the stage for, this book.

Nineteen eighty-six proved a banner year for Piedmont blues, marking the publication of Bruce Bastin's *Red River Blues: The Blues Tradition in the Southeast* and the release of Bowling Green John Cephas and Harmonica Phil Wiggins's *Dog Days of August* album. Bastin's book provided the first comprehensive and accessible survey of southeastern blues, bringing together literature previously scattered in regional journals and record liner notes. Relying heavily on fieldwork (his own and that of Kip Lornell, Pete Lowry, and Glen Hinson) Bastin substantially added to the documentation of the Piedmont tradition.

The *Dog Days of August* record also focused new attention on the Piedmont blues, selling enough to make even the record industry take notice. Produced by folklorists Joe Wilson and Larry McBride, it won the W. C. Handy award for Best Traditional Album of the Year. At the same time, Cephas and Wiggins were designated Blues Entertainers of the Year, an award that had previously gone to mainstream electric artists. The Piedmont style had not had such visible representatives since the heyday of Sonny Terry and Brownie McGhee. These two events served notice to scholars, blues fans, and the record industry that there was more to the blues than electric bands.

This is the first book-length study of Virginia blues musicians, but I don't expect it to be the last. Other researchers have been active.[34] Eventually, the Piedmont blues will be documented as effectively as the Mississippi Delta tradition.[35] Now, with the publication of this book, Archie Edwards and John Cephas have contributed to the documentation of blues in Union Hall, Bowling Green, and Washington, D.C. In the near future, similar studies will allow us to put together a humanistic grassroots history of Piedmont blues, dependent on the memories and experiences of those to whom the tradition belongs.

Notes to Chapter 1

1. For the full text of this original composition titled "My Old Schoolmates," see p. 140.

2. Between 1982 and 1984 we toured on behalf of the Arts America Program of the United States Information Agency, performing in Africa, South America, Central America, and the Caribbean.

3. Scholars may never agree on exactly when the blues form emerged, but evidence shows that a song form consistently termed "blues" began to be reported from 1890 to 1910.

4. Dr. David Evans used the same phrase, "strikingly visual imagery," in his fine descriptive essay, "Structure and Meaning in the Folk Blues," in Jan

Brunvand, *The Study of American Folklore: An Introduction*, third edition (New York: Norton, 1986), pp. 563–593. Obviously, it stuck with me and I acknowledge David Evans's influence as a friend and teacher.

5. Michael Taft, *Blues Lyric Poetry: A Concordance* (New York: Garland Press, 1984), p. xi.

6. See Paul Oliver, Max Harrison, and William Bolcom, *The New Grove Gospel, Blues and Jazz* (New York: Norton, 1986), pp. 36–188; and David Evans, *Big Road Blues: Tradition and Creativity in the Folk Blues* (Berkeley: University of California Press, 1982), pp. 16–19.

7. Barry Lee Pearson, *"Sounds So Good to Me": The Bluesman's Story* (Philadelphia: University of Pennsylvania Press, 1984), pp. 129–136.

8. See "John Cephas's Songs," p. 201.

9. Oliver, 1986, p. 37.

10. For a broader discussion of these pockets of blues activity, see Bruce Bastin, *Red River Blues: The Blues Tradition in the Southeast* (Urbana: University of Illinois Press, 1986). For a fine survey of a local tradition in Mississippi, see David Evans, *Big Road Blues*.

11. My summary of recording activity in Virginia owes a great deal to Bastin, *Red River Blues*, and Kip Lornell, *Virginia Traditions: Western Piedmont Blues* (Ferrum, Virginia: Blue Ridge Institute, 1978).

12. "Chicken, You Can't Roos Too High for Me," *Bowling Green John Cephas and Harmonica Phil Wiggins from Virginia, U.S.A.: Living Country Blues, Volume I*, L & R Records, LR 42.031, West Germany.

13. Kip Lornell, "Tarter and Gay," *Living Blues* 27 (May–June, 1976), p. 18.

14. See "Reno Factory," in "John Cephas's Songs," p. 240.

15. As this manuscript was going to press, I spotted Vaughan Webb's "Styles and Influences in the Southwest Virginia Blues Tradition," *Folklore and Folklife in Virginia* 4 (1988), pp. 66–74. He discussed several musicians, including James Henry "Cripp" Diggs, who was born in Lynchburg and played on the streets of Roanoke. Diggs's repertoire includes several songs that Edwards and Cephas do: "Poor Boy," "Red River Blues," and "Careless Love." Several other artists, banjoist Joshua Thomas, pianist Earl Gilmore, and guitarists Thurman Burks and James Howard Twine, are also mentioned.

16. Samuel Charters, *Sweet as Showers of Rain: The Bluesmen*, Volume 2 (New York: Oak Publications, 1977), p. 137.

17. Discussing banjo players, Lornell noted: "Many of Virginia's black banjo players grew up in an era when the differences between black and white folk music were less clearly defined. They tended to see their music as 'rural' or 'country' and they did not impose the racial connotations on music that it has today. Most of the banjo tunes by black performers that have been collected in Virginia cross racial lines. That is, they cannot be labelled black or white." Kip Lornell, *Virginia Traditions: Non-Blues Secular Black Music* (Ferrum, Virginia: Blue Ridge Institute, 1977), p. 4.

18. Pete Welding, "Stringin' the Blues: The Art of the Folk Blues Guitar," *Down Beat* 32 (no. 19, July 1, 1965). See also Pete Welding's liner notes to *Long Steel Rail: Blues by Maryland Songster Bill Jackson*, Testament Records, T-201, Chicago, Illinois.

19. Charters, 1977, p. 137.

20. Evidence supporting the contention that black guitarists in the Southeast and perhaps elsewhere drew on established banjo traditions continues to

grow. Fieldwork has also shown that blacks continued to play the banjo in North Carolina and Virginia after it went out of fashion in the Deep South. Both Archie and John refer to banjo players, John Hurt could play banjo, and fellow bluesman John Jackson continues to play banjo today. See also Dena Epstein, *Sinful Songs and Spirituals* (Urbana: University of Illinois Press, 1977), and Robert Cantwell, *Bluegrass Breakdown: The Making of the Old Southern Sound* (Urbana: University of Illinois Press, 1984).

21. Bastin, 1986, p. 106.

22. Lornell, *Western Piedmont Blues*, p. 5.

23. Ibid., p. 3.

24. Robert Palmer, "A Night of Piedmont Blues Tradition," *New York Times* (March 11, 1983).

25. Paul Oliver, "Echoes of the Jungle," *Living Blues* 13 (summer, 1973), p. 30.

26. John Cephas performed with Ko Nimo in Ghana in 1982 and immediately blended in with the ensemble as they played "palm wine" music; Cephas accompanied them on the guitar, utilizing his Piedmont finger-picking approach.

27. Obviously, characterizing the degree of difficulty of any performance technique is keyed to subjective judgments. The Piedmont style may be rhythmically easier to master than Delta techniques, but the finger picking is difficult to master. As John puts it, "It's hard to teach. Some get it and some don't." See "Archie Edwards's Songs," and "John Cephas's Songs," for their descriptions of their picking styles.

28. Peter Lowry, "Consider the Wall: Concretization in a Musical Style," unpublished paper, 1984, p. 3. See also Barry Lee Pearson, "Good Times When Times Were Hard: Recollections of Rural Houseparties in Virginia," *Folklore and Folklife in Virginia* 3 (1984), pp. 44–55.

29. See the comments by Pete Welding cited in note 18, and Charles Keil, *Urban Blues* (Chicago: University of Chicago Press, 1966), p. 218.

30. These musicians included Delta, Chicago, and California artists, as well as several Piedmont performers including Edwards, Cephas, John Jackson, and J. C. Burris.

31. Barry Lee Pearson, "Archie Edwards: Barbershop Blues" and "Bowling Green John Cephas and Harmonica Phil Wiggins: D.C. Country Blues," *Living Blues* 63 (January–February, 1985), pp. 14–26.

32. Edwards was born in 1918; Cephas in 1930.

33. For a list of songs not included, see Chapter 6, pp. 262–263.

34. Folklorist Chuck Perdue has been chronicling the life and times of Fairfax bluesman John Jackson and his family since the 1960s.

35. Thanks to diligent investigators such as David Evans, John Fahey, Bill Ferris, Axel Küstner, George Mitchell, Alan Lomax, Jim O'Neal, and Gayle Wardlow, the Mississippi tradition is the best-researched in the country.

2

Archie Edwards's Story

I started playing when I was six or seven years old. See, when I was a kid, my father played and he had some friends that would come past the house on Saturday nights and play the guitar. In those days, people didn't have nothing to do but walk five or six miles and come by his house, you know, and eat dinner, drink whiskey, and play the guitar.

One in particular . . . his name was Boyd Maddox . . . he would do that quite often. And then Steve Patterson, he played a good guitar. And my dad played. But Boyd Maddox, he was the one that inspired me.

Boyd Maddox came by the house on a Saturday night back in the early thirties. On a cold Saturday night we were all sitting in the living room with Daddy, and this fellow playing the guitar. So my mother fixed dinner for them and they went into the kitchen to eat dinner. So when they went to eat dinner, the fellow left the guitar on the bed there in the living room.

So there was one note that was ringing like crazy in my head. It pressed on my mind to go over there, to the bed to where they laid that guitar down, and make that certain note. In those days, you know, children were taught not to touch anything that belonged to anyone else. If you did, you just got torn up. But this note that guy had made sounded so pretty that one mind told me, "Say man, if you can just get over there to that bed and make that note just one time, real low, you'll have it made." I finally got the courage to sneak over to the bed, and I picked up the guitar and I made the note. But I think I dropped down on it a little too heavy, and my daddy heard it.

He says, "Who's in there playing the guitar?" And the fellow said, "Uncle Roy, that's your boy playing the guitar." Well, he was right. It was Uncle Roy's boy and Uncle Roy's boy been playing ever since.

And I didn't get a whipping, so that was the best part of it. It

Archie Edwards at Oxon Hills Farm, Maryland, 1986.
Photo by Mike Joyce.

shocked my dad so much. I guess he figured he better leave me alone. So that's when I started, when I was six or seven. I know if I could just make that one note, I'd have it. That's what you call the "Red River Blues."[1] But that's one thing that my father didn't whip me for. "Now wait a minute, as young as he is, he done made a note like that!"

But the best part was that I kept on playing. And that note still sounds good.

My Father's Music

I was born in Franklin County, Virginia, a little place out in the country called Union Hall. That's near Rocky Mount, kind of between Roanoke, Martinsville, Lynchburg, and Danville. I was born September 4, 1918, and I started playing the guitar when I was about seven, back in the country. My father played the guitar, banjo, harmonica, everything. So I got interested in it from his playing. His name was Roy Edwards and he married Pearl Holland, so my mother's name was Pearl Edwards.

My father was a sharecropper, so I grew up on a farm. There were six brothers and six sisters, that kind of evened it off. My oldest sister's named Thelma, then Sally, who's deceased, then Della, Kate, Agnes, and Eunice, she's the youngest. And the boys... Willie was the oldest, James, me, Robert, Wayman, who's deceased, and Oliver, the youngest. All of us are up here in Washington except for Willie, he's down in Virginia. But the rest of us are in Washington. We contact each other occasionally, not as much as we should, but we do.

But there was no complaining between mother and father because six boys and six girls evened it off. Right?

My mother said when I was a little boy... I guess she said three or four years old... that I would walk about the house singing "Nango Blues." She says she didn't know where I got it from. "Nango Blues." I would sing, "I got the 'Nango Blues.' " She said where it came from she never knew. But that's what I was singing when I was a little fellow before I heard my dad play a guitar. I never heard anybody mention the blues, but I was singing the "Nango Blues." I don't know what it means. Some kid stuff.

She said, "Where in the world did that kid get that title from, the 'Nango Blues'?" But I never heard anybody play a guitar. I never heard anybody sing a song or anything. That was something from my own imagination. So it must have been my calling to be a bluesman.

My dad was the first person that I heard play guitar. And he had a guitar that his nephew gave him. That was way back in the twenties, about twenty-three or -four. I was a tot then. This guy came by the house and said, "Uncle Roy, I got a guitar, but I never play it. So I left it down at John David's." John David had a place where he sold corn liquor and his wife, she cooked chicken and sold chicken sandwiches and whatnot to make extra money, you know? Anytime of the day, of the week, you could go by John David's and get a glass of corn liquor.

So my dad walked from his house down to John David's house one night and brought the guitar back home and tuned it and started playing some of his old songs. So then I got the bug to play the guitar, from what I heard my dad play. So that's way back when I was four or five years old.

My dad used to play a lot of banjo songs on his guitar because he was a banjo picker. He would play "Georgie Buck," and "Stack O'Lee," and "Cumberland Gap," and an old song about the "Preacher Got Drunk and Laid His Bible Down." He used to play all them old things, you know. He used to play "John Hardy"... "They put John Hardy back in jail...." He used to play that on his guitar. They say John Hardy was something like a desperado, something like the Jesse James Boys were. Lived by the gun. They say he killed his buddy for fifteen cents.

He used to play "John Henry," that was his favorite piece, and "Frankie and Johnny," all those old legendary songs.[2] Of course, they had a different way of playing... playing in Sebastapol with a slide in open tuning. He played "That Train That Carried My Girl from Town." That's a slide song like "John Henry."

And he played some of the same songs Mississippi John Hurt played.[3] I think the two of them were about the same age at the time they were playing the guitar, and evidently they were playing some of the same songs, because I know my dad used to play "Frankie and Johnny." And later on I heard the song John Hurt recorded of "Frankie...," so I think my dad and John Hurt was kind of running neck and neck, learning to play the guitar about the same time.

My dad used to play "Take This Hammer," you know, "Nine Pound Hammer," kind of like "John Henry":

> Ain't no hammer in this mountain
> Ring like mine, ring like mine
> Take this hammer, carry it to the Captain
> Tell him I'm gone, tell him I'm gone.[4]

Yeah, that was "Nine Pound Hammer" and John Hurt, he played that too. They played quite a few of the same songs. My dad had a hell of a repertoire. He played "Ruby," that song about "I can hear the whistle blow five hundred miles." Then he played banjo tunes, played the "Fox Chase" on the harmonica, and he even played the accordion, too.

Somebody gave him an accordion and he could play that. He could play anything. And blues, he could play blues for hours. Just go from one song to another. He had a hell of a repertoire for country blues. That's why, when I hear people play songs today I say, "I heard that before," because he used to play them. He knew lots of songs and he knew lots of verses, like that song you sing, "I'm gonna call up China, see if my baby's over there."[5] He played that and another verse, "I'm gonna call up China, tell them everything I know." He knew lots of blues and he would play them on the guitar or on the banjo.

But my daddy was playing harmonica and banjo more than he was playing the guitar because he didn't have a guitar until his nephew gave it to him. But he had a banjo. He could pick banjo. He kept some kind of a banjo most all the time. He'd whip that five-string banjo to death. He could play almost anything on the five-string banjo. Well, anytime he got without a guitar he could play anything he knew on the five-string banjo . . . take the five-string banjo, play the same thing. But he was better on the five-string banjo than he was with the guitar because he could get more out of it.

Yeah, my dad could make that banjo ring. And I'll always remember he had one saying that he would always say when he was playing. He'd holler:

Shout, children, shout
'Cause you ain't going to heaven nohow.

He'd make that banjo sing.

I think if I had a five-string banjo, maybe in five weeks or so, I bet I could rap out some of his tunes, because I still got them up here in my head. But it's funny, my mother always told me to play an even number of strings. See, I used to play the five-string banjo, but she said she always heard it was a sin to play an uneven number of strings, so I picked up the guitar. She never said anything to me about what I played on the guitar. She would love to hear me play the guitar, but she didn't want me to play the banjo. I don't know where that came from. But you know people. It's traditions, handed down through generations. I never heard anybody else say it. But I stopped playing the banjo.[6]

He was really on top playing the harmonica. I wish today that I could play the harmonica like my father did. Boy, that guy could play a harmonica to death. Now there was another guy named Buck Jackson,[7] he could play the harmonica, too. He was a little older than my father and he could play the hell out of the harmonica. My daddy and him used to lock horns, you know, on the harmonica. Do a few free falls to see who was the best. And, boy, they would really go at it. I wish I would have had a tape recorded back then because it was really something. Then I would have something to back up my words. Yeah, they would go at it on the harmonica. I wish they could have gotten in touch with Sonny Terry, because my dad could really blow harmonica. I used to do pretty good with a harmonica myself, but I kind of gave it up.

Old Buck Jackson, he could dance, too. My mother said Buck Jackson could play the harmonica and dance. He never was of any size though, because when my mother first described him to me she said he was a little old skinny boy. When I met him, he was a little old skinny man. Never was any size.

They tell me he could do sleight of hand, magic tricks. Said down in Rocky Mount, Virginia, one night, he was there and the place was full of people. Everybody was dancing and carrying on. Say he did something to all the men, that he had all the men standing in the corner with their pants down. I don't know, he must have fell out with somebody. Say all the menfolk was standing right up against the wall with their pants down, just as crazy as hell. I heard that. I don't know how true it was, but they told me: "Yeah, he had them all standing along the wall, just with their pants dropped."

I saw him one time down at Smith Chapel Church in Penhook, Virginia. Me and my brother, we were youngsters, we went to the meeting with my older brother and we were just walking around. Buck Jackson, he was down there in the woods shooting craps with the guys. Somehow or other something went wrong, and somebody had Buck Jackson running like a rabbit through the bushes. The guy's trying to shoot him, but Jackson got behind a tree.

I said, "Shoot, he may do sleight of hand, but he can run, too." All of sudden you saw leaves flying, people running, and we saw Buck Jackson running up behind this tree. My brother and me said, "Oh, my God!" The people started shooting. They tried to draw a bead on Buck, but they couldn't do it. That's the first time I ever saw a guy pull a gun on a man. If he could have got a bead on him, he would have popped him, but old Jackson was going. That dude could run. But he could blow a harmonica, too.

And then my brother Willie, he used to play the harmonica. He traveled around more than I did because he was older than I was. And he would come home with old broken-up records and old beat-up guitars, you know. That started me, it gave me more encouragement to play the guitar.

When I was growing up they used five-string banjos, harmonica, guitar . . . those were the three outstanding instruments back in those days. And some people take an old wash tub and turn it upside down, and take a broomstick and set that broomstick in the center of it, and

then you would put a cord and fasten it to the tub and the top of the
broomstick and, man, you could make a bass guitar out of that.

Playing music was very common. The only source of music that
they had was a guitar, banjo, harmonica, or something. Because that
was before people was able to buy radios and whatnot, and there
wasn't no television. Quite a few people didn't even have record players.

Around home there were a couple of guys that did a little picking
and singing. One in particular . . . his name was Steve Patterson. I think
you met his brother, Robert Patterson, up there above Rocky Mount
there. Steve Patterson, he played something about "McKinley" back in
those days. He used slide guitar, played in open-E, but he did a lot of
slide work on "McKinley." But he was the only guy I ever heard play
that song about "McKinley." I don't know whether it's local or whether
he wrote it himself and just didn't get any further with it.

He'd come over to my house, you know, when he used to play the
guitar with my father on the weekends, you know. And he would play
"McKinley." I remember a few verses of it:

McKinley hollered, McKinley squalled,
McKinley got shot with a long dungeon ball
Said he's gonna die, he's gonna die.[8]

Dungeon, that means derringer, but I guess that's the way a country boy
like Steve Patterson said it. I don't know if McKinley got shot with a derringer or not.

Robert Muse . . . I know you met him, "Rabbit" Muse. Well, he was
a musician around there. And the Dudley boys . . . Taft Dudley used to
play guitar a lot. I don't know if he ever did anything with his music or
not, but I've gone to several house parties when I was a boy and Taft
Dudley would play.

Boyd Maddox, Taft Dudley, Steve Patterson, another boy, name of
Noel Herbert, did a pretty good guitar, and that was about the only guys
that I heard around there.

A relative of mine had a family reunion here last fall and to my
surprise Boyd Maddox's oldest son was there. His name was Joe Maddox. He married a girl named Rachel Edwards out of Union Hall, Virginia, but she was not a relative of mine. But my brother married her
aunt, so we were all at the same Smith-Edwards family reunion. So I got
a chance to play the guitar for them. When I told this girl that Boyd
Maddox was the first man that . . . the first guitar that I ever played was
Boyd Maddox's guitar . . . telling about how popular he was in the thirties with his guitar, well, she was really shocked to know that I knew
Maddox during the time he was playing the guitar.

But it was really something . . . Boyd Maddox's daughter-in-law. Joe Maddox, he's a preacher now, but, oh hell, he played a lot of guitar, play the five-string banjo, too. He used to do a hell of a lot of playing and dance, too. Country boys used to buck dance and carry on. He was quite a clown when he was a young man.

Then there was a couple of old guys. One guy, by the name of John Cosby, he was a pretty good guitar player. He was a friend of my older brother. In fact, he gave my older brother an old guitar that we kind of started off with. He originally came from down around Acoceek, Maryland, but he came over to Franklin County and married Bertha Edwards. That was my dad's cousin.

He was a great influence on me, and he taught me a few notes in E. He was trying to show me something about professional music, how to make certain chords: E, E-minor, A7, and this chord that we call a crow-foot run. He taught me that. I learned one of his songs, but I never did know the name of it, but I learned it and still play it once in a while.

But I remember he would play it in E, and when he got done he would say, "Darn. Darn, Archie, you're gonna learn that someday." But it wasn't much to it. He didn't have any words to it. He was a guy that would play but wouldn't sing. You know, the old guys played a lot in open tunings and in the key of E and they would do some songs like "Red River Blues," "Poor Boy Blues," and other bottleneck stuff. But the old songs had a pretty good beat to them.

And there was another guy named Lemon Toler who was a heck of a guitar player. He had three brothers and they all played. Four boys. But Lemon, he was kind of like me, the only one who went forward with it. I learned that "Saturday Night Hop" from him. He had some words to it, and I think he called it "Broken Hearted Love." But I can't remember the words because I don't think he sang too much either. He was kind of like my brother Robert. Could play a good guitar, but very seldom would sing anything. He did a little "Red River Blues," but everybody did some of that. "Red River Blues" has always been popular, just like "Key to the Highway." That's old guitar music. But I learned that "Saturday Night Hop" from Lemon Toler. He called it blues, but it's mostly ragtime.

That's as far as I went under their instruction. I met a couple other musicians later on. There was the Wright brothers, Curtis Wright and Wilbur Wright. They were from down the highway near Danville. They played some guitar. My older brother introduced me to them. Then there was one other guy, he was a great guitar player around my dad's age. His name was John Lee Starkey, and he lived in True Vine, Virginia. Everybody knew him. I just met him once, when I came out of the army in 1946. My dad introduced me to him and told me he used to be a great guitar player.

Country Life

Well, when I first started school, we went to an old log-bodied school-house. It had a little potbellied stove in it. So you go to school in the morning, everybody huddled around it. The big kids would get around it and push the little kids back. So I spent quite a few cold hours trying to get there to try to get warm.

About the second year I went to school they built a new school-house. So that was a weatherboard schoolhouse, painted white, and it had bigger stove in the front of it so it was a little better for that.

But anyway, during the school years, I was a B-average student. My teachers always gave me credit for being a B-average student. But the bad part about it...when I got to the eighth grade...that was it. You know, because we had no way of going to high school. So when I left home, two years after I left home, they started running the school buses to the country, picking up the kids and carrying them to high school.

Union Hall, Virginia, 1988.   *Photo by Segrid Pearson.*

So if they had done that a few years earlier, I could have gotten my high-school education. But everybody told me I should have been able to finish my education because they said I had a smart head on myself. But when you got to the eighth grade, that was it. But my report card... I always got A's, B's, A's, B's... very seldom got down to a C. Stayed right up to the A and B class, so they gave me a B average.

My favorite subjects were English and geography and math. I was very good at math and geography. That's the thing that I remember that I've known to become true was the fact of the big cities, countries and things we studied about. After I got to traveling, it was a real thing. We studied a lot about Germany and Canada and I've been to those places. So it became a reality.

On a school day, starting from home you'd have to get up in the morning, do all your little chores that you have to do before you go to school. First thing you have to do is go to the spring and bring up four or five pails of water for Mother, for your parents to use during the day. Bring four or five pails of water. Then you would get out there, bring you some wood or something to keep the fires going during the day. Then you would get yourself cleaned up and ready for school and your mother would fix a little lunch for you. You'd grab your little lunch pails and walk three or four miles to school.

You get to school and the first thing they would do in school, they would have you sing a hymn and then repeat the Lord's Prayer. Then you get into your daily studies which would be, well, math would be the first thing. She'd have you go to the blackboard and work some problems on the board. And then we'd have spelling, learn how to spell twenty-five or thirty words. And then she would have you do reading, read a few pages in your reading book. And then you'd do your geography lesson. One subject to another all the way down to three-thirty, quarter-to-four.

Yeah, you would have your nose pretty well to the grindstone all day. But they do give you a fifteen-minute recess at ten-thirty and forty-five–minute recess at twelve and a fifteen-minute recess again at three o'clock. Then you go home at four.

Take off and go home at four, sometimes you leave at four o'clock in the wintertime... it would be just about dark when you get home. And again, in the morning, you leave home at six-thirty, seven o'clock ... be off to school at eight... sometimes you leave home in the dark.

You get school done, you go to the field and help the old man on the farm then. And that would be plowing the ground, planting it, tobacco or corn... whatever. And then you'd have to plow the ground, cut the weeds, chop the weeds out of it. So you'd work in the fields all day.

But corn and tobacco was about the only field work that we did because they didn't have cotton in Virginia where I lived. So corn and tobacco was the two things that we had to help take care of. But the wheat would grow by itself, but we did have to harvest it later on in the year. We'd plant plenty potatoes, white potatoes, sweet potatoes, and in the garden we'd put the beans, cabbage, beets, whatever. What you'd call the vegetables.

I did pluck a lot of tobacco. We grow tobacco, call it "priming tobacco." Pick off about eight or ten leaves. Rest of it, take a tobacco knife and whack it out, call it "cutting tobacco."

Back in those days, when you're home with Mother and Father, you did what they told you. If you let them know that you hated to do something, they would tear your hind parts up and you did it anyway. So whatever it was, well, you liked to do it because you knew there would be a lot of feedback if you said, "I'm not going to do it." You didn't tell them that you wasn't gonna do it, see what I'm saying. Back in those days you didn't tell your mother and dad, "I'm not doing to do this. I don't want to do it." Because when they got through with you, you wanted to do it then. So I was smart enough to know not to tell them that I don't like this and I'm not going to do this. That was a no-no. You didn't do that at all.

We didn't have school in the summertime. School would close some time around April the fifteenth. School would close from around April fifteenth to the first of September. That's when you're free to help your parents.

The best time of the year was harvesting the wheat because you knew that once you got the wheat harvested, put in those stacks, you know, the threshing machine they call it, would come around. That was a big thing. People from all over the county would come to your place to help thresh that wheat. And always be a big dinner. You'd get some food that you never saw before.

Yeah, my mother would have sweet-potato pies, and fried chicken, and string beans. And, oh God, good food. We'd always love to see that because we'd come up with ice water which you never got a chance to dream about much back in the country. But they'd have a great big tub of ice water, someone have a hunk of ice so big in the tub, you know. Used to take a dipper and dip it up, pour it in a glass, take a drink of ice water. But they told us not to drink too much because it would make you sick.

Yeah, those were the days we looked forward to. Threshing the wheat. And the next thing we looked forward to was having these corn shuckings. You get the corn, bring it up and stack it in great big piles.

Then you invite your neighbors to the corn shucking. And they'd come from miles around. Grown-ups, you know, they'd sit around the corn pile, pull the husk off, toss that corn out there.

Man, the pile of corn that had the husk on it would turn out to be a great big pile of white corn . . . looks just like snow. That was beautiful. We always looked forward to that.

They sang, played guitars, and everything afterwards when you go home to eat the dinners at night. Sometimes they stay up to twelve, one o'clock at night. Playing guitar, drinking corn liquor, and telling lies. And they would do the old square dances, swing your partner and all that. And they had a dance four people would do they called "Swinging the Four Hands." My dad used to play that on the harmonica. Then they would buck dance a lot, jump up and down and kick up their heels. And the womenfolk would get out and do a little jig, shaking their coattails around. I think they called that "sashaying." But it was very little slow dancing, where two people, a man and a woman, dance. No, there wasn't too much of that. It was either square dancing or "Four Hands" or buck dancing.

Of course, I wasn't old enough to get into it, but I enjoyed hearing it. I picked up some pointers about playing the guitar from the old guys sitting around there.

I don't remember too much else as a kid. Mostly I kind of kept to myself. I guess I had the idea of being a musician. But I did play a lot of ball, what they call "sandlot baseball." Back in those days you didn't have a glove or mitt to catch the ball in, they would hold their hat in their hand, you know. That gives you a little protection, but not much.

But that's about the way they did it. But most times they catch it bare-handed. A lot of times they didn't have money to buy a real baseball, so they'd take these wrappings from the tobacco fields. Call it twine. You wrap it. You take that twine and you would knot it together and wrap a big ball of it. Sometimes you put a piece of rubber . . . put an old rubber ball inside of it. And wrap it over and over to get it thick enough and you take a needle and thread and sew it. Well, you can make a baseball with that. Now that would be soft enough to catch with your bare hands.

There was some good ball players, though. I've know a couple of guys to leave home, went to Pittsburgh and became members of the "Homestad Grey's." A guy named Urson Unzer, Garfield Lansdon, and Willie Randolph.

Franklin County was the corn liquor capital of the world. And my daddy, he made the best. Oh, back in the thirties, that was the only thing that he could do for survival, to keep the family going. Because we had several droughts there during the thirties and it was just so hot and dry until you couldn't make anything. So, during the time that he couldn't grow a crop, you know, he would make whiskey.

So that was kind of a shaky survival, but he made it. Yeah, the law was around, looking every day for people making moonshine. But somehow he got lucky enough to make it and get out of the hollow before the law came.

So he was never caught. I don't think he was ever chased. But they had an old guy, named John Cash, he was known to get you. But, I don't think my dad ever had any problems with John Cash. He was always able to get in these hills, hollows, and make just a little corn liquor. He used to work for other people. But then again, after that, he started making some for himself. But he kept a little liquor somewhere around in the bushes there, where a man could come up and if he want a half a gallon or a gallon, he would sell it to him. It kept him in spare change to buy a little groceries with.

Back in the country the only thing you need to buy was sugar, salt and pepper, and a little seasoning for your food, you know. And so he made it pretty well. We used to buy coal oil then. We didn't have any electricity. They'd have this big old lantern with the chimneys on them, you know, shades on them. Fill that with oil and it would last you for about four or five months. You only light it when it gets dark. Most of the time in the country you go to bed before it got dark. So it was very inexpensive life in the country.

So we came over pretty good. Sell our little corn liquor. And me and my brother, we would carry wood for them, and they would give us a little bit. A half a gallon, a big old gallon. Next thing you know, we would have two or three gallons of the stuff saved up.

I was too young to drink it, but I sold the stuff. Somebody come by there to buy some liquor, if my dad didn't have any, well, we'd sell it. That's how I kept myself togged out in new white shoes, summer pants, new shirts, and whatnot. We were pretty sharp walking around with a dollar or two in your pocket anytime you wanted.

We bought our first old Model-T Ford . . . not a Model T, but a Model-A Ford . . . selling whiskey and working in a sawmill. Yeah, we lived a pretty decent life in the country, pretty decent. I call it good times when times were hard, because we used to have fun. So I started off knowing how to handle corn liquor, but we didn't drink it like the older guys did. But I wish we had started sooner, because it was very good. And my dad made the best.

Franklin County was the corn liquor capital of Virginia, but I didn't start drinking the stuff until I left home. Now I get mad with myself every time I get a taste of corn liquor. My God Almighty, I was down there where it was and I didn't drink it! And here I am now, crazy about the stuff. It's like some of the girls I met down there, too. Crazy about them, and I didn't know it until they got away from me. That's life. You never miss your water until the well runs dry.

Learning the Blues

Later on, up in the early thirties, that's when I really started playing guitar.

So one day, along about 1934 or 1935, me and my three brothers were sitting around talking about buying a guitar. We had this brand-new Sears and Roebuck catalog. So I said, "Look man, here's one for five dollars." So my brother said, "How do you know we have enough money?"

Five dollars was a lot of money back then. Sometimes you work a long time to get five dollars. If you have five dollars in your pocket, nobody in the world could tell you that you weren't rich. But me and my brothers, we all grew up around there in the country where they made a little corn liquor. So the ones that was too young to drink saved theirs and sold it. And the ones that could drink, they drank most of theirs. So I had two older brothers that drank most of theirs.

So me and my brothers had some money from selling moonshine. I was the mastermind of everything we wanted to do there, so I said, "Well, the guitar cost five dollars and with four of us, a dollar and a quarter a piece ought to do it."

I said, "Brother Willie, you got a dollar and quarter?"

"Yes."

"Brother James, you got a dollar and a quarter?"

"Yes."

"Brother Robert, you got a dollar and a quarter?"

"Yes."

So we all chipped in and bought this new guitar from Sears and Roebuck, an old Gene Autry guitar, with Gene Autry's horse and a dog on the front of it. So I wrote the order and took it down and sent it to Sears Roebuck.

They sent us the Gene Autry guitar with a little case. They sent that to us with some instruction books and whatnot. I could read and understand a little better than the rest of them, so I was the one that tuned the guitar and started picking out a few chords out of the instruction book. Everybody started playing it . . . but me and my brother Robert were the only ones that stayed with it. After we got to learn to do the C, D, and G-major pretty well, we was off and running then.

I had three brothers played guitar. Well, all of us played something.

The whole family played something. My brother Robert, he was a heck of a guitar player. My brother Willie, he was very good getting hold of people that could play a guitar.

Well, the first guy I ever met in person that could really play was a guy my oldest brother, Willie, met. There was a convict camp about five miles below where I lived. They had those convict camps all up and down Virginia back in those days, clearing the way to build those hard surface highways. So this boy was working on the road there. He was with the road camp, a trustee or something, working with the convicts.

And there was a guy by the name of Alonzo Clemons living not far from us. He had five or six beautiful daughters. So this guy was coming to Alonzo Clemons's house to see one of his girls and my brother Willie was going there, too. My brother met this guy and was telling him how he had a brother that had a new guitar and was trying to learn.

So he came by one rainy day to play our guitar and he played so much like Blind Lemon Jefferson until you could hardly tell the difference. If you didn't know the difference, that it was two different people, you wouldn't have known. I thought it was Blind Lemon.

He said, "No. I play like Blind Lemon. As a matter of fact, I can give Blind Lemon a hell of a time."

So these guys was on the same level. He played this song that sounded like Blind Lemon, about:

> I sent for the doctor and the chief of police came
> You got me in so much trouble, Lord, it's a crying shame
> What do you want with a rooster, it won't crow for day
> What good is a woman, won't do what you say.

Yeah, I learned that song from him. I forgot his name, but he looked like a guy named Rambling Thomas. He looked a lot like that picture in the Heroes of the Blues cards.[9] Oh, he could play anything. Anything you asked, he could play. He played a lot of Blind Blake stuff like "Diddie Wah Diddie." Blind Blake was very popular, too. Everybody liked Blind Blake. And he could play just like Blind Lemon. Yeah, this guy came to my house when I was a little boy and was the man who showed me how to play a song that sounded like Blind Lemon Jefferson. That was one of my idols. Blind Lemon Jefferson, and then John Hurt and Blind Boy Fuller.

Blind Boy Fuller was really big here on the East Coast, one of the hottest things that ever come up the highway with a guitar. And the funny thing, it's a long story about it.

I was walking the highway one evening, me and my brothers and sisters and a couple of kids. We had to walk a couple of miles on an old

Sign for Clayton's in Union Hall.   *Photo by Segrid Pearson.*

dirt road in the country to go to school. So we was passing along this highway one evening coming from school and this little old filling station on the highway. They called it Clayton Barnard's filling station and he sold liquor there.

It's nothing but shrubbery there now. But once upon a time, you used to pull up there and buy gas. You could get a tankful of gas and a pint of liquor. He'd go back and get it, bring it around back to you. He sold gasoline and whiskey.

That's where I was walking along the highway back in those days, in the thirties when I was growing up, when those old highways was secondary dirt roads. This is how I saw Blind Boy Fuller and Sonny Terry. They were in this car with these two white fellows. We were walking along the highway and this fellow took his guitar and played a couple of songs for the people. We weren't close enough to hear what he was playing, but we could hear the sounds of the guitar, the beat of the guitar. So when he finished, he swung it around on his back and the man held up a tin cup of whiskey and he took a drink of corn liquor. That was Blind Boy Fuller.

Sonny Terry, he was walking down the highway. He had on a pair of brown slacks, straight collar open, and he had on a pair of brown suede shoes. At that time, in his younger days, he sported a heavy mustache. I didn't realized then who they were, but I said, "Well, I'll remember that, because I bet that guy is somebody famous." And then I came to find out about thirty-five years later it was Blind Boy Fuller and Sonny Terry.

The way I got most of my music, I listened to Blind Lemon Jefferson, Blind Boy Fuller, Furry Lewis, and Mississippi John Hurt. My sister bought an old record player and we started listening to old blues like John Hurt and Blind Lemon. My oldest brother would go to parties at night and he would pick up old recordings from anybody that he could get them from and bring them home, you know. And we'd put them on the old record player and we would listen to them.

My brother Robert, he and I tutored each other and would swap ideas. So we would listen to the records and try to pick the guitar. If I played something and missed a note, he would show me where I missed a note ... we'd swap guitars. If I made a mistake, he'd take the guitar. And if he made a mistake, I'd take it back. So when we got the song completed, we could both play it as professionals.

Yeah, that's why we got the reputation as being such good musicians, because we were playing stuff that come off the record player. And most people wondered, How did we do it? Well, we did it ourselves just like you would learn to speak a foreign language from a record. So we both learned at home before we were fourteen or fifteen years old.

I just listened to what they were doing, pick it up and play it myself. But it wasn't long after I started playing before I was showing my dad how to play certain pieces on the guitar. When I got to finger working, professional work, I played some songs that he liked. So he was trying to play them himself, so I would show him some chords sometimes. Yeah, he asked me to show him.

We got into it a little deeper than my father because he was never gifted enough to listen to the records, see, and get the chords from the record player like the professionals play. Now, I can listen to a record twice. I'll play it just like the record, like the artist played ... like Blind Lemon, John Hurt. I can listen to those people a couple of times, tune my guitar, and play it. So I kind of learned professional because I grabbed the stuff from an old record player. Barbecue Bob, Mississippi John Hurt, Furry Lewis, Blind Lemon, Blind Boy Fuller, Frank Hutchison, Buddy Moss, all those old-timey dudes, you know. And every time we get a hold of a record, I'll play it around three times and whip it out on the guitar. All the old-timers ... we would play some of their stuff.

And we listened to the radio. I think I heard Blind Blake, he had a fifteen-minute show back in thirty-one or thirty-two, and he was the only black guy that I ever heard on the radio, was Blind Blake in the thirties. But he only had fifteen minutes, so I didn't get much of his music off of it, but I just knew that somewhere, down the line, I would do it too.

We used to go over to Clayton Barnard's service station to listen to it. WJZ, something out of Roanoke. It was a fifteen-minute show came on in the evening around 4:15 or 5:15. And we listened to the "Grand Old Opry." I used to listen to Deford Bailey, you know. He was the guy who played "Up the Country Blues" and "Muscle Shoals Blues," and he was from Tennessee. You know, he was one of the early famous stars of the Nashville "Grand Old Opry."[10]

So I kind of established myself with my father, John Hurt, Blind Lemon, and Blind Boy Fuller, a little bit of Barbecue Bob, Furry Lewis. And then I had to put myself in there somehow. So I squeeze a percent of myself in. A lot of stuff I do comes from their music, but since a lot of stuff is mine, it comes from the same background. All those guys are great musicians, and I try to be as good as they are.

But my greatest inspiration was hearing my dad. So I guess when I got old enough and my dad played and other people played, it just kept building up and building up. So I just kept following through on it and I made it. I grew up listening to that kind of music. Lots of times we would work all day in the fields, the cornfields and the tobacco fields. Come home at night and eat dinner and sit out in the yard. And by the moonlight, my daddy would play the guitar or five-string banjo. He did that until I was big enough to start playing the guitar. Then it changed over. When I started playing, he sat there and listened to me.

He was probably the one that got me out in the public, too, because he said, "Son, you play a good guitar, but don't waste your talent like I did mine. You get out there and do something with it," you know. So I said, "Well, I better do it," 'cause the old man asked me to do it. So I think I better go out there and try, you know. Yeah.

And the stuff I play today is what I heard growing up, you know. Go to a house party, hear someone playing a good tune. I would just keep it. A lot of my early songs were just from hearing it. When I picked up a song, I'd never forget it. I had the best ear for it and the most drive power. So I was determined to do it. And by me having so much determination, I brought the rest of them along pretty good too. But I was determined to play the guitar like the old-timers.

The first prayer I ever prayed in my life was "Lord, let me play the guitar like these old-timers." And so he did it. I'm playing like them. And I said, "They did it and so can I." So I know if I'd keep going, I'd be out there someday. Nobody has ever been able to say anything to me to discourage me. That was a goal that I set my eyes on when I was a kid. So it paid off just exactly the way I planned.

Working at the Sawmill

Then it went from there to after you got old enough to work at the sawmill, you go to the sawmill to work for a dollar a day. Cut timber all day long, snake logs down to the mill or either you would off-bear the lumber you know, from the saw. I started at the sawmill when I was just sixteen. A lot of guys from all over Virginia were working at this big sawmill camp. The name of the place was John Turner's Sawmill.

We would go out in the woods and cut down trees, and you could hear those guys singing the blues all over the woods there. They would sing while they were working cutting down a tree, sing while they were cutting until the tree drops. It was a musical thing. You hear one guy over there singing the blues and the other one answering back. They would sing all along the line. Somebody would be singing all day. It kind of makes you think of the old songs from the levee camps, but they consisted mostly of prisoners. But in the sawmills, the guys had the same spirit. Sing while they work. Of course, they didn't have any guns and dogs on them, but they would just sing the blues alone by themselves.

So I'm listening to all this and I said, "Well, I'm gonna sing these sawmill songs one day." You know they sang "Red River Blues" where it has the verse:

I know, yes, I know
Why the poor boys don't draw no more
Because the line starts at the pay table
And goes straight to the commissary door.

Well, I know about that because this is what really happened. They work all the week and they would buy cigarettes and candy and whatnot on credit, you see. And when the foreman sets up his pay table in a little tent, you go there to the door and call your name. Everybody lines up first, like they do in the army. Line up and you call your name. You walk up and they hand you a little envelope.

Well, the first thing they do then after they deducted out what you owed them, the rest of it they would take and go straight to the commissary and buy cigarettes and sodas and candy. So this is why they say, "I know why the poor boys don't draw no more, because the line starts at the pay table and goes straight to the commissary door."

But the funny thing about this whole thing, my brother James and I, we was working at the sawmill and we didn't take up anything. So the man said, "We can't make any money off those two little Edwards boys because they don't buy anything." So whatever we made, we got it. Wasn't getting but a dollar a day, but at the end of the week we got our five dollars because we didn't owe him a penny. I didn't smoke, didn't drink, didn't gamble. And if I wanted to buy candy, I would pick it up at the little grocery store when I go out and go home.

I did some of all the things there, like cutting logs and off-bearing lumber and working on the yard down at the mill. Most of the times they start you off in the woods, cutting trees and helping load it and get it down to the mill. Then after you work out in the woods for a while, they bring you down to the sawmill and let you off-bear lumber. You know, when they put the big logs on the, what you call the skids, to bring it up to the saw.

When they bring it up, the saw hits it and cuts off a slab. You have to take that off and throw that on the slab pile. And then the lumber you take off and carry it and stick it on the lumber pile. Sometimes you have four or five guys there, because if the saw man, if he's a real saw man, now he keeps you busy. Now he'll rip a log in two in a hurry. So by the time you get this piece of lumber and walk away with it, by the time you drop it down and come back, it's another one waiting for you.

So sometimes it's five or six of us off-bearing lumber. But it was fun. Very seldom you have a piece of lumber big enough to double on. So they was cutting from inch boards, eight-by-tens, and then they cut some cross ties for railroading and also they cut some heavy timber for building houses, you know, for foundations for big houses. So those eight-by-twelves, it takes three good guys to move those. It was oak logs, eight inches by twelve inches, and sometimes it's twenty feet long.

So when the skid comes up there, you take a hold on it and the other guy get a hold of it, the next thing there's three guys got it and you walk away with it.

And they had an old slogan at the sawmill: "Eat beans and don't grumble / And walk steady and don't stumble." Because, beans was the main course of meal there. Beans and corn bread, or maybe a piece of fatback. And, buddy, if you was walking away with one of those big eight-by-tens or whatever, and if you stumble, somebody gets hurt. They say: "Eat beans and don't grumble / And walk steady and don't stumble." That was the slogan around the sawmill.

The work conditions was very pleasant. Frankly speaking, the sawmill is a pleasant place to work because you're with different people, and the work is not so bearing that it puts a lot of pressure on you. You can work with a free mind. You're out there in the fresh air and the sunshine. The boss is not hard on you. So you just get out there. And you have three guys together. One guy to pick the tree we gonna cut down. He will clear and clear around it with the ax, cut the shrubbery around it. Then you have to cut a little lead gap in it. Then me and my brother would saw it. But if you cut a tree down without putting a lead gap in it, it's not gonna fall the way you want it to fall.

See, you have to figure out how you want it to fall without falling on some of the other workers or falling against another tree and letting it hang up there, you know. Then it would have a chance to fall later on and kill somebody. So you have to figure out which way it should go so it will hit the ground. So it was a man with an ax and two guys with the saw. The man with the ax would clear the way around the trunk of the tree and then he would cut this lead gap in it. And the saw men will saw it down with a crosscut saw.

When you cut the tree down you measure it. If you want it twenty feet, then you measure it twenty feet, and then you cut it in twenty-feet blocks. If you want it thirty or whatever, well, you have a tape measure and you block it off in so many feet and you cut it. And snaking logs, you got a big chain with something like arms on it, you know. And we would pick this chain up and come back and grab the butt end of the log in it and fit those spikes, call them chain dogs. Sometimes you take a hammer and drive them in and then when you do that, you hook it to the tractor or the horses and you drag it down through the woods to the mill.

But these chain dogs, you got to have them to grab it. Those spikes are about so long and sharp on the end, see. You drive them in so they won't come out and then, buddy, you hook them to the horses or your tractor and down through the woods you go. That's what you call "snaking it."

And then you would pick up some country blues from there. A lot of guys from different parts of the country would be around the sawmill. I learned some good stuff from the sawmill. We'd play at night. We had this big old house there, something they called a shanty with a lot of bunk beds. It just so happened that my bunk was at the bottom, so I'd sit at the side of my bunk and play the guitar. Yeah, sometimes stay up until two or three o'clock in the morning playing guitar.

Sometimes two or three guys in the group have a guitar. One guy in a corner playing some blues, another guy in another corner. Or we would trade back and forth. Yeah, kind of swap songs, like I'd play a number or so, another guy would pick it up, play a song or two. You'd go around just like we do here in the barbershop. Only thing about it, we didn't have no corn liquor or stuff to drink. But it's the same old tradition, and I got pretty popular at the sawmill camp with the guitar.

There was one guy there that was a pretty good musician. I think his name was James Coker. He played pretty good guitar. He played the "Lovin' Spoonful" in the key of G. And there was another guy by the name of T. J. Pace and he would sing some pretty blues. And I learned one of Blind Boy Fuller's songs from another boy. So I learned a whole lot at the sawmill. Some boys would play poker, some would pitch horse-shoes, but I would sit around and pick the guitar and listen to the other guys play. They would play blues, songs like "Red River Blues," "How Long Blues," "Going Up the Country," "Poor Boy Blues," and "Stack O'Lee," "John Henry," "West Virginia Rag," "Coney Island Blues," songs we heard on the radio. And then the next day we had nothing to do but go out and cut wood.

We'd work from Monday morning until Saturday. It's a five-and-a-half day week. Knock off at twelve o'clock Saturday, then you'd go home.

Me and my brother James used to walk from the sawmill home on Saturdays. Leave at twelve o'clock, then we'd get home about one-thirty, two o'clock. That's when he and I were together, by ourselves. But we had one guy that was working there with us, the Mr. John Cosby that I was telling you about. Now he walked like a snail. Man, he leave at twelve o'clock, it will be good five o'clock getting home. Many times me and my brother James tried to walk away from him. But he'd holler, "Hey, wait a minute, wait a minute." I'd say, "Oh my God. We got to stand here and wait until he catches up." But he was a good old guy. A very comical old man.

House-Party Days

About the only livelihood we had on the weekends was just house par-ties. That was the only thing except going to church. Going to church on Sunday was a must for a lot of those people there.

Frankly speaking, my first early church experiences was something that I probably picked up myself. My father, he didn't go to church and my mother, she went occasionally. But we never went to church to-gether. So when my mother used to go to church, I was too little to go. See, I had to stay home.

So I was up around fourteen or fifteen years old, kind of venturing out on my own, when I first started church. And so I went to church Sundays and Sunday school on Sunday morning for a while. And shortly

after that I made up my mind to become a member of the church and
so I joined the church. My mother and father, they weren't there when I
did that either. So I kind of been on my own doing the things I thought
was best for me. It was a little church, called the Union Hall Baptist
Church in Union Hall, Virginia.

My mother had been a member of that church before me but
Daddy, he didn't get into the church for a long time. He didn't join the
church until I brought him to Washington, D.C., a few years before he
died. He was an independent thinker and had his own way of doing
things. He was semireligious, but he never attended church. But he
wasn't a stone devil. He had some respect for God. Later on, when I
brought him here from Virginia to Seat Pleasant, he became a member
and was baptized there. You know how people live a moral life by just
being themselves, tending to their own business, and not bothering anybody. Of course, he would get upset every once in a while and say a few
curse words, but that's about all. Maybe take a little drink. He was what
you call a regular guy.

Well, I left Virginia pretty soon after I got big enough to get into
church. I attended church very regularly in Virginia before I left home,
and I attend church here. I'm a member of the Baptist Church, the
Highland Park Baptist Church, the big church on the highway. I've attended for years.

Back in Franklin County, we didn't play guitar in the church. Most
country churches, they didn't have any music like guitars or pianos. You
went there and you just sing old hymns. But as far as taking an instrument in the church, no, they didn't do that. But the church people didn't
interfere with you if you had the desire to be a musician. I didn't have
much of a problem there.

On Sunday, the religious people went to church, that was their big
day, church on Sundays. But for the youngsters, Saturday night party
was a must. You must get to that house party because you'd meet different people and get a chance to converse with them and swap ideas with
them. If you wanted to play the guitar or hear somebody play a guitar
and get a chance to run off a little steam, you went to a country party.
They would have them maybe twice a month or sometimes every Saturday night.[11] This family maybe give a party this Saturday night; people
eat, drink, dance, and have fun. And the next week or so, someone else
would throw a party. It just kind of rotated around.

Now, they didn't give those parties where everything was free.
Whoever gave a party in the country sold a little something. They had
the party to pick up a little change and they wasn't rich enough to have
a party say, "Come on in man, it's free." No. You come in there, a cold

soda was five cents, which was just about the same thing as at the store. But when they sold them at the house party they did it for the purpose of making a little extra money. They all charged a little something.

They'd catch a couple of chickens and wring their necks off and cook them so they had hot fried chicken and homemade biscuits. They sell them for, oh, you could get a chicken thigh and a biscuit for about fifteen cents back in those days. And they had sodas, go to the store and get them some big Nehi drinks and have a big old tub under the table, put some ice in it, and sell them for five cents.

But the biggest thing they had to sell was whiskey. They had maybe three or four quarts of corn liquor there. You go in there, buy a soda, and if nobody is in there that looks like they might be a law official or something, you say, "Give me a shot." And they get that corn liquor out from under the table and pour a little glass of it. A shot of liquor was ten, twenty-five cents.

Well, they didn't get rich off it. But they might make twenty or twenty-five dollars. Back in those days, twenty or twenty-five dollars was a big deal. So they went and bought a few sodas, killed a few chickens, baked a few biscuits, and sold a couple of half a gallons of corn liquor. Well, that's a big night, you know. Come up with a pocket full of change the next morning. Money was kind of hard to get. If a man wanted to buy his wife something or do a little something, maybe give a little party, might wind up making twenty dollars.

I started playing the guitar at house parties when I was very young. I had a brother named Willie, my older brother, and he bought an old Model-A Ford. He would just frequent these house parties, and the only way that I could get a chance to go to one at my age . . . my brother would go to the party and start woofing at the older musicians and tell people about him having a little brother at home in the bed sleeping that could beat them playing the guitar. So they'd say, "OK. Go home and get him." You know. They'd send him home after me.

So he would come home at twelve o'clock, sometimes one o'clock, two o'clock in the morning, and ask my mother. Say, "Mama, can Archie go to the party, nobody's there that can play the guitar." You know what I mean, but he was saving his butt because the people say, "You go get him," or else they're gonna kick his butt. She would say yes.

Now this is how I got a chance to be exposed to the public when I was about twelve or thirteen. I got one song, in particular, an instrumental that I run together I used to call the "Saturday Night Hop," simply because I used to hop out of bed every Saturday night and go somewhere and play that song.

I'd hop out of bed, grab my little old guitar and jump in the car with him. We go click-clunk down the road, across the wood, to the

Willie Edwards in Union Hall, 1988. *Photo by Segrid Pearson.*

house party. And when we get to the house party, there's old musicians there. Tough guys. But by me being young and stupid, I guess I was too stupid to be afraid, so I'd buck up against them. And I played with them. I played along with them.

But in the meantime, I was learning from them. So it helped me a lot. Got me to the point where I wasn't afraid to appear in public, and it gave me something to look forward to. It instilled in me to become a musician. Today, I thank him for it, because he helped make me what I am today.

But with all the lies he told, it turned out he's a preacher now. If he's saved, I'm saved. Yeah, everything works out good for those that trust God. I used to laugh, man, that guy come home that time of night, get me out of the bed to go and play guitar, it's got to be something behind it. But he became a preacher, though. Now I know that anything can happen. He used to be a devil, my older brother. My older brother used to be a devil . . . whoo!

But my brother Robert, he was a youngster just like me. Our parents didn't let us out at night. Biggest thing we would enjoy would be getting out from home, getting out from home and being able to meet the public and play the guitar. Sometimes them old schoolgirls might be there, give you a chance to look at her and say something, you know. Little country girls round there, you get in there and buy them a soda or two. You drink a little soda and dance a little.

So I enjoyed going to parties to break the monotony and get a chance to meet the public. Yeah, we always enjoyed getting out on Saturday night after working on the farm all day, all the week. Get home on Saturday night, clean up, get out and meet the public and play the guitar. Sometimes there'd be four or five people that could play, sometimes just me and Robert. But most of the time there'd be some pretty good guitar pickers. My older brother, he would play, sit down, do a set, couple of songs. Might play for a while, put his guitar down. He might even leave, get a couple drinks in him, get in the car and ride off to another party somewhere.

At a party I would play until I got tired, then I'd hand Robert the guitar and he'd play. But he won't play now, and he never would sing. If we had two guitars, we'd play together. If we had one, he'd play after me.

We used to go over at Willie Edwards's house, we had the same name, but we weren't related. We used to play the guitar and he give us a cold soda, chicken leg, and a biscuit, something like that. Back in those days there wasn't no money. The people didn't have much to pay you, and I wasn't old enough to drink whiskey. So the proprietor, or whoever was in charge, would give us cold sodas, a couple of pieces of hot fried chicken and I was satisfied. That was really the only entertainment back in the country. If someone didn't give a house party, they had no entertainment. It was a really good time. I call it good times when times was hard.

Robert and I were sidekicks. He could play anything I could play, but he wouldn't sing. That's how people could tell us apart. Every time somebody would be having a party they ask, "Who's playing?" Archie and Robert. So we made a good reputation for ourselves around home. Archie and Robert. You can go down home now and find some old people who will say, "Well, yeah, I remember them boys when they were growing up. They're mighty good guitar pickers." Yeah, you can find people that knew me and my brother when we were sixteen or seventeen years old.

Once you in a little community where everybody got to know everybody, they can get together, have some fun. Now the thing about it, the guys ten, fifteen, twenty miles away would hear about it. They'd come in and try to take the girls over and then that would be the problem. Down in Union Hall, if they had a community party, you wouldn't have any problem. But sometimes guys from Roanoke or thereabouts say, "Let's see if we can find a country party." They'd stop and ask questions, "Anybody giving a party tonight?" And then they crash the party. They ain't got no women with them. They come into the party, get a few drinks, next thing you know they corner somebody's girl over there, you know. Dudes get tough on it, have a few little fistfights.

But in those days news couldn't travel too fast. You could drive through a little town and didn't see no one to ask questions 'cause people went to bed. So you could drive right through the town and not see a damn soul, so you didn't know nothing. "Hey man, who's giving the party tonight?" Nobody's giving a party tonight because they don't want you there. But then, if somebody was to say, oh yeah, such and such a person's having a party, somebody may want a ride. "Jump in, I'll take you there." The dudes coming bring in four or five buddies.

Those country dances in Union Hall, I enjoyed them though they were rough in certain parts of the state. Now it never happened to me, but I have known other people tell me that they have been to parties where the husbands or boyfriends of some women would get jealous, angry with the musicians because he might play a song that some of the women might like and they might smile at him, say something to him, and there might be a fight over that. But I guess it never happened to me because I was too young to cut my eyes back at them.[12]

I was playing the guitar pretty good at that time and I had another brother, James; boy, that guy would fight all the time. He's here in Washington, D.C. My brother Robert and I used to go to parties to play the guitar, but we couldn't play because people would run in the house telling us, "Archie, your brother James is outside fighting."

We were trying to play and sing and he was outside fighting, you know. Sometimes I wish we had known to put boxing gloves on him and put him in the ring to become a prizefighter. We could have made some money on him.

But he fought all the time. Yeah, my brother James fight all the time. The last time I was going on a vacation, before my mother and father were disabled to work, I was supposed to be down in Virginia two weeks. But I had to leave there early because my brother James had been in a fight and the law was looking for him. Some guy done bit his thumb halfway off. I said, "Mama, I got to go, because I got to get James away from here." "Yeah, take him on, Archie. Take him on home."

So my brother got in the back seat of my car in Rocky Mount, Virginia. He was laying down in the back seat with something over him, scared the police was looking for him. About forty miles up the highway he sat up in the back seat and said, "I don't want to go back there." I said, "I don't blame you. I wouldn't go either, because you sure caught hell while you were there." Always in a fight. Always in a fight. I don't think he's gone home more than once or twice since then.

Then we had this younger brother, Wayman. They named him "Switchblade Boy." Oh, my brother Wayman would cut you. I don't care what you say or what you did. If you made him mad, he was gonna cut you. Yes, indeed. He was known to cut you.

The last time my brother Wayman got into a fight my brother said, "If you do it again, I'm going to cut your guts out." So the guy did it. So my brother took his knife and, whoosh, cut him across the belly and the guy reached in there and caught his guts. So my brother Wayman, I never deal with him too much. But he was one that was known to cut you.

And some people today will tell me, say, "Archie, you mean to tell me you're a brother to Wayman and James?" They say, "Unbelievable." There are people living today that would never be convinced that I was James and Wayman's brother. My brothers Wayman, James, and Willie was kind of on the rough side. And there's three on the good side. Me and Robert were the two that grew up together, never had any trouble. Never did anything wrong. We grew up and left home clean. My baby brother, Oliver, he's clean. He's a little preacher too. But Willie, James, and Wayman was the three that the people says, "They're not related to Archie, Robert, and Oliver." But we're brothers. You can't convince people that we were brothers. There's just that much difference.

But we all got along. Robert and I, we didn't try to be like the other brothers because we decided the easy way was the best way. We didn't have any real bosses among us, and we understood if one of my brothers was disagreeable we didn't bother him. So, I guess that's why it always ended up with me and Robert together, because we were the only two that could really see eye-to-eye and get along. The rest were hot-tempered. James was hot-tempered, so I didn't bother him too much. And Wayman, he was younger than me, so I didn't have time, a chance to bother him, because I left home real early. And my brother Robert left too, because the war came.

So that was another part of my life story. These things make me feel pretty good, to sit down and reminisce. Think about, backtrack, and retrace yourself. You trace your life this way. But there's not too many people can do these things. Things that happened to me when I was a kid don't fade out too fast. It seems like to me something tells me, "Remember this, because it's gonna be history someday."

Leaving Home

Around '37 I left the sawmill and worked for a doctor, a fellow named Dr. Doss. I used to work around the house for him, cut the grass, even drive his car a little bit from to time. But, frankly speaking, I looked forward to getting old enough to leave home. Get out on your own to try to get someplace. Because the parents back in those days, they didn't have too much, but they gave you encouragement so you wanted to do something for yourself. See, you wanted to better your condition. You grew up on the farm and had plenty of food, plenty to eat, a place to sleep and everything. My mother and father made everything as comfortable as possible. But after they feed you and clothe you to get to be a certain age, you go to school and get what education you can. Then you learn in school about what you call the distant lands, you know. And you're crazy to go there, to see what's over there, to see if it's better. Then, when you get there, if it's better, you keep on going.

But when I got ready to leave home, I didn't have any money. Me and a friend of mine, named Douglas Poindexter, we were old school buddies, went to school together, ran around together, courting, going to see our girlfriends, everything. So the last thing Doug and I did together, or next to the last thing, we decided to go and sign up for the CC Camp. Three C's, you know. So we signed up for the CC Camp. But the lady said it would be about six weeks before there would be another vacancy.

So, during the time we had signed up, between the time that she was going to call us, Douglas Poindexter and I decided to make a little run, you know, make some corn liquor, so we could have a little spending money. So we went and bought the corn meal and we bought the stuff that my dad needed to put us up a little run. So he put us up a little run and ran it. Doug and I, we split the expense and we split the whiskey. So I sold my whiskey.

So that's always been what my encouragement was, to better your condition, see, to make out with what you got until you get better. So, when I got old enough to leave home, I left. And I just kept climbing... kept climbing... kept climbing.

My oldest sister, Thelma, was living in New Jersey and a friend of ours, about my sister's age, was living in New York. He was coming down to Virginia for two weeks' vacation. And in the meantime he had found a job for an errand boy, somebody to run errands for a dry-cleaning plant in New York. So he told my sister about it because he was working there himself. So he told my sister, "I'm gonna bring your brother Archie back up when I come because he's smart. I think he can handle the job."

So my sister called me, said, "Eddie Edwards wants to bring you back to New York with him." And she says, "You think you can handle this job?"

I said, "I don't know. Maybe."

She says, "Well, go on back with him and if that job don't work out, I'll get you a job over in Jersey where I am."

So this is what happened when I get to New York with my buddy, Eddie Ewards. We were both Edwards, but we weren't related that I knew of. But anyway, we get to New York and the man had filled this vacancy. He had found some city boy to take care of the job. When I got there the man says, "I hired a boy the other day, but keep in touch and maybe something will come up and I'll give you something to do."

I said, "Well, that's OK."

So, I stayed in New York for a while and got kind of homesick and was planning on coming back to Virginia. So I called my sister over in Jersey and told her, "The man has got somebody for this job." She said, "Hang on over there with Eddie for a week or so. If nothing shows up, I'll see what I can do over here."

That was because my sister was working for a private family, and quite a few people was friends with the lady that she worked for. And she had a pretty decent reputation, you know. So after I didn't get the job, she said, "I know a lady by the name of Mrs. Dean that's a good friend of Mrs. Gaffny's. She has a boy and a girl, school age, and they live pretty close to school but she wants somebody to help her around the house a little bit and drive the kids to school. You think you can handle it?"

"Yeah, I can handle it. I can drive."

So I went over there to Park Ridge, New Jersey, to work for Mrs. Dean. I got my driver's permit and drove the kids to school and helped Mrs. Dean around the house there. In the meantime, she taught me to be a hell of a good cook. I don't let people know that I can cook, but I can cook.

So about two years I stayed around there working as a chauffeur and a butler, you know. It's called, back in those days, a chauffeur and a butler. Working in the kitchen, serving dinners and helping with the dishes and whatnot.

Sometimes I would go back home to visit. Take the bus from New Jersey and get off in Rocky Mount, Virginia. They did have one little place in Rocky Mount where there used to be music. It was run by a cousin of mine named Grant Poindexter and we called it Grant's Place. Now one guy was booked in there pretty often. I met him even before I went to New Jersey. He was named Noah Davis. Now his real name was Noah Lewis and he said he was Furry Lewis's half brother, but, see, his daddy was a Davis.[13] Now I had heard about him from my brother because he and his wife played in there. She played piano and he played guitar and harmonica.

So I met him one day. Me and my brother were driving and here he come walking and hopping up Tank Hill. His feet were hurting him, so I told my brother that he wanted to rest. So we called him over. He said, "What can I do for you, son?" I told him, "Get in the car."

He had his guitar with him, a hollow-body cutaway guitar, so he played us a couple of pieces and then asked if I could play. So I played a tune and he said, "Son, you're doing pretty good."

But he said he was Furry Lewis's half brother, and he used to play around there at Grant's Place. Later on the name of the place was changed to Joe's Grill because Grant had a half brother named Joe Edwards, and he took it over. Then when he died, his brother, Eddie, took it over. That was the same man, Eddie Edwards, that carried me to New York back in 1938. See, there were two families of Edwards, but they were not related. Eddie had another brother who was blind named Clayborn Edwards, and he was a pretty good musician. He was older than me, but we were friends and I used to lead him around and we would hang out together.

The last time we played music together was back in 1939. I came back to Franklin County one time for a vacation when I was working in New Jersey. So on a Sunday night I was waiting for the Pan American Bus, that's an express, runs from New York to Florida, to take me back to New Jersey. And it used to stop in Rocky Mount about eleven o'clock in the evening. So I was in this restaurant, Grant's Place, and I had my guitar and Clayborn Edwards had his guitar. So we played together on songs like "Meet Me in the Bottom," "Undertaker Blues," until I had to leave and catch the bus.

But the funny part, there was a girl who was working there that night. Her name was Susan Gravley. So my mother went in there some time later and she was still working there. So she told my mother, "Aren't you Pearl Edwards, got a boy that can play the guitar? Oh, I heard that boy. I'd rather hear that boy play the guitar than eat when I'm hungry."

Yeah, she talked about me and my mother told me about it.

But most all those places are gone now. The old family home burned down in the early seventies. My cousin, Moses Spencer, lives out where it used to be, but it's all changed now. The store is still there, J. H. English's place up the hill from the service station on the way to Willie's place. I played the guitar up there not too long ago.

But the house is gone and Clayton's station is gone, and when I went back I found out that Joe's Grill is gone, too. It closed five or six years ago. I went down there and drove around the other day. It was raining like hell, so I stopped and asked the man, "Where's Joe's place at?" He said, "Man, it's gone." So I jumped back in my car and kept going.

But we used to go into Rocky Mount a lot. We used Rocky Mount, that's the county seat, as our home address. Those other little places, well, most people don't know a thing about Union Hall, but if you say Rocky Mount, Virginia, well, some of them don't know about Rocky Mount. They say, "North Carolina?" "No, Virginia."

They all work in Rocky Mount, you know. All my nieces and nephews, all started out working in Rocky Mount. So I guess I'm one who grew up and left there. But I worked in Rocky Mount. My oldest brother, he worked in Rocky Mount. My brother Wayman, he worked in Rocky Mount. So just about the whole family did. Left from Union Hall up to Rocky Mount and worked there, then went on to other places. Like I did when I worked in New Jersey.

So I kept on working in New Jersey, and after I did that for about two years it dawned on me one evening, "Now, wait a minute. This is not a real man's job, man. You're young. Get out there and face it. You know, face it." So I said, "Hell, I'm gonna leave here."

So I wrote Mrs. Dean a note: "Mrs. Dean, I've been around here for two years now and I really appreciate what you have done for me, but I am going to get me a man's job." And I jumped me a bus and came back to Roanoke, Virginia. Worked in Roanoke for a little while. The man that I worked for there, he was something like the president of the Lindsey Robinson Milling Company, did a lot of milling of flour and meal and for hog food or whatnot. So I worked for him for about six months. It was the same type of job that I'd had in New Jersey. I didn't like that, so I said, "Well, time to move again."

Army Life

So I went down to the Greyhound bus station and caught me a bus to Columbus, Ohio. Went to Columbus, Ohio, stayed there until Mr. Roosevelt said, "You got to do a year's service."

After I got to Columbus and started working in the hotel, the Deshler Wallace Hotel in downtown Columbus, everywhere I went there was a man, Uncle Sam, saying, "I want you! I want you!" I said, "Oh hell, I'm sick of that." I wasn't old enough. But I worked there for a while and one boy in Columbus, Ohio, that encouraged me a lot, his name was Roger Donaldson. He was twenty-seven years old. He was about eight years older than I was, but I wasn't yet twenty.

Then, in 1940, President Roosevelt decided all young men from the age of twenty-one up would have to register for the army, see, and I wasn't old enough. I volunteered because my buddy, he was drafted and he said he would go in and do his one year and he was coming back to Columbus, you know, and start life over again.

Well, we was such buddy buddies. I said, "Well, since you been drafted, I'm gonna enlist so I can come back with that behind me." So I said, "Well, Roger, I'll tell you what I'm going to do. I'm gonna enlist and go and do my year and come back at the end of the year, and we'll be back at the same time. We can be buddies again." But the funny part about it, after I enlisted, just before I completed my year, the Japs bombed Pearl Harbor. I was hoping we would do our year and come out, but the Japs hit Pearl Harbor, December 7, 1941, and, buddy, that was it. That was it. Four years and nine months and twenty-six days later I came out. And I haven't seen Roger Donaldson since. Never seen the boy since. So it played a trick on me. So that's the way life works out.

That's when I wrote "Pittsburgh Blues."[14] See, an old girlfriend of mine, she had moved to Pittsburgh. When I found out where she was, I said, "I'm going to Pittsburgh." But I never did get to Pittsburgh because when I went in the service, I didn't see her no more.

When I first went in the service they sent me to Camp Blanding, Florida. I used to hang out in Jacksonville and Gainesville, a couple little towns in South Florida. I was around through Florida in my army days. I was in the military police in Camp Blanding, so I used to do a lot of pounding the beats in Jacksonville, all up and down Duvall Street.

I used to like Florida, but one thing about it. The guys that were familiar with Florida came up with a great big alligator and tied it right in the mess-hall yard, up to a big, old oak tree. And he would play possum on you, looking at you when he's asleep. And they'd say, "Don't get too close to him, buddy, cause he'll snap you." I didn't trust anything that laid in the yard with all these people around. I didn't trust him because he had his eyes shut. Now, anybody can tell you that with all that noise he gonna lay there with his eyes shut? Anybody would know he's playing possum on you! So, if you get close to him, he's gonna grab you.

No, I don't trust nothing with his eyes shut. Because if he's that close to being dead, they should bury the dude. But, he's laying there, under the shade tree, with his eyes shut. And you're supposed to walk right past him in the chow line. I said, "No way."

I had quite a few experiences while I was in the service. One of the greatest experiences that I had in the service during the time I was in Camp Blanding, the guy, Howling Wolf,[15] was down there in the same camp that I was in. So I got a chance to play his guitar and he heard me play and he advised me to continue because he liked what I was doing, so that made me feel pretty good.

Then they sent me over to Van Dorn, Mississippi. In the back of my mind I knew one day I would meet Mississippi John Hurt, so I kept picking the guitar. And I was stationed in a little town called Centreville, Mississippi, and I asked a lot of people if they knew Mississippi John Hurt. Well, some of the old-timers around there knew him, but they didn't know where he was. He had kinda faded out. So I stayed in Mississippi about two, three years, and didn't find John Hurt. I didn't find John Hurt, but I always had it in my mind I would meet him.

They sent me from there to Breckinridge, Kentucky, and from Breckinridge, Kentucky, they sent me to Fort Warren, Wyoming, and from there I went to Arizona and then on to Seattle, Washington, and from there to Hawaii, and finally to Okinawa. I ended up on Okinawa after the war ended. That's where I was in 1945, in the mud holes on Okinawa. That's when I wrote "Duffel Bag Blues."[16]

But we had a president then who wasn't afraid of people. That was Harry Truman. President Roosevelt had just died some months before and we were down there on Okinawa ready to invade Japan, which I don't know if we would have made it or not. But Harry Truman dropped the bomb. He dropped the atomic bomb on them so we came home. I'm down there in the mud, so I said, "Thank you, Mr. Truman."

So I went in the service, came out four years, nine months, and twenty-six days after. I came out in January 1946. But then I re-upped and went back in, about six or eight weeks later, in order to get that two-hundred dollar bonus. I stayed in one more year and got out around the first of January 1947, sometime after Christmas.

And then, during the Korean War, I was in the reserves and Mr. Truman called up all the reserves. But I didn't go overseas because of all the time I had been in the service before, when I had already been overseas. I spent a year training troops in Fort Lee, Virginia, with the 972d Quartermaster Laundry Division.

You know, my brother Robert, he also went into the service during World War II. He got five battle stars because he was in five battles in Europe, from North Africa to Italy. So he came back with five battle stars plus a souvenir. He was in a foxhole one day and the Germans was watching him. He came up real slow and they shot a hole right through his steel hat. That's a souvenir. But, if he'd come up a little faster, he wouldn't be here.

I was a military police officer. The military, the army, it was all right at the particular time, because you didn't know any better. It was Jim Crow. Yeah, very Jim Crow. But today you would say it was hell, because you go to town on the bus and they had certain areas for black soldiers to sit. Certain parts of town that you could go, other parts of town you couldn't go. And the barracks on the post, you know, you have a certain area over here for the black soldier, over here for the white soldier. So we had to go to different recreation centers, and all that stuff, you know. It was—now sitting here listening, talking, telling about it—it was really hell. But at the time, you know, change hadn't come. We hadn't gotten educated to the fact that we were being pushed around and less thought of than the white soldiers, because we were in there for the same purpose. It was different then. But General Eisenhower, he broke that up after the war ended.

After leaving home I played off and on. Some of the time I would have a guitar available and some of the time I wouldn't. So, every time I had a chance, I got a hold of a guitar and I would play some. I know the last guitar that I had that I bought from a guy . . . I think it was on Okinawa . . . I kept it for a while, then turned around and sold it to a fellow. Then after that I didn't get any guitars from 1945 up until 1952.

The worst time was when I was in the service. I didn't play a lot, but I never felt discouraged. No. My life, as far as my music was concerned, it was just like a good interesting book. You could read so many pages, lay it down, you go back and pick it up. That's the way it was when I was in the service. It was so many years that I didn't play the guitar. But I had my mind set on it that when I got loose, got back to civilian life, I would play my guitar. So I did.

I bought another guitar, that old Harmony with pearl inlaid in the neck. I bought that for forty-nine dollars, for a Christmas present in 1952. But a comical thing happened when I got out of the service and bought my first guitar. I couldn't play a note. Not one note. Everything was blocked out. Army life had blocked out everything.

I said, "Wait a minute. I know I used to play the guitar."

So, I went to bed that night and kind of concentrated on my music. I woke up the next morning, and picked up the guitar, and started playing...just like that. All of a sudden it just snapped back to me, just like turning on a light. I was right back in the old slot with my guitar. So I've been off and running ever since.

Washington, D.C.

So, after I got out of the service, my older sister, the one that was in Jersey when I went to New York, she had moved to Washington. So when I got out of the service, I came directly to Washington. I landed here in 1946. So I've been here ever since.

After I came to Washington, I went to school on the GI Bill, and took up brick masonry. That was too hard work for me. I went to Richmond for a while, and took up barbering and came back and passed the exam. I got my apprentice license and I worked my apprenticeship out in two years under another barber. Then I went back and got my master's.

I worked for the government first as a truck driver. I started December 2, 1951, and worked for a long time, maybe twelve or fifteen years. And then I left the government and went to work for GEICO, Government Employees Insurance Company. I did everything. Laborer, truck driver, even worked in the mail room for a while. Then I went back to the government around 1969 and got on the security force as a guard. I worked as a security guard all around. At the District Building, the Municipal Center, and finally at the Welfare office. That finally got to me, and I retired back in 1981. So I gave the government thirty-something years.

Then I bought the barbershop on Bunker Hill Road back in 1959. That was about thirty years ago. It's many changes have taken place in this area. Used to be a drugstore next door there, a very nice drugstore. Doc Ballerton and his wife, they were nice people. You could go there and have a bite to eat. Anything you wanted to get, you get it on credit if you wanted to. Doc Ballerton was a fine man. But some of his little helpers that he had working for him undermined him, set him up, had him robbed and beat half to death. And, eventually, they shot a guy over there, robbed the place, and killed a man over there, one of his pharmacists. So when that happened, down the hill went Bunker Hill Road.

From 1959 to 1967 the barber business was fine. But then after 1969 things started to taper off a little bit. Everybody went to long hair, beards, and didn't care about getting a shave, haircut, or anything.

But I like to come over here to the barbershop because so many people in the neighborhood that I've been knowing since 1959, seems like to me to be a part of family, in a way of speaking.

The John Hurt Era

Now, Mississippi John Hurt, there's a story about him that you will never believe to save your life. I learned to play his pieces when I was a kid, "Stack O'Lee" and "Candy Man." I learned them in about 1931 or

Archie Edwards, Frances, and family, circa 1950s.
From Archie Edwards's private collection.

1932. And from then until 1964 I still played his songs. And I had a feeling in the back of my mind that I would meet him one day. I had looked for him in Mississippi, but I didn't find him. But I always had it in my mind that I would meet him because he was my idol.

The whole thing started in the John Hurt era. Mississippi John Hurt was rediscovered in the sixties, early sixties . . . sixty-one or -two. I had admired John Hurt's music all my life, since I was a kid. But after growing up, going in the service, and being sent to Mississippi, I took it for granted I would meet John Hurt. But I didn't meet him.

So later on, after I got out of the service and came back and settled down in the Washington area, I moved over to Seat Pleasant, Maryland, where I am now. So one Sunday morning, I was sitting out front there, sometime in June or July. A beautiful Sunday morning. And I was sitting there waiting for the little newspaper boy to bring the newspaper.

And he was late that particular day. Later on, way by and by, I saw him come dragging up the street. Here he comes with his bag over his shoulder, looked like every step was going to be his last. When he got up to my gate I got up off the doorstep there, walked down to the gate, and reached over and got the paper from him. And during the time I was standing there, a friend of mine that lived on the end of the block came up the street and said, "Archie, come on, let's go for a ride."

I said, "Man, I can't go for a ride."

He said, "Come on, I'll be right back."

I had just moved out there, and didn't know the city and the countryside or nothing, and he was gonna show me around. Plus he had a six-pack of Budweiser. You know I was going!

And so I said, "Oh, well, OK. I'll go."

I told my wife, I said, "Take the paper upstairs and put it on my side of the bed in the chair and don't let nobody bother with it because there's something in the newspaper that's gonna mean a lot to me."

And she stood there like she's saying, "What in the world is in this paper that he knows is gonna mean so much to him?"

But she did as I asked her to do. She carried the paper upstairs and put it on my side of the bed in the chair. So no one interfered with the paper.

On a Thursday evening I came home from work, and finally get to that Sunday paper. I was sitting out on the front porch, same place I was sitting on that Sunday morning. And I'm reading the paper, fingering through the paper. Every time I stopped to look at something, something say, "A little further, a little further," you know.

And, lo and behold, I finally flipped the page, saw this man sitting there with a guitar . . . "Mississippi John Hurt now appearing nightly in Washington, D.C. at the Ontario Place!"

I jumped up just like somebody that was going crazy. I ran into the kitchen. "Look honey, look honey, this is what I was telling you about. Look, look!"

She said, "What is it? What is it?"

I said, "This is Mississippi John Hurt, the man I was telling you about all my life."

She said, "Oh."

I said, "This is what was gonna mean so much to me."

She said, "Why you think that's gonna mean a lot to you when he's a professional and you're just nobody, in a way of speaking."

I said, "I don't care. I'm going there to meet him and we're going to have a time. You don't know John Hurt like I do."

And sure enough I did.

I called the club to check it out. I picked up the telephone and called the Ontario Place and asked them if it was true that John Hurt was down there. He said, "Oh yes, he's here. Every night, just like the paper stated." He said, "Do you know John Hurt?"

I said, "Yes, I sure do."

"Are you from Mississippi?"

I said, "No."

"How you know John Hurt?"

I said, "Well, I learned to play the guitar when I was a little boy and I learned to play 'Stack O'Lee' and 'Candy Man.' "

He said, "Oh, so you play guitar."

I said, "Uh-huh."

He said, "Well, you got the right man. Come on down here and tell him about it."

So I went down and told John about it and that was the beginning of mine and his friendship. I had laryngitis that night, but I told him who I was and everything. "Well, brother Arch," he'd say, "I'll tell you what. We'll get together sometime and when you can talk, we'll play and sing some."

It was a beautiful thing between me and John Hurt, 'cause for the last three years of his life he'd come to my house when he wasn't on the road, or I'd go to his house. Or we'd go to the barbershop, and we'd sit and play all night long until the sun came up. We just had ourselves a hell of a good time. When I met him it was like I'd known him all my life. We sounded so much alike. Now John and I had several things that we were doing just alike, even though he was from Mississippi and I was from Virginia. Most people thought I was his understudy, but I was playing that way before I met him. That knocked him for a loop. He didn't know anybody was still picking the guitar like him.

I worked with John Hurt for about three years then he went back down to Mississippi and passed away. I used to go down there on Rhode Island Avenue and pick him up because he lived at #30, Rhode Island Avenue, Northwest. So if he wasn't on the road, I would call him and tell him, "John, I'll come down and pick you up. We can go to the barbershop."

So we would go over there and he would sit and play the guitar for my customers. Sometimes we'd have a whole barbershop full of people. We've had them all the way out in the street, in the back and the front. I would be cutting a head of hair and if he played a song I felt he needed some backing on, I just put the tools down and pick up the guitar and follow him.

So we had a lot of fun there. Big audiences would come to hear me and John play and the people tell me about that now sometimes. "Man, I remember a time back in the sixties when you was doing big business here and John Hurt would come in here and play. A lot of people come to the barbershop just to hear you and John Hurt play."

I used to shave him and cut his hair. But the funny thing about John Hurt, I brought him past there one morning and he needed a shave. He said, "Brother Archie, let me use one of your razors. I want a shave." I said OK and let him have a straight razor and he must have been a little nervous because he lathered his face and started shaving and cut himself a couple times. He got to shaking. "Brother Archie, Brother Archie, please take this razor and finish shaving me." I said, "Yeah, I better, John, before you cut your throat."

But when we got together, we had some fun. We drank up many half pints. I didn't say nothing about that. But it's a shame, so many dead men go to the trash can. I never heard him use a curse word and I never knew him to do anything to anybody. But he would take a drink and smoke cigarettes. That's as far as he would go. I never knew him to speak an evil word against anybody. He was a very cool guy. You can't take it away from him. John Hurt could play the guitar. So it was an honor to meet a man like that.

I used to talk to his wife now and then, call her in Mississippi. His little granddaughter, Ella Mae, she came to Washington and stayed out in Seat Pleasant with me and my wife when she went to college.

We'd have Saturday night gatherings at the barbershop. The Gaines brothers, Leroy and Willie Gaines,[17] different people sit around, play the guitar, drink a few beers, a little whiskey. Willie Gaines, boy, he had a voice on him, like a bullhorn. He could holler so loud that your windowsills would rattle. Good Lord say, "Willie Gaines, get out there on that mountain and holler!" He'd wake them up. Yes, sir, Willie Gaines get up on some mountain and yell, he'd wake up everybody down in the valley.

That boy had a voice on him, and he was so stout he could take his
guitar strings and he could strip the strings off it, come back on it, and
pull the strings off it. He ruined so many guitar strings on me that I
said, "Wait a minute. My guitar strings don't wear out like this." I said,
"Willie, you're so strong that when you pull back, you tear the dad-
blamed strings up." Yes, sir, he was something. And Willie could dance,
too. He was an all-around guy.

Mother Scott used to come out to the shop. And Skip James.[18] He's
been here at the barbershop and played and sang with me. Back in
1964, Dick Spottswood had me on a contract with John Hurt and Skip
James, and we played at NIH, the National Institutes of Health.

I was a little late getting there that night and when I got there, Skip
James was on stage. Spottswood rushed me, got me ready to go on, and
so I went on before John Hurt. Now on my way there I had it in my
mind to play John Hurt's guitar, but it worked out that I played before
John Hurt. I had just bought a brand-new Gibson, one-fifty Gibson, so
when I come offstage, John Hurt asked me to let him play my guitar. So
I did. And I said, "Well, I'll tell everybody John Hurt played my guitar."
So that was the first time I performed for the public under contract with
other professionals.

I had met him before that. We had worked some at his house and
down here at the barbershop quite a lot. But the first time I hit the public was with John Hurt and Skip James. Skip James, he was a character.
We had another time when Mississippi John Hurt, Skip James, and me
were doing shows at the Ontario Place. John did a show, next week
Skip did a show, then it was my turn to do a show. Skip called me up
to come with him on his show, but I told him if I played on his show
then the people wouldn't come out to see me on my own show.

Anyway, I went down with him and you know, he got so drunk I
wound up doing his whole show. He fell off the stage and was lucky he
didn't break up his guitar. So I had to do the whole show. And the next
week, when I did my show, nobody showed up. They said, "We already
saw you last week." I think about ten people showed up.

After John Hurt went back to Mississippi and passed away, I kind
of retired from playing in public for a while. See, after I worked with
him for three years he asked me to carry on his work for him. So I
thought, "What has this guy done to me now?" Because that was a big
order, you know, carry John Hurt's work on for him. So I stayed at
home for about two years, didn't go out in public and studied and pon-
dered what to do. I said to myself, I can't face the public and tell them
that John Hurt asked me to carry on his work because they don't know
me. I'd be the laughingstock of the music world. "Who is this guy, coming out here claiming he was with John Hurt?" They would think I was

trying to steal his glory. So finally I decided I would write a song to show that I knew him and that's when I wrote "The Road Is Rough and Rocky." Then I was ready to face the public again.

Back in Action

I started going out again and played for a time with a group named The Travelling Blues Workshop.[19] This was John Jackson, John Cephas, Phil Wiggins, Mother Scott, Flora Molton, and some other musicians. It wasn't always the same group, but we would get together and put on a show.

I worked off and on at some clubs: McGuires up on Pennsylvania Avenue, Southeast, and Food for Thought. I also played for different festivals around the country and for the Smithsonian Festival here in Washington.

Then in 1978 I ran into Axel Küstner from Germany and he helped me record my first album, *Living Country Blues U.S.A., Volume Six: The Road Is Rough and Rocky* for the German L and R label, which came out in 1980. I have another album to be released in Toronto, Canada, but they're dragging their feet for some reason. But it will be on the market sooner or later.

Anyway, it's a funny story how Axel found out about me. He heard about me through Flora Molton.[20] Now, I first met Flora Molton at the Ontario Place. She came down there to see John Hurt, and that's how me and Flora became acquainted. Flora and her little band had gone down to New Orleans, out of the clear blue sky had made up their minds to go to New Orleans. They had no gigs down there, they just went.

When they got down there, there was a festival going, so they did pick up a few gigs and made a little money. So at the time Axel Küstner from Germany was over here scouting and looking for new talent. After he heard Flora Molton and her little group play, he wanted to know where they were from. So they said from Washington. And he asked them if there were any good blues players around Washington and they said, "One of the best."

"Who is this?"

"Archie Edwards."

So he said, "I'm going back to Washington with you." So he did. He came in here on Saturday night about 11:30. Me and the boys, you know, the Gaines brothers, was sitting here playing the guitar and drinking a little bit. We had the door locked and somebody knocked on the door. So I went to open it, and it was Axel Küstner, and Phil Wiggins.

They said, "Archie, this is Axel Küstner. He's from Germany. He's scouting for new talent." He says, "They tell me you play the guitar."

I said, "I play enough to suit myself."

He said, "Well let me hear you play something."

So I played a couple of songs for him and he just got around me and got his tape recorder and his camera and taped me and snapped my picture. He said, "I don't know why somebody hasn't discovered you. I'm going to take you to Germany if it's the last thing I do. You will be in Germany. I'll get you there."

Well, I thought he was kidding, but he meant it. After he left there that night, about two years later, I get this great big picture of me. It says, "Archie, this is the picture I took of you." He said, "I posted it all over Germany. I'm getting you into this blues festival in Germany. Come to Frankfurt." He had made all the arrangements.

So two weeks after I retired, I jumped on a plane and went over there and it was beautiful. European audiences, when they see a billing of a bluesman coming over there, I guess they they start asking questions. They know more about your background most of the time than you do, because they can say things that you have to think and say, "Wait a minute. Yeah, that happened."

We played all over Germany and then we went down to Barcelona, Spain, for a couple of nights. Switzerland, Vienna, Austria. But you know, East Berlin, it really amazed me, going behind the Iron Curtain. We were treated better behind the Iron Curtain than we were any place else.

I don't know how the real life is, but it was beautiful the time we were there. Big crowds, and every time we would do a show the girl would go put a great big wreath of flowers around our necks. It made me think of Hawaii.

Yeah, we had a hell of a show over there. The American Folk Blues Festival was put together by Horst Lippmann. That's Lippmann and Rau who put out my record on L and R label. That's their label. We traveled all over, country blues and Chicago blues. It was John Cephas and Phil Wiggins, James Son Thomas from Mississippi, Carey and Lurie Bell and the Sons of the Blues out of Chicago. Yeah, we really had a time.

After I got back from Europe, I thought about putting some musicians together so we could tour. See, when John Cephas and Phil Wiggins became partners, it kind of left me dangling. I said, "Well, Mother Scott is dead. John Hurt's dead. John Jackson has his son, James, working with him. John and Phil have teamed up. So that leaves me by myself." I said, "What am I going to do?"

Archie Edwards, publicity photo, 1988.
Photo by Axel Küstner.

So I thought maybe I should get a little group together. So the first I thought about was Flora Molton. Over the years I had kept in contact with Miss Flora. We were almost as good friends as me and John Hurt were. The only difference is Flora, she can tell a big lie, but she won't take a drink of liquor with me.

Flora plays gospel music and she had a little group that worked with her. At one time she worked with Tim Lewis, Phil Wiggins, then Larry Wise, and a backup guitar player named Ed Morris. He was a good friend of mine. But then Ed died and Flora didn't have a guitar player to work with her.

So one night I was playing up at Food for Thought on Connecticut Avenue, and Eleanor Ellis was there working as a waitress or a dishwasher or something. So I said to her one day, "Do you play a guitar?" She said, "Oh, a little bit." I said, "That's exactly what I wanted to hear you say. A little bit." I said, "I know a lady that needs a guitar player. She had a fellow playing with her, but he died. Now, she's a nice lady and she needs a guitar player. I wish you could get in touch with her." The next time I saw Eleanor she was playing with Flora. So I said, "That's exactly what I wanted." Then we hooked up together and we have a hot little group. Even John Cephas says, "Archie, I swear to God, you, Flora, and Eleanor have made a hell of a team."

Flora, she sings a song about a little rejected stone, and for a while I thought I felt like that rejected stone. But then I was on the road again. And raising some hell, too, Jack. We're raising hell. Flora Molton, Eleanor Ellis, and me. But we don't try to do anything together. Everybody has their slot, you know. It goes in circles: one, two, three.

Yeah, we got a hot little group going, blues and spirituals. We've toured all over the country: North Carolina, Southern Carolina, Pennsylvania, New York, Canada, and Europe. We did a tour of Europe in 1987. I got this second tour through a guy named Rolf Schubert who had heard me perform the first time I was over there with the American Folk Blues Tour. So he wrote me a letter, said he liked what I was doing and asked if I knew anyone else. So I mentioned Flora and Eleanor and told him what a dynamic duo they were.

He said send him some tapes and pictures. So I did and he wrote back and said, "I've got all three of you booked for a tour of Europe." So we went and toured Europe with Charlie Musslewhite and another guitar player.

It always works out for the best, though. Regardless of how many stumbling blocks you have, hang with it. It will smooth up. You know the song "The Road Is Rough and Rocky"? Well, it will smooth out. Sooner or later, somewhere along the line, it will smooth out. Everything's going pretty good right now.

You know my brother Robert? He's very proud of what I do. Every time I go somewhere and have a good success, when I come back, he says, "I'm going to get my guitar. I'm going with you." But he never goes. It would be a great thing, though, if I could get him to get back into playing. Then we could go back down home there as the Edwards Brothers on blues guitar.

I think he's too bashful to play in public. But I know he could play if he practiced. It's a puzzling thing to me. You're not bashful as far as getting up and going to work and facing the public. You work for the public, you work in the public. You drive an automobile and all this stuff. You buy a home and you get married and all these kind of things. If that doesn't embarrass you, then sitting up in front of somebody, playing a guitar, shouldn't embarrass you. I just can't figure out why people think that playing the guitar for the public is embarrassing. To me it's a great lift to show that I can do what these other people have done.

Friends and Memories

Over the years I have met a lot of musicians. That's me and Mance Lipscomb[21] over there. He was a tough man. We were both there at the Smithsonian Festival down on the Mall in 1970. I got acquainted with Mance, and we sat and had a long conversation.

A few years ago I was coming through Georgetown one rainy night and I was cruising along there with nothing to do, and this bellboy came out to the corner and flagged me, you know. So I stopped for him and he said, "Follow me in here to the hotel." He said, "Follow me and wait. I'll bring you a passenger out." So he went in and came back out and I saw this blind man and this lady with him. So he gets in the cab and says, "Take me to the Cellar Door."

So I asked him, "Who's playing at the Cellar Door tonight?" He says, "I am. I'm Sonny Terry." I says, "Sonny Terry? Man, I been knowing you for the longest time." He says, "How do you know me?"

I told him back in the thirties, I was coming from school one evening and I passed by a place called Clayton Barnard's filling station and the guy sold liquor there. I saw these two white fellows in a '30 Chevrolet coach, and they had these two colored fellows with them. And the blind boy with the gray guitar, solid metal guitar, was Blind Boy Fuller. I know this because about thirty years later I was at John Hurt's house one day and we brought up Blind Boy Fuller's name and so I asked him, "What kind of guitar does Blind Boy Fuller play?" He says, "Blind Boy Fuller plays a solid metal gray National." And the other guy was

Mance Lipscomb and Archie Edwards, 1976.
Photo by Jesse Winch.

him, Sonny Terry. He was the young man that was waving at us, you know, walking past the highway.

I say, "Well, I saw you when I was a kid." It's true, and when I told Sonny Terry about this he says, "Man, you got a better memory than I have. But I know you, too, though. You're the man that plays that old steel-pan Gretsch guitar and sounds like Blind Boy Fuller."

I says, "Yeah."

He says, "Come down to the club, tell them you're my guest and see the show." So, I went down and saw the whole show and he sent me over beer and everything.

A few years ago I was down at Ferrum College in Franklin County, Virginia, and I met a guy there. He and I both went to school together. His name was John Tinsley[22] and I hadn't seen him for about thirty-five or forty years. So when I got down there, looking at the billing of the program, I saw John Tinsley's name. I said, "Darn, I know this guy. We went to school together."

After a while we met on stage, and he was wondering whatever happened to me. And I said I wondered whatever happened to him. So we were both doing the same thing, still playing the guitar. That was a great thrill to meet him after almost forty years. Both playing the same style guitar and sounded just almost identical to each other. He's still playing down in Franklin County.

But last year I had one of the greatest experiences of my life. I was called by the Smithsonian Institution and they asked me would I take part in the Folklife Festival down there. They had this group of people from Philadelphia called themselves "The Philadelphians." They had everything they needed, except a blues guitar player. They had two guys, old guys. One of them was called "Spoons," he played spoons, and one of them was called "Washboard Slim." They needed somebody to play the guitar for them. But when I met the guys they were telling me that I sounded like Blind Boy Fuller. And Washboard Slim was a guy that played washboard for Blind Boy Fuller, when Blind Boy Fuller was a youngster, you know.

I said, "What a coincidence." Here I am playing guitar for the man that played washboard for Blind Boy Fuller. That was really a coincidence. Yeah, I got a kick out of that.

My wife and her whole family, once they found out I played the guitar, they started mentioning Luke Jordan. I had no idea that I would run into anyone that knew Luke Jordan. But my wife, she knew of him ever since she was a baby, a little girl. She used to see him on the corner in Lynchburg playing his guitar. So when they found out I was from Virginia, playing the guitar, they thought I knew Luke Jordan. They said, "Archie, you sound something like Luke Jordan." And my wife and all my sisters-in-law and brothers-in-law would always tell me how they used to see Luke sit on the corner playing the guitar and singing. One of his favorite songs was "Pick Poor Robin Clean." Another one of his songs was "Church Bell Blues." Those songs were pretty popular back in the thirties, late twenties and early thirties. Somewhere down the line I have met people that knew just about all the old guys I try to represent.

You know, the guitar is pretty famous here on the East Coast. So I think you can find lots of blues players around here, like John Tinsley, the Gaines Brothers, Willie and Leroy, John Cephas, Flora Molton, John Jackson and his son James. They're all from Virginia. I think you might find some more blues around those old country towns where boys get together on Saturday night, drink some whiskey, and stomp their feet.

But I really never heard of too many who played here in Maryland, except Buster Brown.[23] Now I heard he was living out in Capitol Heights for a while before he died. He was the boy that came up with that harmonica thing about "Fannie Mae." It's not too many around here who played blues, but there's guitar players. Roy Clark, he lived up the highway. He's a local boy, but he's more country or bluegrass man on guitar, banjo, and just about anything. And Roy Buchanan,[24] he's a rock and roll man. He plays blues, but not country blues. They all got farms out there in Prince George's County, out near Palmer Highway.

Taking it Easy

Me and this old steel-pan guitar have made it pretty good. It has brought me a lot of recognition, so I decided I would give it a name. It's a funny story.

My wife's name is Frances and this guitar is Frances. The reason I named this guitar Frances, after I went to Europe the first time and came back, she says, "Well, now you got in the famous stage of life with your music, which one of your guitars are you gonna name after me?"

I said, "Wait a minute, let me figure out something so I'll get a little argument out of this." I looked at all my other guitars, which was practically new and everything, and I said, "Honey, I got to tell you I got to name that old beat up one after you." Now, why did I say that? She got so upset. I said, "Wait a minute now, let me explain something to you. This guitar is the best guitar that I have and I will not sell it for any price because it's brought me fortune and fame. When I went to Europe, everybody went crazy about me and this guitar over there."

I said, "No way in the world anybody could buy this guitar from me. So this is the best. The rest of them I could probably sell, but this one, no way." So I got out of that one. So from now on this guitar is "Frances."

I've backed up other musicians or had them back me up at times, but usually I play by myself. Me and my guitar. John Hurt, he told me, "Play by yourself. If you do good, you know who did it. If you mess up, you know who did it. And if you make a lot of money, you don't need to give anybody any of it." So that makes sense. He said, "With your repertoire you can carry a show on yourself." Said anything you can do by yourself, "if you don't need anybody, don't use them. Leave them alone." If you get in a band and you got a big gig coming up somebody might get a drink or two and start an argument and won't play his part. You're messed up. So if you don't get drunk yourself, you got it made, right?

With a group each man has a part and you get accustomed to having the guy do his part. Then what happens? "I can't make it." Or either you get there and, "I need a drink to get myself together." Give the joker a drink and he gets drunk. Then it takes the rest of the band to get him

together. They have big fights, and what happens? Nobody gets paid.
Everybody's in jail. You have to call somebody to get you out of jail.

So I decided to do it myself. I don't do a lot, but whatever I do, I'm
gonna try to do enough of it to make people think I'm all right. And if I
make any money, I don't have to give anybody any except when I get
home and my wife says, "You been playing the guitar?" "Yeah, baby," I
have to come across and share it with her because after thirty-four years
I don't think I'd want to try to start all over. That's too far down the
road. So, I'll give it to her.

My son, his name is Dana Andrews, like the movie star. He's working out in California now. He doesn't play the guitar. I never could get
him to play. I had him pick the guitar one time and he made a beautiful
note on it, but he stopped. He was crazy about Michael Jackson when
he was growing up, but I don't know whether he cares for him or his
music now. But I think Michael Jackson is great. I saw him on television
the other night and he is one hell of an entertainer and a great dancer.
But my son's a good dancer and a singer, too.

And smart, let me tell you. He was here in the barbershop with me
once when he was about three or four years old. I had a pellet gun I
used to hunt squirrels, and all around the barbershop, on the walls,
they had mirrors hanging up there. I walked outside one day to wash
the car or something and when I came back that boy had taken that BB
gun and, man, he had shot one of those mirrors to death.

I said, "Boy, you done ruined my mirror." I grabbed him, about
getting ready to spank him. He said, "Wait a minute, Daddy. Wait,
Daddy. Look up there at that good shooting."

So I looked and said, "Dog, if that isn't good shooting." This is so
true I had to laugh. He had made a straight line from the bottom of that
mirror all the way to the top. And in a space six inches apart, bottom to
top. You know I couldn't have done it to save my life. I looked at that
and said, "Son, that is good shooting."[25]

Sometimes I'm sitting in that barbershop and I look at that mirror
and I think, "Man, that guy was smart from the time he came into the
world, because he knew I was gonna tear him down. But he knew it
was good shooting, too."

My wife was married to a Connyers, so my stepdaughter's name is
Gloria Connyers; then Bobby Connyers, that's my eldest stepson. I have a
grandson, Kevin, which is my oldest daughter's son. And I have a
granddaughter, my oldest boy's daughter. And I have foster grandkids.
There's Alonzo Sutherland, Theresa Sutherland, Raegene Sutherland,
and my youngest foster daughter, Mary Ann Ederland.

I brought up a bunch of foster kids, but none of the kids tried to play anything other than just this last little grandson. He jumped right on it, the first he heard as soon as he was big enough to look at me and hear me play, and he's only two years old. He saw me on television one morning, and that set him off. Oh, he's got to do what Granddaddy was doing.

His name is Antonio, but we call him Chinny Chin, because when he was a baby he had a big double chin. He still goes by that. Now he is going to be a musician! Yes, indeed. And I bought him a little toy guitar. Every day, if I'm around the house there for any length of time, he just has to have two jam sessions. I have a baritone uke I keep upstairs in my room and every day he comes, "Come on, Granddaddy. Come on, Granddaddy, let's go. Come on!"

We go upstairs, walk in my bedroom. He walks over in the corner to get my baritone uke and hand it to me and pat the bed for me to sit down. I sit down, he reaches and gets his little guitar. Comes back and stands right in front of me and waits, waiting for the count down. When I start, he starts patting his feet and goes crazy! Singing away. He watches television and sees how those guys play the guitar and turn and do this and that. He does all of that.

But he'll get his two jam sessions in. Once we do that jam session, he applauds and takes my ukulele and puts it in the corner. Puts his guitar in the corner with mine and he won't touch it again until the next jam session.

Yes, he's gonna be a musician. He's the only member of my family so far that really makes me believe that he's gonna make it.

Now I'm my own boss. I work at the barbershop and play my music. But that's really not work. Working with something that you love, you don't worry about it. And I love to play the guitar. I'll play for hours and hours. That's something that I want to do. Enjoyment takes the stress and strain out of whatever you're doing. If you like to do it, no problem. But anything that you do, if you don't like to do it, it will drive you crazy.

Like I quit that job as a police officer. I made up my mind to get that burden off of me because it was worrying me to death. I was doing my job, but other people wasn't doing their job. When the clients come into the building, instead of the workers coming downstairs to see them, to help the clients so they can go about their business feeling good, they'll wait to the last minute. They wait until the client starts raising hell, then they want me to get the client out of the building.

Why, you got to be crazy! I'm not gonna use no physical stress and strain on this client. They got to see him. Throwing him out of the building is not gonna solve the problem. Give him a chance to go get a gun, come back and shoot everybody. See what I'm saying? I say, "You see the guy before he leaves here. I'll see that he doesn't harm you, but you see the guy before he leaves here."

So, a lot of people didn't like me. They call downtown, tell the captain that I was working against them. I say, "Captain, I'm not working against these people. I'm working with them. They want to work against me, though. They want me to tussle and fight with the clients because they don't have anything to do but come and talk to the clients. That's why the clients come here. They wouldn't come here if they didn't need to come here. They come here, they lost a check or something. They come in to get somebody to help them straighten it out."

But the workers upstairs, they want me to throw that client out. Why throw him out when he's got to come back? If they throw him out because he's done with all of it, then all right. But you don't throw a man out of the building when he's mad and hungry, because he's coming back. Right? He gonna shoot up somebody when he comes back. People got to be crazy. I ain't nobody's fool to fight and tussle with nobody when he has the right to be there, too. That's stupid.

So now I think I'll hang out at the barbershop, do some barbering, teach a few students, and keep on playing. I got to keep a little bit of money rolling in.

I went overseas and came back home with a pocketful of money. I just knew I was gonna have a good time, take off about a month and not do nothing. But no sooner than I walked in the house, my wife said, "Look, honey." I looked in the back room and she had a fireplace put in the back room. She had the house done up inside with flagstone and on the outside. Thirty-five hundred and some dollars! Whew!

I said, "Baby, why didn't you call me and tell me that you were doing all this? I could have stayed on over there for a few more weeks and had enough money that we could have gone out to dinner or something." But being good-hearted, I just run my hand in my pocket and started counting one-hundred-dollar bills until I give her a little over a thousand dollars and said, "Here, baby."

So every time I make a little money, I'm helping her pay for the fireplace. But me and this old guitar been bringing it on in. But really, nobody makes too much money playing this type of music. So I play for my own enjoyment and to let people know what the old type of blues is about. I think about the best time that I ever had and the most money that I ever made for a short period of time was at the Philadelphia Folk Festival. They had me booked to play up there, but it was so many musicians I only had ten minutes. But I got two hundred dollars for ten minutes. So I said, "Now this is the kind of money I should be making."

But you don't get enough requests for country blues to get rich. You can make a few dollars, but that's not rich. You can put out a few albums, but people don't buy it like they buy that wild crazy stuff. People don't have common sense today like they used to have, so they're all way out there with this eardrum-busting music. But the good stuff, country blues and country spirituals, they don't go for it. Oh, it's coming back a little bit, but not as it should. The country blues ought to be the country's second national anthem because this is where the music comes from. Back in the early days folks like Ma Rainey, Bessie Smith, and Jimmie Rodgers, he's a white fellow but he played the blues, got into it and developed a beautiful thing. But now they won't realize that everybody got their ideas from blues and spirituals. So you don't get rich from playing it. I don't expect to get rich.

But even if you do get paid, the money doesn't go anywhere today. It's not worth much. I said once before that, back in the old days, those were hard times when times were good. But now, I have never seen a time as bad in my whole life before. Now we got bad times when times are good. Because you can make money now, but people is so rough out there that after you made it, you got to try to sneak away home. Because if they see it, they'll try and get it.

God said man will destroy himself and, buddy, if they ain't working on it. If only they would try as hard to keep peace on earth as they try to destroy it, it could be a different story. Really, I think man is getting too smart, like when they sent that thing up in space and it blew up. I think that's telling us something.

God put man on the earth. When you die they bury you back in the ground; and when God sends for you, then your spirit goes out there. Jesus, when he left here, his spirit got on the wings of a cloud and moved out. He went out there into the heavenly bodies. Now, what reason does man have to be out there? Wait until he calls for you.

I was born on earth and when I die I'm gonna let them put me down in the earth. But my spirit, I want it to get on out there and then I'll find out what in the hell people want to go out there for. But I know it will be beautiful. Because nobody can bother you. Man, you get out there, you got it made. When you get out there, they'll be no fussing and shooting. It's peaceful. Right?

But until then I'll keep busy doing things I want to do. I might go down in the country, kill me a bunch of squirrels, and drink corn liquor. I don't need too much. A shot of whiskey and a beer, a cigarette or cigar, that's enough for me. In my life, that's enough. I say to myself that any man has a right to his own way of thinking. But a lot of things I see people do, I wish that I could have some influence on them. To encourage them not to do it. But I usually just say, well, he'll turn around some day.

What I do is what I like to do, but I hope the things I do won't interfere with what you do. Because I don't want what you do to interfere with what I do. That's the way I see it.

You know when I first started playing the guitar again, blues was fading a little bit. Anybody that played them, people would poke fun at you. So it made me a little embarrassed. But I just kept playing for myself. I said, I don't need those people. I like it, so I'll play it. To me it was fine and I'm glad I did play it.

People used to say, "Why don't you play jazz guitar? Why don't you do rock and roll? Why don't you go to school and study and get into this deep stuff?"

I say, "Oh, no, this is deep enough. This is actually deeper than you think." See, most people don't know actually how deep blues is, and once you know how to do it yourself, you'll know how deep it is. 'Cause it's the next thing to a spiritual.

Music has a tendency to go in certain trends. It will blossom and it sinks, you know. So the blues has been faded so far back for such a long time until right now it seems like everybody has gone as far as they can go with music. So I believe that there's a turning point. It has to

Archie Edwards at the barbershop, 1986.
Photo by Lisa Falk.

come back to home base and start again. It's gone so far out it don't have no other place to go. So it has to come back home and start all over again.

Jazz and rock and roll, that's a wide field. Everybody's in that, just about. So I decided to get back in something that everybody was looking over. They were looking over the blues. Everybody had tossed the blues in the corner, just like those old guitars over there. People were beginning to feel a little bashful, ashamed of the blues. They figured that if you played the blues that you were telling somebody that you worked on a farm or had to eat corn bread and beans three or four times a day or something like that. They thought that people were thinking that you were hard up, you know. And they said that it was passing away. If they hear you playing the blues, people said you were "old down home."

But it's coming back now, and the people are gonna really like it. Even if the blacks don't bring it back, the whites are gonna bring it back. So it's coming back. Yesterday I heard them playing the blues, Sonny Terry and Brownie McGhee, on the black station. So that's telling the people we are getting into our own stuff again. That's good.

So this is about the best thing I've done in my life. Hung onto the blues. The greatest feeling that I have is to be able to sit here and tell people that I did it myself. It's good to be able to say that the thing I believed in all down through life is beginning to come back to the front again. It brings you up.

So I'm trying to keep the blues, what you call black heritage, I'm trying to keep it rolling. Yeah, and it doesn't matter who I teach it to because Mississippi John Hurt asked me, he said, "Brother Arch, whatever you do, teach my music to other people." He said, "Don't make no difference what color they are, teach it to them. Because I don't want to die and you don't want to die. Teach them my music and teach them your music."

Notes to Chapter 2

1. See the full text of "Red River Blues" on p. 111 and references to it as a work song on p. 39.

2. Archie Edwards uses the phrase "legendary songs" to refer to old songs, usually ballads, that tell of the exploits of legendary figures like Stack O'Lee. Coincidentally, scholars also use the phrase. For example, Roger Abrahams wrote of legendary songs: "Another group of songs often known as ballads are those which center not on events, but on a legendary personage and tell a series of verse long stories about his life" (Roger Abrahams and George Foss, *Anglo-American Folksong Style* [Englewood Cliffs, N.J.: Prentice Hall, 1968], p. 89).

3. As will become apparent later, John Hurt played a major role in Ar-

chie's life, as a musical model off of records and much later as a friend and teacher. Archie tends to compare John Hurt and his father, musically and personally.

4. For further discussion of "Nine Pound Hammer," see John Cephas's version and the notes, p. 222.

5. Archie is referring to a song I play entitled "Dust My Broom," written by Robert Johnson and popularized by Elmore James. The verse should now be considered traditional.

6. I am not at all sure what to make of this obscure reference. It may reflect a folk belief concerning the banjo and other instruments associated with secular music. It may indicate the shift away from the banjo, with its minstrel-show connotations, to the guitar as the major folk instrument, or it may simply have to do with the fact that Archie's dad played the banjo and one banjo player in the house was enough.

7. University of Maryland folklorist Gladys Marie Fry has collected numerous accounts of the exploits of Buck Jackson and similar characters with alleged magical or supernatural powers. Her research focuses on the region where Archie comes from and she interviewed him several years ago.

8. The verse Archie Edwards recalls comes from a well-known song called "Whitehouse Blues," or "McKinley Blues," which describes the assassination of President McKinley. On another occasion he remembered two other verses:

Jumped on a horse, picked up the rein
Told the horse to outrun the train
From Washington to Buffalo

The doctor came out of the operating room looking sad
Said your president's been shot, he's shot mighty bad
He's gonna die, he's gonna die.

The song has been recorded by Charlie Poole, Riley Puckett, and the Carter Family.

9. Archie Edwards is referring to a set of trading cards portraying major country blues artists, illustrated by R. Crumb and put out by Yazoo Records, a major blues label. According to the card, Number 18 in the series, Thomas died in Memphis, although he is associated with the Southwest. It is difficult to determine at this late date whether Thomas was jailed in, or worked in, Virginia. It's certainly possible, but musically he is known for his great slide style, as opposed to the stylings of Blind Lemon or Blind Blake, but who knows for sure. Musicians traveled extensively and were often jailed for vagrancy or simply to provide entertainment for the local officials and fellow prisoners.

10. I have been unable to corroborate any radio show by Blind Blake although many other traditional artists, including the Tennessee Chocolate Drops, had radio slots. Deford Bailey, on the other hand, was a mainstay on the "Grand Old Opry" and influenced countless black and white harmonica players.

11. For further discussion of the house-party tradition see: Barry Lee Pearson, "Good Times When Times Were Hard: Recollections of Rural Houseparties in Virginia," *Folklore and Folklife in Virginia* 3 (1984), pp. 44–45.

12. Archie refers to an African-American tradition in which "cut-eye" refers to a look or expression of hostility. See John R. Rickford and Angela E. Rick-

ford, "Cut-eye and Suck-teeth: African Words and Gestures in New World Guise," *Journal of American Folklore* 89, No. 353 (July–September, 1976), pp. 294–309.

13. A Noah Lewis played harmonica with Cannon's Jug Stompers and other Memphis and Ripley, Tennessee, musicians in the late 1920s and 1930s. I don't think this Noah Davis, or Noah Lewis, was the same musician. Furry Lewis was one of Archie Edwards's early heroes and the source of his "Everybody Blues." See p. 120.

14. "Pittsburgh Blues" is the second of three autobiographical blues which Archie composed years ago. See p. 128.

15. An outstanding bluesman and Chess recording artist, Howling Wolf, born Chester Burnett, spent the first half of his life in Mississippi then moved to Chicago in the 1950s.

16. "Duffel Bag Blues" is the last of Archie's autobiographical blues triad. See p. 129.

17. Brothers Leroy and Willie Gaines were fellow Virginia musicians who lived in the Washington, D.C. area.

18. Blues legend Skip James was a gifted Mississippi musician who, along with John Hurt, was "rediscovered" during the folk revival. As Archie implies, at times Skip James could be difficult. See John Cephas's discussion of Skip James and his music.

19. This informal assembly of local musicians played in and around the D.C. area during the 1970s.

20. Archie's friend Flora Molton, or Miss Flora, as he sometimes calls her, plays gospel music on the streets of Washington, D.C. A fine musician, she has several albums to her credit and has toured Europe with Archie.

21. Texas songster Mance Lipscomb is remembered as an outstanding guitarist whose repertoire, like John Hurt's, bridged the nineteenth and twentieth centuries. Born in 1895, he died in 1976.

22. See the reference to Tinsley in Chapter 1, p. 9. For further information, see Bruce Bastin, *Red River Blues: The Blues Tradition in the Southeast* (Urbana: University of Illinois Press, 1986), p. 299.

23. Harmonica player Buster Brown came from Georgia and recorded a number of popular blues hits in the early 1960s. He died in the mid-1970s.

24. Roy Buchanan is best known to rock fans as a fine guitarist. According to Chicago bluesman Byther Smith, Buchanan taught guitar for a Lyon and Healy music store in Chicago during the early 1960s. Buchanan committed suicide in 1988.

25. For further discussion of this narrative see Pearson, *"Sounds So Good to Me,"* pp. 39–42.

3
Archie Edwards's Songs

Archie Edwards refers to himself as a country bluesman or, on occasion, a blues guitar player. His emphasis on guitar-playing skill reflects a regional bias as well as his own personal feeling that a bluesman or blueswoman should be able to play competently. Despite the fact that he plays ballads, spirituals, and old-timey country songs, he refers to his music as "good old country blues," often adding "like the old-timers used to play." His instrumental and vocal approach has deep roots in rural Franklin County, and from his perspective his music has changed very little over the years.

The following section focuses on his music, including his thoughts about his own tradition, blues in general, composition, and, finally, forty-four selections from his repertoire.

I have included what Archie Edwards and I consider to be his most representative songs, drawn from his expansive repertoire. These are the songs he commonly plays and uses to represent himself, his primary influences, and his regional tradition. These songs come from Franklin County musicians, more recent acquaintances, phonograph recordings, and his own creative imagination. Most are blues, but there are also non-blues songs drawn from a common stock of traditional material shared by both black and white southeastern string-band performers. These non-blues come primarily from his father and John Hurt, whom Archie links together as representatives of the generation of musicians who preceded him.

Several of these non-blues have been recorded by white artists who either consciously played in a black idiom, like Frank Hutchison, or who simply included black material or blues in their repertoire, like the Carter Family. Edwards professes color blindness when it comes to music, listing Jimmie Rodgers, Uncle Dave Macon, and Frank Hutchison as sources of his songs and influences on his music. In fact, he never knew Frank Hutchison was white until he recently saw an album jacket photograph. However, we should note that even though the recordings in Archie's Franklin County home included material by white country artists, Archie's generation was a blues generation and the majority of the songs he learned were blues, as are all of his own compositions. After his father and John Hurt, his major influences were bluesmen Blind Lemon Jefferson and Blind Boy Fuller. He also learned songs from recordings by Barbecue Bob, Furry Lewis, Jim Jackson, Buddy Moss, and others.

While he takes pride in his early ability to learn from recordings and to play in the manner of the artists he emulates, particularly John Hurt and Blind Lemon, what he plays bears his own musical signature, which is rooted in the Piedmont tradition.[1] Although he incorporates musical figures, guitar runs, or other stylistic techniques he ascribes to other artists, the overall sound remains his own, even in his musical tributes.

Over the last ten years, I have watched his repertoire slowly expand as he perfected songs recalled from his younger days, composed new songs, or reworked and expanded fragments of traditional lyrics. Nevertheless, he has maintained a relatively stable repertoire of songs which he actively performs or, in his own words, "chooses to keep alive," and these are the selections in this book. However, before proceeding, I should explain my editorial role regarding song order and the manner in which each song is presented.

I initially considered several options—original compositions first, then the songs of the artists who influenced him, strict chronological order according to when he learned a song, and other meaningful and orderly systems. However, each of these schemes created problems. In spite of his remarkable memory, Archie doesn't remember when he learned all of his songs. Furthermore, he has been composing songs for forty some years, and early compositions precede and then alternate with material derived from recordings. The John Hurt material comes from two stages of his life, early recordings and later personal contact.

Realizing that whatever scheme I used would be somewhat arbitrary, I finally decided to organize the songs according to source. That is, according to whom he learned them from and to whom he pays tribute when performing them. First, we have the songs he learned from his father, then the songs from his local community, followed by the songs learned from John Hurt, Blind Lemon Jefferson, Blind Boy Fuller, and others. The final grouping, in chronological order when possible, includes his own compositions and songs he reworked from traditional fragments. I felt that his own work should come at the end, representing, in a sense, his maturity as an artist and his lifelong immersion in the blues tradition. Although he wrote songs throughout his life, most of his compositions are more recent. As he says, he doesn't listen to records much any more and has reached the point in his life where he is comfortable creating his own songs. This order reflects his own assessment of his repertoire as a little of his father, a little John Hurt, and a little of himself.

Finally, Archie's songs generally include spoken commentary, whether he is onstage or off. In contrast to John Cephas, who most often lets his songs speak for themselves, Archie introduces his materials with some type of exposition regarding source, story line, or applicable moral lesson. This stylistic trait shows off his storytelling skills and easy knack for improvisation, linking him with artists such as Leadbelly and Big Bill Broonzy, who also liked to talk about their songs. Moreover, Archie's sense of this book as a type of historical record further encouraged him to comment on the songs, a tendency I noted in an earlier book, *"Sounds So Good to Me": The Bluesman's Story*, which deals with blues life story in general.[2] There, I offer multiple examples of Archie's storytelling skills and a discussion of the tendency to develop narratives or commentary about songs. Quite simply, Archie likes to talk about or frame his songs with anecdotes, and his storytelling skills serve him well.

His Thoughts on His Music

I play what they call the old Piedmont style, but I call it East Virginia blues because that's where I learned it when I was growing up in the country. It's finger picking, where you use your thumb and your fingers, but I don't use any picks. I just play with my fingers. John Hurt, he played about the same way, but he called it cotton-picking style.[3] Now, we never had any cotton where I grew up, but I did pluck a lot of tobacco.

Anyway, that's the way the old-timers played. Back in the old days, if you wanted a little bass you had to do it with your thumb because they had nobody to play bass for you, or drums, either one. Back in the old days, you did it all; bass, treble, melody. Back then the guys had no one to help them out, so they had to do it all themselves. So that's the way I learned, from watching other musicians and listening to those old records. That's how I learned and that's how I play today.

But nowadays it's mostly bands. You run down and pick up someone on bass, somebody on drums, and everybody plays a part. They got urban blues, Chicago blues, Mississippi Delta blues, but a lot of it is the type of blues that you take and dress up a little bit. Now, what I play is the Piedmont country blues. But you take somebody, get a horn and set of traps, it will change the tempo and change the sound of it. That's the urban blues. And way down in the Deep South, people play a different style of guitar, call it the Delta blues. But very few people come out with the finger-picking blues, Piedmont blues.

But when you start adding to it, it's blues, but I call it "dress-up" blues. You take a country boy from the country, he come up to New York or different places, he gets a little group, and the next thing you know they're playing it, but it don't sound like it used to sound. They dress it up. Just like a country boy will leave the country in his dungarees, go to New York and get him a job and the next thing you know he's got on sharp-toed shoes and all that stuff. He's the same old country boy, but he just don't look the same, right? That's the same with the blues. It's blues, but it's dressed up. It just don't sound the same. It's the same old song, but the next thing you know it's messed up so you don't know it when you hear it.

But you don't find many people sitting down and picking it out with their fingers. This is how the old guys did it, country style, where you sit down and cross your legs, pat your foot, and put your glass of corn whiskey close by you. Play a song and take a sip of corn whiskey and go right back and play some more.

Oh, I have an electric guitar at home and sometimes I'll plug it in and play some blues. I used to do a little rock and roll, but I quit it. John Hurt said, "Brother Archie, rock-and-roll players gonna be ten cents a dozen pretty soon, so you stay where you are." So I'm sticking with the old country blues.

This guitar, it's probably older than I am. But it is a wild-looking guitar, an old guitar. It's what we call antique, very antique. It's got a resonator, that's the first form of amplification that they put into the guitar. All guitars used to be like this wooden guitar, hollow body with a sound hole. Then they decided to improve the sound of it, so they cut this hole out, put a piece of pan in it. Then later somebody got smart and put an electrical device on the inside, stuck a plug in it . . . boom! . . . they electrocuted the guitar.

But this old Gretsch, it's something I looked for all my life. I had a chance to play one when I was a little boy, and I could have bought it for ten dollars. But, you know, ten dollars was like a million then for me. So I couldn't buy that one. That kind of broke my heart, you know, 'cause I really wanted the guitar. So I said to myself, "If I ever get old enough to leave home and get a job and go to work, I'm gonna buy me one." So this one is the first one I seen since I left the country, and I bought it. And guess what I paid for it? Twenty-two dollars and fifty cents!

I went down to the pawnshop, man said, "What you looking for?" I said, "I'm looking for an antique guitar." He said, "You just a day late. We took all those guitars and smashed them and burned them up." I said, "Man, you got to be kidding!" He said, "You're just a day late."

So I stood there, and he said, "Wait a minute. Go back there in the back room and look up there on the top shelf. I think I remember putting a couple of old guitars up there." Man, I walked back there and reached up, and I could feel this guitar neck, but I couldn't reach it because I was too short. I got me a chair and pulled it up there, and got it down and it was just what I was looking for.

So I carried it out there and said, "Man, what are you asking for this?" He said, "Twenty-two fifty." I said, "What?" He said, "Yeah, twenty-two fifty." I had two dollars in my pocket. I gave him the two dollars and told him, "You hold that until I come back."

Man, I jumped in my car and I think I ran red lights and everything. Went home to get the rest of the money. But in the meantime, I had an old guitar like this. I give a little young white guy five dollars for it. I met him one Saturday night. He said, "Man, I'm broke as hell. Let me sell you this guitar." "What do you want for it?" He said, "Ten dollars." I said, "Man, I don't have no ten dollars in my pocket." He said, "What you got?" I said, "Five." He said, "That's OK." I took the five-dollar guitar, carried it back to the music store. The man said, "I'll give you ten dollars for it." I said, "Good." So I gave him ten-fifty and I got the guitar.

So when I went out in public and played the guitar, a man walked up to me and said, "I'll give you a thousand dollars for it." I said, "You've got to be crazy." He said, "What do you mean?" I said, "If this guitar's worth a thousand dollars to you, what do you think I would make with it by me just coming out in the blues world with my type of music? This thing blends with my type of music."

I've seen others like it that start at seven hundred and go up to fifteen hundred dollars. I've had other people offer me a thousand dollars for it, but I said, "No. I'm gonna hang on to it because I'm not hungry and I'm not broke either."

I play it in standard tuning, what John Hurt used to call regular auditorium tuning. The way I learned my chords, I listened to other people and after a while I would figure out the chord. You just built it yourself. Then way later on, I got a couple of old guitar books and learned a few chords and found out I had learned the right way by myself.

My dad played guitar, banjo, and harmonica, so I learned all that from him, and I learned some slide from him. He never could learn to play chords, but he could slide like crazy. See, back in the old days, they had the type of music they call bottleneck guitar. They take a string and soak it in gasoline and tie it around the neck of a bottle. Strike a match to it and it will make a ring around it. You tap it and it will break off, make a bottleneck.

But my first type of slide, you take a piston out of an old Model-T Ford. You take a hammer or something and beat on it and beat on it until you break it all to pieces, see. Then you take that little seal out of there and use it on your finger. But later on in life I found out that the blow-down pipe on a hot water tank was the very thing. If you could steal a blow-down pipe and get you one of those pocket pipe cutters, one of those small ones you keep in your back pocket, next thing you know, it will drop right in two. So that's what I use now.

But then I let that style go for quite a while. Now I do quite a few songs in slide, like "John Henry" and "That Train That Carried My Girl from Town." My father played those. I play "I Called My Baby Long Distance" with a slide and I wrote that. And I've been putting some music to my brother's song with a slide to make it sound like Blind Willie Johnson. I'm gonna put a little more emphasis on that slide stuff. I used to do a whole lot of Blind Willie's stuff, but after you grow up you kind of get away from it. So you have to put your mind back on it and work with it.

I don't really try to change my old songs. The stuff I started out with as a kid, it's basically the same. Because once you learn something as a youngster you don't get too far from it. Now, I might change something around a little bit that I wrote recently. Add something to it, put a little something in. But most of my songs, coming back to home base, stay basically the same.

But I still play a lot of the songs I learned when I was a kid. I picked up on all the old-timers. When they played a song I just never forgot it. It just continued to ring in my ear. So when I got a chance to pick up a guitar, I played it. So the songs stuck with me.

If I can think of a song that I heard when I was a little boy, if I just concentrate hard enough, it will come back to me. I call it my computer. Press a button, and it will come up. It may take a long time, but it will come up sooner or later. Like a file cabinet. You put some things in there and file it away. When you need it, you come back and look for it.

But one thing back then, you didn't have much to think about, so once you heard a song it never left your mind. See, it was my determination to become a musician. So I figured out the only way to do it was to catch it in my head and keep it there. I can play songs now I learned fifty years ago, with never anything written down on a piece of paper.

If it was good, I grabbed it and remembered it. I don't care who did it. If it was good, I remember it today. I listened to Uncle Dave Macon, Riley Puckett, and Ola Belle Reed when she picked that five-string banjo. When it came down to music with me, there was no color.

Anything that I heard that wasn't worth a shit, I don't care who it was, it didn't have no effect on me. All the good ones, white or black, I grabbed it. Like Jimmie Rodgers. I loved him. That's why I call him the Elvis Presley of the 1930s. If I liked it, I learned something about it, and I respect them. I'm a playing guy. If you ain't no good, I'll just tell you, you ain't with it. There ain't no color there. It's whether you're there or not.

So I learned a lot when I was younger from the old-time musicians, but some just seemed to hit me harder than others. Especially Mississippi John Hurt and Blind Lemon Jefferson. I listened to them when I was learning and tried to play the way that they played and I still try to play it the way they played it today. I learned John Hurt's style on songs like "Stack O'Lee" and "Candy Man" from the record player thirty-five years before I met him. So when we met I knew his style. I don't care what he played, I backed him up on it.

Back in 1933 or 1934 my brother borrowed that record, "Stack O'Lee" and "Candy Man," and he brought the recording to the house and put it on the old record player and played it. But the speed he was playing was a little too fast for us to catch all the sound and all. So we improvised a method of slowing the old record player down to where the man would talk just above a mumble. Then we would listen to the guitar, trying to follow the guy.[4] If I made a mistake, my brother would tell me where I made my mistake at. So I'd give him the guitar and he would fill it in. So we did that for a couple of weeks and when my brother carried the record back to the owner, my brother and I had stolen all the music. We could play "Stack O'Lee" and "Candy Man" as good as John Hurt. So I never had to rehearse on it when I met him, because I had already learned his style. But then he couldn't play my songs because he didn't know me. When I got into my sack he was lost, because he didn't know my songs the way I knew his.

And today, if I'm going to play John Hurt's music, I'm gonna try to play just as close to his style as I can. The same with Blind Lemon. I play just the way that I learned from them. See, that way I keep the guys alive. I don't try to take anything from anybody. If I try to twist it around and make it mine, see, it wouldn't be right. But if I'm going to represent Mississippi John Hurt, I'm going to say, "I'm going to play such and such a song by Mississippi John Hurt." And I'm going to play it just as close to him as possible so everybody can hear it and say, "That is Mississippi John Hurt."

Now other artists, I don't play in their style at all. I may have

**Archie Edwards and author in the classroom, University of
Maryland, 1979.**   *Photo by Cheryl Brauner.*

learned a song from them, but I do it more in my own way. It's just a
few that I really try to play like John Hurt, or my father, or Blind
Lemon. And some guys, I like their music, but it just doesn't fit in the
way I like to play.

Skip James, he never did faze me too much. That's why I didn't pay
much attention to Skip's music. It put you in a type of mood that I could
never get myself into. I just couldn't never get myself in that slot too
well. That boy was a hell of a musician though. He was a musician
from the heart. And I'll tell you somebody that learned his music pretty
good, John Cephas.[5] But you kind of had to fit yourself into his slot,
where you could dig what he was doing.

Now today, quite a few people are stealing what they can from me
and playing the life out of it. They can put the ingredients in, but they

can't put in what I've got in my mind, because they can't think like me. See, I put anything into a song that I want to put in, but they can't do that. They have to put what they know into it. That's the difference.

Music is like baking a pie. You can get a good pie crust; that's the basics, the chords. But once you get that pie crust you can put in any filling you want to as long as it's good for the pie. That's the way I summarize playing blues. Anything that you can put in there to make it sound better, put it in there. But if it isn't gonna sound any better, don't put it in. So that's my philosophy. There isn't anybody out there that plays my music the way I play it. They can get some of the stuff that I do, but they can't get it all, see. Because they don't think like me.

But really, I don't mind teaching what I know. And it doesn't bother me if people take something from me unless they mess it up. Sometimes I say, "Lord, look what they done to my music. They just ruined it."

Frankly speaking, I don't listen to many records anymore. I call up what I have in my computer. Anything comes across my mind I'll just concentrate on that until finally I build it. If I don't get the song just right, I'll build the pieces. The part that I don't hear, I'll make it myself, build it up myself. Quite a few songs I've done by knowing maybe one or two words.

And then I start studying and try to piece that with something that will blend with it and build a song out of it. So sometimes I'll take stuff that I've heard and rearrange it. But most of the stuff that you hear me do today, if I say it's mine, it's something I did myself. Something I picked out of the blue sky.

I've been writing my own songs for a long time. So when I met John Hurt I had already written songs like "I Had a Little Girl, She Was Sweet as She Could Be" and "Pittsburgh Blues." But he encouraged me. John Hurt said, "You cannot become famous playing other people's music." He said, "One good song that you write and put on the market yourself will do you more good than lots of other people's material." They say that what other people have done has been done before, but what you do, well, it's the first time. So I try to write some things that have never been done before, and I have quite a few that I play.

For me it's not that hard to write a song. My father and Boyd Maddox, they kind of planted a sound in my head and it stayed there. Throughout life, I got to traveling around and certain things I've seen in life, certain things I've done in life and certain things I wanted to do it in life, well, I got it together and made a blues out of it. Hard work or whatever, you don't forget those things, the good part of life and the bad parts of life. So it's no problem to write the blues. All you have to do is put it together just like you write a poem. You do a song and then you take up the guitar and try to find the chords that will play with it. And after a while you got the blues together.

Sometimes you're just sitting around reminiscing, thinking about what happened to you in life. You think about an old girlfriend or something and you just say, "Well, I'll just kind of put together some of the things that happened to me." So, it's just reminiscing about whatever pops into your mind.

But the blues have a great meaning. It's not just the idea that it's expressing hardship. It's something that's there. Somebody has to do it. Because it's something that we all have at times and we need it. There has never been a man or woman that didn't have some type of blues in their life. So even if you don't sing it, if you think it, you're still in the bag with me.

If I play it and sing about it, I'm letting the people know about my experiences and how I feel. But rather than walk around with it all bottled up here inside me, well, I just wouldn't do that. Whatever has happened in my life, I don't mind telling about it. And I'm proud to be able to play the old country blues because it's about a part of life that everybody comes in contact with sooner or later. I've never seen a person that didn't have the blues one way or another. I've known the times I've seen a dog sit on the hillside in the country and just howl his poor heart out. So it dawned on me later on in life that the guy had the blues. Everybody gets the blues sometime, sooner or later.

So it's just the mood you're in. When you're moody, you sing a moody song. You're happy, you sing a happy song. So it's not really something that you have to be down and out to do. It's just something that's been handed down from generation to generation, and I'm happy to carry it on.

Some of it is actually everyday living. Some of it is the hard times, hardship that people go through. And then again sometimes you just sit down and start imagining things. You might not have ever seen it. That's like when I wrote that song with the line, "... call my baby long distance 'cause I want to talk to her so bad. When the operator asked me for my money, took every cent I had."[6] Man, I didn't ever do nothing like that, but I was just imagining if I was in that predicament. Like an artist paints a picture, sits down and starts to thinking about certain things. I might start writing a song about it, but I don't experience it. You can imagine the blues. Any person that has a cultivated mind can sit down and imagine yourself to be in the worst predicament in the world and not have it be true.

You can imagine yourself being a bum, standing on the corner, no shoes on, but have a pocketful of money. You can imagine that and start writing. It all depends on what you want to concentrate on, what predicament you imagine yourself in. Or you see somebody, you know such and such a person's having a hard time, so you start writing. An artist might draw a picture. Everything they put on the paper is not real, but they can imagine it. And some person come and looks at it, say, "My

God, look at that expression on his face. Look how he's dressed. He's had a hard time in life." But an artist puts his on a piece of paper. You put yours through your body, out your fingers, and on the guitar.

But most of the blues did originate from the living everyday trend. Now if you sing a song about your wife or girlfriend, that may be true life. If it's good or bad, it's true life. Blind Lemon Jefferson, he plays "Bearcat Mama Blues," "Eagle-Eye Mama Blues," all that stuff. Now that may be true life. He lived it. All those old guys sing about their wives or girlfriends or whatnot. Women, whiskey, or money. That's what you can sing about, right? Because you take a bluesman, they think alike. Somewhere down the line, they think alike. It is something that they've seen or done or had done to them. So bluesmen, their life kind of coincides. But, I'll tell you one thing, my wife, regardless of who I sing about, she knows who's got me. And she says she'll never let me loose. So I say, well, that's the bottom line. She'll never get away from me.

So some blues come from true experience and some come from imagination. Like, take that song I wrote, "Baby, Won't You Please Give Me a Break." I was sitting in my barbershop one day and I just decided to write a song. Well, I had put some things together and was looking for a title and then this sweet young thing walked by and I said, "Uh-huh, there goes my title." When the little girl walked down the street, well, I wasn't worried about anything. But you know older men. I mean, I'm not an old man yet, but older men might look at her and say, "Baby, please give me a break." Because she's looking just the way he would expect a young woman to look. It's like Furry Lewis, back in the twenties, wrote a song called "Everybody's Blues." So this is something like an everybody thing. You might see a good-looking woman coming down the street, you're afraid to say anything to her. But you're gonna say, "My God, baby, would you please give me a break?" Right? My age and her age, if anything happened between us, she'd have to give me a break. See what I mean?

So you can use your imagination or think about your own experiences. Everybody can get the blues. And if you don't have the blues, you just think about some of your old love affairs and you'll get the blues.

Repertoire

East Virginia John Henry

"John Henry," that's a song my father used to play. It was his favorite song and he played it on the five-string banjo and on the guitar in Sebastopol with a slide. That's the way I play it, too. But I call it "East

Virginia John Henry." That was my dad's favorite song, and if it was good enough for him, it's good enough for me to play.

It's an old legendary song and it was supposed to have happened over in the Big Bend Tunnel. That's what the song says. John Henry was a steel driver and he worked with his shaker. A shaker, he's the guy that sets the spikes and holds it so the steel driver can drive it down. John Henry was such a steel-driving man that if he hits it two or three times, it's all the way down to the cross tie. So the shaker, he holds it and the other guy pounds it. So that's why John Henry told the shaker, "You better pray." Because if he missed the piece of steel, tomorrow would be his burying day. So, naturally, the guy was kind of shaking, too. That's why they call them shakers.

1   John Henry walked into the Big Bend Tunnel
       His captain was by his side
       The rock was so tall, John Henry was so small
       Lord, he laid down his hammer and he cried
       He laid down his hammer and he cried

2   John Henry told his captain
       A man ain't nothin' but a man
       And before I let that steam drill beat me down
       I'll die with my hammer in my hand
       I'll die with my hammer in my hand

3   John Henry told his shaker
       Shaker, you better pray
       If I miss that piece of steel
       Tomorrow be your burying day
       Tomorrow be your burying day

4   John Henry had a little woman
       Her name was Polly Ann
       John Henry got sick and he couldn't get well
       Lord, Polly drove steel like a man
       Polly drove steel like a man

5   John Henry had a little woman
       The dress she wore was red
       Said, "I'm going to the track and I'm never coming back
       I'm going where my husband fell dead
       I'm going where my husband fell dead"

6   When I was in Roanoke City
     Coming down Fifth Avenue
     Met a little girl, she was dressed in red
     Said, "Honey, I'm crazy about you
     Honey, I'm crazy about you"

7   Ain't gonna tell you no story
     Ain't gonna tell you no lie
     If I don't get the girl I love
     Gonna take morphine and I'll die
     Gonna take morphine until I die

"John Henry" may be the most popular as well as the most re-searched Afro-American ballad. Most Americans have heard the song or are familiar with the story of the steel-driving man who proves that a special type of man is greater than a machine. Over the years scholars such as Guy Johnson, Louis Chappell, Richard Dorson, and Lawrence Levine and Brett Williams have sought the song's origins and discussed its symbolic importance. Currently, the best survey of the related litera-ture can be found in Norm Cohen's excellent survey of railroad songs, *Long Steel Rail*. Both Archie Edwards and John Cephas, as well as John Jackson, another well-known local artist, perform the song and testify to its popularity in the rural black community up to at least the 1940s. Its prevalence in field collections and songbooks further attests to its com-mon distribution. Countless recordings of the song are also available by both black and white musicians, blues artists, old-time country musi-cians, and popular singers.

Archie Edwards notes that it is an old legendary song and its leg-endary qualities have obscured its historicity. Nevertheless, local musi-cians tend to place the event in West Virginia and include references to the Big Bend Tunnel. Archie's version further localizes the ballad by adding what amounts to blues verses at the end of the song. Although he adheres to a fairly standard narrative, he switches to personalized verses following the first five verses, in effect beginning as a ballad and finishing as a blues.

While the song does not employ a common blues structure, the shift from narrative ballad content to common blues ideas leads me to call the song a "blues ballad." For our purpose, the term "blues ballad," first coined by D. K. Wilgus, tends to de-emphasize narrative continuity and strict chronological development in favor of commentary about the protagonist—the legendary figure—personal observations from the sing-er's perspective, or other traditional blues verses. This tendency toward personalizing narrative songs is fairly common to blues singers who happen to include several ballads in their repertoires. Furthermore, we should note that in the Southeast, certain ballads tended to serve more as dance songs, shifting the purpose away from storytelling. More concerned with meeting the needs of the dancers, musicians extended the song through improvisation or interpolation of traditional verses, such as Archie Edwards's final verse of "John Henry," more often associated with "Frankie and Johnny." Local musicians also contend that other participants, dancers, and audiences also added verses of their own.

For further information see B. A. Botkin, 230–239; Sterling Brown, 219; Louis Chappell; Norm Cohen, 61–69; Harold Courlander 1963, 280–286; Courlander 1976, 383–392; Richard Dorson 1959, 231–232; Zora Neale Hurston, 309–312; Guy Johnson; G. Malcolm Laws 1964, 246; MacEdward Leach and Horace P. Beck, 273; Alan Lomax 1960, 551–553, 560–561; John and Alan Lomax 1934, 3–10; Alton Morris, 182–183; Howard Odum and Guy Johnson 1926, 221–240; W. K. McNeil, 150–153; Paul Oliver, *Songsters*, 1984, 231–235; Walter Raim, 152–153; Art Rosenbaum, 188; Carl Sandburg, 24–25; Happy Traum, 36; Newman Ivey White, 189–191; John Work, 242–243; Brett Williams. Archie Edwards's version can be heard on LR 42.04. See also John Cephas's version.

Stack O'Lee

My dad played "Stack O'Lee" on the five-string banjo. That's where I first heard it. But I also learned it from John Hurt. He played it on the guitar. I learned it off a record when I was a kid because John Hurt was one of our idols. I bet when Stack O'Lee shot Billy De Lyon it wasn't over no more than a nickel or a quarter. Back in those days they didn't have no big money. You didn't steal nothing or cheat nobody back in those days. You did that, you take your life in your hand. Yeah, that was a real story, just like John Hardy. He killed his buddy for fifteen cents. Back in those days, fifteen cents or a quarter was big money.

The way I visualized it, Stack O'Lee was a bad man. Somebody that nobody would want to be bothered with, nobody would want to meet. I thought he was something like the Devil. You know, when you meet him you've had it. So that's the way I figured it. You'd never want to meet a man like that. It's like what we have today with these drugs. I just might write a legendary song about people murdering each other over drugs.

1   Police and officers, how can it be?
     You can arrest everybody but cruel Stack O'Lee
     He's the bad man, old cruel Stack O'Lee

2   Stack O'Lee, Stack O'Lee, please don't take my life
     I've got two little babies and a very lovely wife
     But he's the bad man, old cruel Stack O'Lee

3   What I care about your two little babes and your darling loving
          wife
       You stole my Stetson hat and I'm bound to take your life
       He's a bad man, old cruel Stack O'Lee

4   "Boom, boom, boom, boom," went a forty-four
       When they found Billy De Lyon, he's lying dead on that barroom
          floor
       That bad man, old cruel Stack O'Lee

5   Gentlemen of the jury, what do you think about that?
       Stack O'Lee killed Billy De Lyon about a five-dollar Stetson hat
       That bad man, old cruel Stack O'Lee

6   Standing on the gallows, Stack O'Lee let out a curse
       Judge says, "Let's hurry up, and kill him before he kills one of us"
       That bad man, old cruel Stack O'Lee

7   Standing on the gallows, had his head up high
       At twelve-o'clock they killed him, all glad to see him die
       He's a bad man, cruel Stack O'Lee

    "Stack O'Lee," or "Staggerlee," is another of America's best-known
black ballads. The story and the character may have some basis in reality, but so far nothing concrete has come to light. In most versions of the
legend, the bad man or bully, Stack O'Lee, kills Billy Lyons or De Lyons
over a gambling dispute. In John Hurt's 1928 version, which serves as
Archie's model, Stack is brought to trial and pays for his crimes. Other
versions embellish or curtail the details of the narrative, focusing on the
sheriff's and deputies' fear of Stack O'Lee, or adding motifs in which the
bad man goes down in hell and competes with the Devil. One odd version of "John Henry," by Silas Pendleton of Rappahannock County, Virginia, recorded in 1947, includes a spoken section in which Stack O'Lee
and John Henry have a set-to, with Stack O'Lee shooting the ties off John
Henry's shoes and the buttons off his shirt.
    John Cephas sings a fine version of the ballad and, according to
both men, the song was quite popular when they were young. White
bluesman Frank Hutchison, whom Archie admired, also performed the
piece. A rhythm and blues hit by Lloyd Price in 1959 served to fix the
song as a rock and country standard. Stories and narrative poems about
Stack O'Lee have been collected with some frequency, indicating his status as a folk hero.

See also: Roger Abrahams 1963, 129–142; Abrahams 1970, 45–47; B. A. Botkin, 122–130; Sterling Brown, 214; Robert E. Buehler, 187–191; Olive Wooley Burt, 202–203; Harold Courlander 1963, 178–179; Richard Dorson 1954, 160–162; Donald Garwood, 38; Stefan Grossman, Stephen Calt, and Hall Grossman 1973, 148; Bruce Jackson, 188–194; G. Malcolm Laws 1964, 253; Lawrence Levine, 413–415; Alan Lomax 1960, 559, 571–572; John and Alan Lomax 1934, 93–99; W. K. McNeil, 66–67; Howard Odum and Guy Johnson 1925, 245; Odum and Johnson 1926, 196–197, Paul Oliver, *Songsters*, 238–241; Art Rosenbaum, 104; Eric Sackheim, 255; Dorothy Scarborough 1925, 92–94.

See Archie Edwards, LR 42.036. For related recorded versions see Mississippi John Hurt, "Stack O'Lee Blues," Okeh 8654, December 28, 1928, reissued on *Mississippi John Hurt 1928 Sessions*, Yazoo 1065; Frank Hutchison, "Stackalee," Okeh 45106, 1927, reissued *American Folk Music: Volume One, Ballads*, Folkways FA2951; and John Cephas, FF 384.

Frankie and Johnny

"Frankie and Johnny," I first heard that from my dad. He played it on the guitar in open tuning, called it Sebastopol. But that's an old ballad, the old love story of Frankie and Johnny. Now that's been done so many different ways by so many different people. But I first heard it from my dad and from a record back in the thirties when I was a kid. John Hurt, he recorded it back in about 1929 under the title of "Frankie and Albert." He was the guy that recorded it, but people changed it. You know how people change the name and say, "This is mine."

But it's not yours. Somewhere down the line it goes back to the original owner. See, I know that. When I played it, John Hurt said, "Archie, I recorded that in 1929."

See, that was called "Frankie and Albert." But my daddy played it as "Frankie and Johnny." So this song represents two people that I admire ... my daddy and John Hurt. Of course, my dad and John Hurt were about the same age so they were hearing the same song about the same time. But my dad was in Virginia and John Hurt was in Mississippi. All them songs, "Stack O'Lee," "Frankie and Johnny," my dad played them on the five-string banjo. So when John Hurt came in to my view the songs he was singing, see, my dad already put those songs in my mind. But "Stack O'Lee" and "Frankie" was my daddy's favorites and he played them constantly.

1   Frankie and Johnny were lovers
      Oh Lord, how they did love
      They promised to be true to each other
      Just as true as the stars above
      Johnny was her man. Lord, he treats Frankie wrong

2 Frankie went down to the barroom
  Eyes were filled with tears
  She said, "Tell me, Mister Bartender,
  Has my loving Johnny been here?
  He's my man, but I think he's treating me wrong."

3 Bartender says, "I don't want to cause you
  Trouble, Miss Frankie
  I don't want to tell you no lie
  I saw your love about an hour ago with an old gal
   called Nellie Bly
  He's your man, all right, Lord, he sure been treating you
   wrong"

4 Frankie went back to her house
  She got her forty-four
  She went down to Nellie Bly's house
  She shot "boom, boom, boom" through that hardwood door
  Johnny was her man, she caught him treating her wrong

As widespread as "Stack O'Lee," "Frankie and Johnny" or "Frankie and Albert" supposedly commemorates an altercation between a St. Louis streetwalker and her boyfriend. Often treated comically, the song exploits the role reversal, uncommon in folksongs, where a woman is the murderer. Equally well-known in black and white traditions, the song and story have even been the subject of an Elvis Presley film. The song was well-known among blacks in rural Virginia, and Archie's version can be traced to his father, although it is similar to the Jimmie Rodgers version and perhaps supplemented by verses from Mississippi John Hurt. John Cephas also remembers it as a standard at country dances, recalling the fragment:

 Frankie and Johnny were lovers
 True as the skies above
 She shot her man, 'cause he was doing her wrong.

Another Virginia version was collected from Rappahannock County native Silas Pendleton in 1947.

For an excellent analysis of the John Hurt version see David Evans, 45–46. See also Harold Courlander 1963, 182–184; Courlander 1976, 394–396; Donald Garwood, 47; Stefan Grossman et al. 1973, 156–157; G. Malcolm Laws 1964, 247; MacEdward Leach and Horace P. Beck, 257–284; Alan Lomax 1960, 557, 569–570; John and Alan Lomax 1934, 103–110; John and Alan Lomax 1936,

192–201; Alton Morris, 126–128; Paul Oliver, *Songsters*, 1984, 235–238; Vance Randolph, 125–136; Eric Sackheim, 231; Carl Sandburg, 80–85; Newman Ivey White, 213.

Related recorded versions include: Mississippi John Hurt, "Frankie," Okeh 8560, February 14, 1929, reissued *Mississippi John Hurt: 1928 Sessions*, Yazoo 1065; and Bill Williams, "Low and Lonesome," Blue Goose 2004, 1970.

The Longest Train I Ever Saw Ran on The Red River Line

My father used to pick some songs about trains on the banjo. He had one he always played called "Ruby" that mentioned something about "You could hear the whistle blow five hundred miles." That's like the song John Cephas sings. But my favorite, the one I remember best, was "The Longest Train I Ever Saw Ran on the Red River Line." Man, I used to be crazy about that when I was a kid. I don't remember all the verses he did, but it had a whole lot of verses. Seems like in the old days, they'd take one song and stretch it out a mile long.

1   Said the longest train that I ever seen
       Ran on that Red River Line
       Said the engine came by at eight o'clock
       And the caboose came by at nine

2   The prettiest little girl that I ever did see
       Lived on that railroad line
       She had red-rose cheeks and coal-black hair
       And the curls hang down her back

3   True love, true love, what have I done
       That you should treat me so
       Look up, look down, that lonesome road
       Before you travel on

Archie's short version represents a song popular among black and white string-band musicians in the Southeast. John Cephas also performed a fragment of the piece:

The longest train I ever saw
It was on the Georgia Line
The engine passed by at six o'clock
And the cab came by and by

Archie refers to Cephas's song "Reno Factory," which he connects with his father's "Ruby" or "Reuben's Train." "Reno Factory," discussed later, also shows a similarity to Atlanta singer Peg Leg Howell's "Rolling Mill Blues" (Columbia 14438-D, 1929), which is considered a variant of "The Longest Train," which is probably the same song as "In the Pines"—all of which demonstrates how malleable this lyric song is. Coincidentally, another version of the piece was collected from a Kentucky musician named Uncle Ira Cephas, back in 1952. John, however, disavows any relation to him.

For further references see: Norm Cohen, 491–502; Judith McCulloh; and Bruce Buckley.

The Train That Carried My Girl from Town

My dad used to play that on the guitar. That was a slide song similar to "John Henry." He learned it off a record that we got from a fellow out in Virginia. It was by Frank Hutchison and I remember the other side was "Coney Island Blues." My father learned to play it pretty well and I'm trying to play it in the same way he did. But he was a little more professional on that one because he could play slides. That's what he mostly played when he played the guitar.

1   Take that train carried my girl from town
    Yes, if I knowed that number, sure would have flagged him
        down
    Hey, I hate that train that carried my girl from town

2   Hello, Central, give me six, oh, nine
    I want to talk to that girl of mine
    Hey, hey, hey

3   Wish to the Lord that train would wreck
    Kill the engineer, break the fireman's neck
    I hate that train that carried my girl from town

4   Take that train took my girl from town
    If I'd have knowed her number, I'd soon flag her down
    Hey, hey, hey

5   There goes my girl, somebody call her back
    She put her hand in my money sack, hey, hey
    I hate that train that carried my girl from town

West Virginian Frank Hutchison was a white guitarist who recorded in the late 1920s. Norm Cohen credits him with the dissemination of this song. "There is no question that this beautiful bluesy song was preserved only through the recordings of Frank Hutchison, one of the best white blues guitarists of the 1920's." Archie's version uses four of Hutchison's nine verses and his testimony corroborates Cohen's assertion. Cohen further notes that Hutchison drew on traditional verses found in other black folksongs.

See Norm Cohen, 426–430, and Frank Hutchison, "The Train That Carried My Girl from Town," Okeh 45114, April 29, 1927, reissued on *Frank Hutchison: The Train that Carried My Girl from Town*, Rounder 1007.

I'm Gonna Send You Back to Your Mother Payday

My dad played that a long time ago on the banjo and on the guitar. I play it in Sebastopol with a slide, but that was an old song. Uncle Dave Macon, he played it on the banjo. I got that verse:

> Honey, if you say so, I'll never work no more
> I'll hang around your shanty all the time

I got that from an old Uncle Dave Macon record, but the other verses, those were ones my daddy played. John Hurt, he played that, too. So I learned it from all of them.

1   I tried and I tried, but you're never satisfied
    I'm gonna send you back to your mother one of these days
    Hey, babe, Lord, please stay
    I'm gonna send you back to your mother's one of these days

2   There's a rabbit in the log, but we don't have a dog
    And we can't let this rabbit get away
    Get away, no, get away
    And we can't let this rabbit get away

3   Honey, if you say so, Lord, I'll never work no more
    And I'll hang around your shanty all the time
    All the time, all the time
    I will hang around your shanty all the time

Tony Russel links this song with other fiddle/banjo tunes, "Send You Back to Your Mother's," "Rabbit in the Log," and "Keep My Skillet

Good and Greasy." The short version could be expanded with other couplets if it were still functioning as a dance song. As it stands, Archie's recollection demonstrates the shift from banjo to similarly open-tuned guitar as a vehicle for the older fiddle and banjo tunes.

See: Stefan Grossman et al. 1973, 118–119; Tony Russell, 29.

John Hurt, "Payday," Vanguard CRS 9220, 1964; Uncle Dave Macon, "I'll Keep My Skillet Good and Greasy," BB 5873, January 22, 1935; Henry Thomas, "Shanty Blues," Vocalion 1139, October 1927, reissued *Henry Thomas Sings the Texas Blues*, Origin Jazz Library OJL3; Dock Boggs, "Sugar Baby," Brunswick 1188, 1928, reissued *Anthology of American Folk Music, Volume Three: Songs*, Folkways FA2935; and Eli Owens, "Rabbit on a Log," *South Mississippi Blues*, Rounder Records 2009.

Candy Man

That "Candy Man" was the first song I learned of John Hurt's back when I was a kid, back in thirty-three or thirty-four. "Stack O'Lee" was the other song I learned from him. From those two songs I followed John Hurt from Virginia through Mississippi and finally wound up meeting him in Washington, D.C. That was the greatest thing that ever happened to me.

1   All you ladies, gather round
     The candy man is back in town
     He's your candy man, candy man

2   Big stick of candy, don't melt away
     Just gets better, so the ladies say
     He's your candy man, candy man

3   All you ladies, gather round
     Candy man is back in town
     He's your candy man, candy man

4   You and the candy man is getting mighty thick
     You must be stuck on the candy man's kiss

Like so many blues songs, "Candy Man" employs a sexual metaphor initially made even more comical by John Hurt's innocent delivery. Archie learned his version from a 1928 recording with "Candy Man" on one side and "Stack O'Lee Blues" on the other.

For John Hurt's lyrics and music, see: Donald Garwood, 40; Stefan Grossman et al. 1973, 205; Eric Sackheim, 229; Mississippi John Hurt, "Candy Man," Okeh 45106, 1928, reissued *Mississippi John Hurt 1928 Sessions*, Yazoo 1065; and Babe Stovall, "Candy Man," *South Mississippi Blues*, Rounder Records 2009.

Lovin' Spoonful

John Hurt played "Lovin' Spoonful," only he called it "Coffee Blues." That's Maxwell House Coffee, good to the last drop, he said. So you know where those boys out of Canada, you know, John Sebastian and the Lovin' Spoonful, got their name. They had a group, but they didn't have a name, so they heard about this old bluesman from America coming to perform in Ottawa. They said, "We'll go down and hear this guy play because he's supposed to be pretty good."

So they got down there and when they heard John Hurt play "Lovin' Spoonful," that became their title. So I know that John Hurt is the real Lovin' Spoonful Number One. And he asked me to carry on his work, so that must make me the Lovin' Spoonful Number Two, right?

1   I've got to go to Memphis
     From there to New Orleans
     I got to find my baby
     Get my lovin' spoonful
Chorus
        A spoonful, my lovin' spoonful,
        I just can't do without my lovin' spoonful

2   My baby packed her suitcase
     She went away
     She had to come back
     To get her lovin' spoonful
Chorus
        A spoonful, my lovin' spoonful,
        I just can't do without my lovin' spoonful

3   Said old preacher in the pulpit
     He was jumping up and down
     Laid his Bible down
     To get his lovin' spoonful
Chorus
        A spoonful, my lovin' spoonful,
        I just can't do without my lovin' spoonful

4   Good morning, baby
        How'd you do this morning
        I don't feel so fine
        Need my lovin' spoonful
Chorus
        A spoonful, my lovin' spoonful,
        I just can't do without my lovin' spoonful

According to Don Kent's notes, Papa Charlie Jackson's 1925 Paramount recording "All I Want Is a Spoonful" was based on a popular black song with pre-blues origins. Since this initial recording of the piece, there have been a variety of blues songs called "Spoonful." For example, Chicago bluesman Howling Wolf did a song by that title, written by Willie Dixon, which has become a standard in the Chicago idiom; and Texas songster Mance Lipscomb recorded another very different version. "Spoonful" is a traditional sexual metaphor, although it can have several meanings, which is a common trait in blues poetry. Archie's version follows John Hurt's song entitled "Coffee Blues."

See: Donald Garwood, 40; Stefen Grossman et al. 1973, 58–59.
    See also: LR 42.036; and John Hurt, "Coffee Blues," *Mississippi John Hurt Today*, Vanguard VSD 79220; Papa Charlie Jackson, "All I Want Is a Spoonful," Paramount 12320, September 1925, reissued *Papa Charlie Jackson 1925–1928*, Biograph Records BLP 12042; and Charley Patton, "A Spoonful Blues," Paramount 12869, June 14, 1929, reissued on *Charley Patton: Founder of the Delta Blues*, Yazoo L1020.

Monday Morning Blues

"Monday Morning Blues," that's John Hurt. That song tells a story and I really like it myself. I had several requests for it before I made up my mind to learn to play it. But learning it was no problem because I already knew how to play "Lovin' Spoonful" and all of his other stuff. So I just said, "Well, I'll add another one of his."

So now the next time you see me, I may be adding another one and then the next time I may be doing his whole repertoire. But he asked me to do it, so I have nothing to do but work on it.

1   Oh Monday morning blues
        Oh Monday morning blues
        Oh Monday morning blues
        Feel it all through my bones

2   Been laying jail
      Been laying jail
      Been laying jail
      Six long weeks today

3   But tomorrow morning
      But tomorrow morning
      But tomorrow morning
      Gonna be my trial day

4   I asked the judge
      I asked the judge
      I asked the judge
      What might be my fine?

5   He said, "Get a pick and shovel"
      He said, "Get a pick and shovel"
      He said, "Get a pick and shovel"
      Man, let's go down in the mine

6   That's the only time
      That's the only time
      That's the only time [Lord]
      That I ever felt like crying

7   I woke up this morning
      I woke up this morning
      I woke up this morning
      With the Monday morning blues

8   Mister, please change a dollar
      Mister, please change a dollar
      Mister, please change a dollar
      And give me a lucky dime

John Hurt is the source of this song originally recorded for Okeh, February 14, 1928, but unissued. Archie considers this piece to be a story song, and it does imply a story line. This song is unusual by blues standards, actually a single line with the first half repeated three times. In this respect, it has characteristics of early blues, where a single line can be repeated three or four times.

See John Cephas, "Going Down That Road Feeling Bad," for another example. And for John Hurt's version, see *Mississippi John Hurt: Monday Morning*

Blues, 1963 Library of Congress Recordings Volume One, Flyright FLY 533. This piece is somewhat similar to Virginian William Moore's "One Way Gal," Paramount 20309-1, January 1928, reissued on *Ragtime Blues Guitar: 1928–30*, Matchbox MSE 204.

Take Me Back Baby

I learned that from John Hurt. I didn't try to change that. See, John Hurt told me, "Play my music. Talk about me every way that you know and that way I don't die. You teach people my music and teach them your music and that way you'll pass it on. When you're gone, somebody will be carrying your work on for you."

So I got to pick up and find me somebody to carry my work on for me. I guess I'll find a beautiful little girl and teach her how to play. That would be enjoyable, knowing that a cute little woman is going to carry my work on for me. Now his version is the same as mine. I don't know if he had a different title, but this is what I learned from him.

1   Take me back, baby, try me one more time
     Take me back, baby, try me one more time
     If I don't treat you right
     I'll kill my fool self trying

2   There's no more potatoes, mama, the frost has killed the vine
     There's no more potatoes, mama, the frost has killed the vine
     And the blues ain't nothing, man,
     But another man's woman on your mind

3   You tell me pretty mama, is there something going on wrong
     You tell me pretty mama, is there something going on wrong
     You went away last night
     And you stayed out all night long

4   Take me back, baby, try me one more time
     Yes, take me back, baby, try me one more time
     If I don't treat you right
     I'll kill my fool self trying

I can't find a song with this title among John Hurt's recorded works. However, the second verse is also the second verse in John Hurt's "See See Rider."

See: Stefan Grossman et al. 1973, 154. Archie claims the only other song he does that John Hurt also did was "Keep A-Knocking But You Can't Come In."

Chinch Bug Blues

My uncle bought that record. He came out of the army in something like 1920, and about six years later Blind Lemon Jefferson began to be pretty popular with blues. My uncle, he liked the blues, and he bought this record and brought it home, "Chinch Bug Blues." I listened to it on the old record player. Once I heard it a couple of times, well, I've had it ever since then. It's the first song by Blind Lemon that I learned. I've been playing it since I was fifteen or sixteen years old. It's just like my daddy used to say, I got a memory like an elephant and that's just about right. I never forget a song. Yes, I played that at the same time that my daddy used to play back when I was a kid. Nothing was written down, but any time I heard a song, and I liked it, I stayed with it and never forgot it.

1   I wonder if a chinch will bite in Beaumont
    Like they do in Beale Street Town
    I wonder if a chinch will bite in Beaumont
    Like they do in Beale Street Town
    Since I stayed in Memphis
    Chinch bug turned the bed around

2   Well, my wife has quit me
    What's sweet-pea daddy gonna do?
    Well, my wife has quit me
    What's sweet-pea daddy gonna do?
    I'll just hang around here all alone
    Sing these chinch bug blues

3   Had to get the people with the pistols
    Keep the chinch from taking my life
    Had to get the people with the pistols
    Keep the chinch from taking my life
    Old chinch bug got my number
    Wrote a sweet letter to my wife

4   That must have been a bedbug
    'Cause a chinch won't bite so hard
    That must have been a bedbug

'Cause a chinch won't bite so hard
I asked my baby for fifty cents
Said, "There ain't a dime in the yard"

Through his phonograph recordings, Texas bluesman Blind Lemon
Jefferson influenced both black and white musicians in the Southeast as
well as throughout the country. Jefferson's impact also demonstrates
how recordings changed local or regional repertoire and style. Dick
Spottswood tells me that "chinche" is the Spanish word for bedbug.

This version derives from Jefferson's "Chinch Bug Blues," Paramount
12551, Chicago, October 1927, reissued on *Masters of the Blues: Blind Lemon
Jefferson, Volume 2: 1926–29*, Biograph BLP 12015.

One Thin Dime Blues

I learned that off a Blind Lemon Jefferson record, but Willie Gaines, he
played it, too. I caught it from a record at my aunt's house back in 1934
or 1935. But Willie Gaines played it at the barbershop and I was surprised anyone still played it. So when he played it, I sat down and we
played it together because I had heard it years ago, and had been playing it all along. Yeah, Willie Gaines, he was tight on that, "One Thin
Dime Blues." But I used to back him on it.

1   I'm broke, ain't got a dime
     I'm broke, ain't got a dime
     I'm broke, ain't got a dime
     Just a poor boy and, Lord, it happens all the time

2   I was standing on the corner of Cairo City one day
     I was standing on the corner of Cairo City one day
     I was standing on the corner of Cairo City one day
     One dime was all that I had

3   Oh, mama, don't treat your little girl mean
     Oh, mama, don't treat your little girl mean
     Oh, mama, don't treat your little girl mean
     She's the meanest old woman that the poor girl's ever seen

4   I'm broke and I ain't got a dime
     I'm broke and I ain't got a dime
     I'm broke and I ain't got a dime
     Just a poor boy and it happens all the time

5   One dime was all that I had
        One dime was all that I had
        One dime was all that I had
        And it done got late and cold

6   I'm broke and I ain't got a dime
        I'm broke and I ain't got a dime
        I'm broke and I ain't got a dime
        Every poor boy gonna have hard luck sometime

Versions of "One Dime Blues" have been collected and recorded throughout the United States, testifying to the popularity and the staying power of the 1927 Paramount recording by Blind Lemon Jefferson. Elements of the song may have been traditional before Blind Lemon recorded the piece. Kip Lornell notes a similarity to William Moore's "One Way Gal" cited in the notes to "Monday Morning Blues." Both Archie and John Cephas do the song. In fact, Cephas does a fast and a slow version. Other Virginians, Willie Gaines (whom Archie mentions) and James Lowry, from Bedford, Virginia, also perform it. W. C. Handy in "East St. Louis Blues" employs the line:

Walked all the way from East St. Louis
And I didn't have but one poor lousy dime

Like "Monday Morning Blues" and Cephas's "Going Down That Road Feeling Bad," it employs a four-line verse. On another occasion Archie added the verse:

You gonna call me your dog when I'm gone
You gonna call me your dog when I'm gone
You call me your dog when I'm gone
But when I come back with that hundred-dollar bill
Say, "Where you been so long?"

This verse, associated with "Black Dog Blues," led back into "I'm broke and I ain't got a dime."

See: W. C. Handy and Abbe Niles, 53; Alan Lomax 1960, 586; John and Alan Lomax 1936, 131–135; Kip Lornell 1978, 11; Blind Lemon Jefferson, "One Dime Blues," Paramount 12578, October 1927, reissued *Blind Lemon Jefferson: The Remaining Titles*, Matchbox MSE 1001.

Bearcat Mama Blues

Blind Lemon Jefferson had a lot of trouble with his girlfriends, but he came up with one that I really liked, "Bearcat Blues." A Bearcat Mama is nothing but a young woman that watches everything you do.

A lot of us wake up in the morning feeling fine, but then have to go out on the streets to get some bread together to take care of that woman of yours. Well, this is what Blind Lemon was trying to tell you, if you listen to the song. You see why he was sneaking out the door? He didn't want to wake her up, so he'd hear her "yap, yap, yap" anymore. You know, "yak, yak, yak" all day. Yeah, he was sneaking out the door, but I think she caught him. "Old Bearcat mama / Don't want to hear her mouth no more."

You know, some of these girls, they "yak, yak" all night and, man, you don't get no sleep. You get up, try to sneak out.

"Where you going?"

That's life. That's why he called her a bearcat mama.

1   I waked up this morning
     Lord, I sure was feeling fine
     I waked up this morning
     Lord, I sure was feeling fine
     Said had to walk the streets all over
     See that bearcat woman of mine

2   She was fussing, she was fighting
     She was acting like a doggone fool
     She was fussing, she was fighting
     She was acting like a doggone fool
     Said she was heeing, she was hawing
     Acting just like a balky mule

3   Bearcat and wildcat
     But she won't stay home at night
     Lord, bearcat and a wildcat
     But she won't stay home at night
     But when it comes down to squabbling
     That girl sure know how to scratch and bite

4   I was standing on the corner
     Said I was thinking about that old bearcat news
     I was standing on the corner
     Thinking about that old bearcat news

Yeah, that old bearcat mama
She ran me home to the bearcat blues

5   I waked up this morning
I said I was sneaking out the door
I waked up this morning
I said I was sneaking out the door
I didn't want to wake up old bearcat mama
Don't want to hear her mouth no more

One of Archie's favorite and most frequently performed songs, "Bearcat Mama Blues" comes from Blind Lemon Jefferson's "Balky Mule Blues."

Blind Lemon Jefferson "Balky Mule Blues," Chicago, Paramount 12631, October 1928, reissued on *Blind Lemon Jefferson: Early Years*, Olympic Records 7134, n.d. Archie Edwards's version is on LR 42.030.

Eagle-Eye Mama Blues

There were a couple of guys from Texas that I heard when I was growing up. There was one guy named Texas Alexander; Blind Willie Johnson, he was a spiritual singer; Blind Lemon Jefferson; and then later, Lightning Hopkins. I listened to all their records.

Blind Lemon, he was a blind man, but he had a lot of girlfriends. He couldn't see, so I guess he imagined a lot of things that weren't there. He had all kinds of woman blues, "Eagle-Eye Mama Blues," "Stocking Feet Mama Blues." But he wrote that "Eagle-Eye mama . . . watching him all day and night. Kept those eyes on him until the good Lord broke daylight." So you know that was pretty tough.

1   My woman got eyes like an eagle
Lord, she watch me all the time
She got eyes like an eagle
Lord, she watch me all the time
She keeps her eagle eyes on me
Till the good Lord breaks daylight

2   There's a dog in my backyard
Oh, Lordy, how he can howl
There's a dog in my backyard
Oh, Lordy, how he can howl

I'm trying to quit the eagle-eyed woman, man
And I don't know how

3   My eagle-eyed woman
Got ways, Lord, that I can't explain
My eagle-eyed woman
Got ways, Lord, that I can't explain
But I know if I ever leave her
That gal would go insane

4   There's a dog in my backyard
Lord, how he can howl
There's a dog in my backyard
Lord, how he can howl
I'm trying to quit this eagle-eyed woman, man
And I don't know how

See: Blind Lemon Jefferson, "Eagle Eye Mama," Paramount 12739, January 1929.

Screaming and Crying Blues

Blind Boy Fuller was one of the biggest things going back years ago. I learned some of his songs. Now, "Screaming and Crying," I heard that after I had grown up, sometime back in the mid-1950s. I was grown and married and had been in the service. I got hold of one of his old records from somewhere and I learned it.

1   Say, I lay down last night laughing, mama
I waked up screaming and crying
I lay down last night laughing, mama
I waked up screaming and crying
I was worried about my little baby
Lord, she's gone and left me behind

2   She's gone and left me
Left me sick and on my bed
She's gone and left me
Left me sick and on my bed
She left me without anybody
Lord, to hold my worried head

3   I don't care where you go mama
    Don't care how long you stay
    I don't care where you go, mama
    Don't care how long you stay
    It's my good kind treatment, mama
    That's going to bring you home to me again someday

Born Fulton Allen around 1907, Blind Boy Fuller died a young man in 1941. Despite his short life, he was the Piedmont region's most recorded and most influential blues artist. Assessing the Piedmont tradition, blues scholar Paul Oliver concluded, "Of this considerable body of folk talent, anonymous and legendary alike, none was more famous than Blind Boy Fuller." With an output of more than one hundred songs on a variety of labels, he was also, as Sam Charters noted, "the best selling of all the East Coast bluesmen."

Fuller worked with and recorded with other major Piedmont artists, including John Cephas's hero, Blind Gary Davis, and harmonica virtuoso Blind Sonny Terry. Cephas and Archie either learned directly from Fuller recordings or from other artists who were influenced by Fuller. Irrespective of his terrific influence, Fuller was not really the wellspring of the traditional Piedmont style. Rather, he was a popularizer in the best sense and a synthesizer who assimilated and reinterpreted the musical traditions of his region as well as those available from blues recordings. In this way, I consider him to be similar to the Mississippi Delta artist Robert Johnson.

Archie has an old 78 RPM version of "Screaming and Crying," with "She's a Truckin' Little Baby" on the flip side, in his barbershop today. Generally, he no longer owns recordings he learned from. See "Screaming and Crying," Columbia 37155 (SC20), originally recorded on Vocalion 04603, October 29, 1939. Reissued on *Death Valley: Blind Boy Fuller 1907–1941*, Oldies Blues OL 2809.

You're So Sweet, My Woman's So Sweet

You know my wife, Frances, I played her this song before we got married, and she liked the song. So she said, "You will never get rid of me."

I thought she was kidding, but thirty-four years later since that, I don't believe she's kidding me. Now, I've seen her a few times where I wished I hadn't played that song, but it worked out. It was worth it all. Yeah, we're very happy. Yeah, it paid out pretty well. I believe if I had to do it over again, I'd do the same thing.

1   Hey, woman, hey, gal, don't you hear me calling you
     You're so sweet, yes, you're so sweet
     Woman's so sweet

2   I love my little woman, love her to the bone
     Till it breaks my heart sometimes
     Just to see the little woman go home
     She's so sweet, yeah, she's so sweet
     My woman's so sweet

3   When you see me with my woman, man
     Don't you get so smart
     'Cause I will cut your liver out, man
     And I'll plug your heart
     She's so sweet, yes, she's so sweet
     My woman's so sweet

4   I'd walk a many miles for you, good woman
     I'll even rob a little bee
     'Cause the woman I love, she's the sweet thing
     In this whole round world to me
     She's so sweet, yes, she's so sweet
     My woman's so sweet

This popular Fuller song has become a blues standard. It is one of the few songs that both Archie Edwards and John Cephas perform. Fuller's version has been singled out as being reminiscent of the field-holler tradition. In fact, it was recorded by Frederick Ramsey, Jr., from an Alabama singer as a field holler. On one hand, this may be a case of a man singing a blues song while out in a field (you can hear a tractor and birds). On the other hand, it shows a free-form holler approach leading Paul Oliver to note of Fuller: "That he remained close to the roots of the blues is clearly evident in the echoes of the field holler that are to be heard in his recording of 'Little Woman You're So Sweet.' " Archie, however, used it as a praise poem and love song in an obviously effective manner. Musically, the song is related to "How Long, How Long Blues."

See: Stefan Grossman et al. 1973, 180; Oliver, *Blues*, 1984, 98; Blind Boy Fuller, "Little Woman You're So Sweet," Vocalion 05476, March 6, 1940, reissued *Blind Boy Fuller 1936–1940*, Old Tramp OT-1202. See also John Cephas's version, p. 227.

Baby Let Me Lay It on You

I learned that from Blind Boy Fuller, but he didn't really make it up. He was one of the stealingest dudes in the world. Memphis Minnie called it "Baby Let Me Do It For You" and he took it and called it "Baby Let Me Lay It on You."

1   Baby let me lay it on you
     Baby let me lay it on you
     I'd give anything in the whole round world
     Baby let me lay it on you

2   Baby let's go across town
     We can get drunk and clown
     Get drunk and clown all night long
     Baby let's go 'cross town

3   Buy you a brand-new suit
     I'll cut your throat to boot
     I'll do anything in the whole round world
     Baby let's go across town

4   Baby let me lay it on you
     Baby let me lay it on you
     I'd give anything in the whole round world
     Baby let me lay it on you

Archie's version of this well-traveled song, also known as "Baby Don't Tear My Clothes," derives from Blind Boy Fuller's "Mama Let Me Lay It on You," ARC 6-08-54, April 28, 1936. Also available on "Death Valley," *Blind Boy Fuller 1907–1941*, Oldies Blues OL 2809. Archie's version has not been recorded.

Cherry Red River Blues

That's an old song that I picked up during the time I was working at the sawmill. I would hear guys singing it out in the woods while they were working, and this song just stuck in my ear. It's an old song, one of the most popular here on the East Coast. But I took the old "Red River Blues" and called it the "Cherry Red River Blues" and play it in my own style. But it was one of the first songs I ever heard.

1   I love my little woman
    She's low and little, too
    That woman is three times seven
    But she don't know what she want to do

2   Which way, pretty woman
    Do the Cherry Red River run
    From my back window
    Straight to the rising sun

3   Go down on the corner
    Tell my brother Bill
    That that woman he's loving
    Lord, sure gives me a thrill

4   I know, yes, I know
    Why the poor boys don't draw no more
    Because the line from the pay table
    Goes straight to the commissary door

5   Which way, which way
    Do the Cherry Red River run
    From my back window
    Straight to the rising sun

It comes as no surprise that the most extensive study of blues in the Southeast is titled *Red River Blues*. Researcher Kip Lornell notes, "This song is a favorite among musicians in the Southeast and has been for fifty years." Although it is also known in Mississippi and Texas, along with "Crow Jane," which is very similar, "Red River Blues" could be considered the Piedmont blues national anthem. Notable versions were recorded by two of the most popular Piedmont musicians. Josh White did it as "Blood Red River" in 1933 and Blind Boy Fuller as "Bye Bye Baby Blues" in 1937.

The song's verses are interchangeable with those of other eight-bar blues songs that are sometimes referred to as related to the "Crow Jane" family. In this manner, performers of songs such as "Red River Blues," "Crow Jane," "How Long, How Long Blues," and "Key to the Highway" may draw from a common pool of traditional blues verses when and where he or she thinks they work. For example, John Cephas doesn't play "Red River Blues" by that name, but he does play a version of Big Bill Broonzy's "Key to the Highway," which concludes with the verse:

Tell me, tell me
Which way the Red River run
It runs from the back door
To the rising sun

This practice of using traditional verses is likewise common with twelve-bar blues and was initially noted by scholars in relation to African-American ballads.

See Archie's comments in the work-camp section, p. 39. For further information see: Bruce Bastin; David Evans, 151, 268; Kip Lornell 1978, 13; Paul Oliver 1969, 128; Oliver, *Blues*, 1984, 95–98; Walter Raim, 56–57; Eric Sackheim, 349.

For several East Coast versions see: Josh White, "Blood Red River," Banner 32858, August 15, 1933; Blind Boy Fuller, "Bye Bye Baby Blues," Vocalion 04843, 1937, reissued *Blind Boy Fuller with Sonny Terry and Bull City Red*, Blues Classics 11; John Jackson, "Red River Blues," Arhoolie 1047; and Bill Jackson, "Blood Red River," Testament Y-201.

Poor Boy a Long Way from Home

"Poor Boy a Long Way from Home" was an old song we used to play at the logging camp. Lots of guys played it when I was a kid. They played in open tuning, Sebastopol, with a slide. Now, the one I do, I don't use a slide. I learned it from a Barbecue Bob record that my brother brought home. I didn't do too much of Barbecue Bob, but any song I liked, if it registered in my ear and I liked it, I played it.

1 I'm a poor boy
   A long way from home
   Yes, I'm a poor boy
   A long way from home
   Got no place to lay my weary head

2 Mama, tell me
   What you gonna do
   Oh, Mama, tell me
   What you gonna do
   Sometimes I think I'm gonna lose my mind over you

3 I'm the poor boy
   Stood on the road and cried
   I'm the poor boy

Stood on the road and cried
Didn't have the blues, but I couldn't be satisfied

While Archie's version stems from the Barbecue Bob 1927 recording, the song "Poor Boy a Long Way from Home" is probably two decades older. Howard Odum uncovered a version which he published in 1911, noting that it was often a knife or slide song. It appears to have been one of the earliest blues to have a relatively stable melody that coincided with rudimentary slide or bottleneck chord positions on an open-tuned guitar. Kentucky guitarist J. T. Adams told me, "My daddy played a piece about 'Poor Boy a Long Way from Home' in bottleneck when I was a kid, so I know it's old."

One of the earliest blues, the song was also widely disseminated and recorded in the Memphis area and in Texas. In the Southeast, Atlanta bluesman Robert Hicks recorded it in 1927. Perhaps more telling, fellow Atlanta musician Blind Willie McTell alluded to it by title and by playing the signature musical phrase in his 1929 recording "Travelin' Blues." His allusion implies his audience would be familiar with the piece. Some versions of "Poor Boy" are "one-verse songs," an older, pre-blues form where a single line is repeated three times. Archie's short version combines Barbecue Bob's first and third verse in its first verse, expands and rhymes up Barbecue Bob's one-line second verse, and closes with a personalized interpretation of Barbecue Bob's fourth verse. Paul Oliver provides a short comparison of four versions of the song, including Odum's and the Barbecue Bob recording. Zora Neale Hurston presents a song titled "East Coast Blues" with the words "Po' gal long ways from home."

See: David Evans, 268; Zora Neale Hurston, 314; Howard Odum and Guy Johnson 1925, 169; Paul Oliver 1969, 27–29. Barbecue Bob, "Poor Boy a Long Ways from Home," Columbia 14246-D, June 16, 1927, reissued on *Barbecue Bob 'Brownskin Gal'*, Agram Blues AB 2001; and Blind Willie McTell, "Travelin Blues," Columbia 1484, October 30, 1929, reissued on *Blind Willie McTell 1927–1933: The Early Years*, Yazoo L-1005.

How Long Blues

That was done by Scrapper Blackwell and Leroy Carr, but I kind of made my own version. That used to be my favorite song at the sawmill camp, so I played it a lot of times. Some of the guys got up the next morning, say, "Man, if you'd of played that song a little longer, the sun would have come up shining on my little butt going down that road in the morning. I'd been leaving here."

1   How long, pretty mama, how long
     Do you think I'm gonna let you treat me wrong
     How long, how long, baby, how long

2   You a dirty mistreater and you ain't no good
     Why do you think I would worry if you left the neighborhood
     For so long, so long, baby, so long

3   If I could holler like a mountain jack
     I'd go up on some mountain, call my baby back
     She been gone so long, so long, she been gone so long

4   I'm going to the pawnshop, I'm gonna put my watch in pawn
     Don't want nothing in my house, tell me how long my baby
        been gone
     She been gone so long, so long, yes, my baby been gone so long

Indianapolis-based piano and guitar duo Leroy Carr and Scrapper Blackwell were very popular at the end of the 1920s and during the 1930s. According to blues scholar Jeff Titon, their recording of "How Long, How Long Blues" was one of the best-selling blues records of any period. Like other hits of the era, its success led to follow-up versions, "How Long, How Long Blues" Parts Two and Three.

Archie attributes his version to Carr and Blackwell, but it only shares the third verse with the original. His other verses may come from Carr follow-ups or, more likely, from a local cover. One possible contender would be Blind Boy Fuller's "I Don't Care How Long." Like other eight-bar blues, it has been linked to the "Crow Jane" / "Red River" family.

For a fine survey see Norm Cohen, 437–440. See also: Bill Ferris, 192–193; Alan Lomax 1960, 589–592; and Jeff Titon 1977, 89–92.

Leroy Carr and Scrapper Blackwell, "How Long, How Long Blues," Vocalion 1091, June 1928; Carr and Blackwell, Parts Two and Three, Vocalion 1241, 1279; Blind Boy Fuller, "I Don't Care How Long," Vocalion 05273, June 12, 1939.

Sitting on Top of the World

I love the old blues number "Sitting on Top of the World." Most everybody has done it, but they don't do it right. Les Paul and Mary Ford, they did it, but they jacked the song up so high until it was higher than the moon. It didn't have anything to do with "Sitting on Top of the

World," to put it back in its slot. It was written way back in the 1920s or 1930s by the Mississippi Sheiks. I learned it in the 1940s and it's one of the favorite songs I do. But I rearranged it. It's one of the old type, but nobody played it the way I thought it should sound. So I figured I would blues it. Back in the 1930s you had no money, didn't have a job, and your girlfriend was about the only person you could rely on. And when she put you down, you really had the blues. This is my version of "Sitting on Top of the World."

1   Here you come running, holding out your hand
    I can get a woman, faster than you can a man
    Oh, now she's gone, but I don't worry
    Because I'm sitting on top of the world

2   It was in the spring, one sunny day
    When my little girl left me, Lord, she's gone to stay
    Now she's gone, but I don't worry
    Because I'm sitting on top of the world

3   I'm going down to the station, gonna stand in the yard
    Gonna catch me a freight train, Lord, times done got hard
    Well, now she's gone, but I don't worry
    Because I'm sitting on top of the world

4   Worked all the summer, I worked all the fall
    Now I'm gonna spend my Christmas, Lord, in my dirty overalls
    Oh, now she's gone, but I don't worry
    Because I'm sitting on top of the world

Originally recorded by a popular black string band called the Mississippi Sheiks, "Sitting on Top of the World" was another best-seller known to both black and white artists. Credited to Walter Jacob and Lonnie Carter, also known as Walter Vinson and Lonnie Chatmon, the song was immediately covered by dozens of competitive versions, and on the East Coast it has been recorded by Blind Boy Fuller as "I'm Climbing on Top of the Hill" and by the Two Poor Boys and Sonny Terry and Brownie McGhee. Other influential versions are associated with Bob Wills and Bill Monroe, the respective kings of Western swing and bluegrass. To this day it remains a standard. Archie feels he has personalized this song which, to him, tells a real story that captures the spirit of the time in which it was written. According to Robert Palmer, the first songs Muddy Waters learned from recordings were "How Long, How Long Blues" and "Sitting on Top of the World."

See: Robert Palmer, 111; Mississippi Sheiks, "Sitting on Top of the World," Okeh 0784, February 17, 1930, reissued on *Stop and Listen: The Mississippi Sheiks*, Mamlish S 3804. Archie recorded it on LR 42.042.

Kansas City Rock

Jim Jackson wrote the old "Kansas City Blues" a long time ago, and recorded it in '26 or '27, sometime in the twenties. We had the old record and it had the same song on both sides, Part One and Two. Somewhere along the way I changed it around and put a little more beat to it. So I call mine the "Kansas City Rock."

1   My mama told me; Pop, he told me, too
     Don't let them smile in your face, son, make a fool of you
     Because we move to Kansas City
     Yes, you got to move to Kansas City
     They got to move to Kansas City
     Because everybody's doing the Kansas City Rock

2   Mississippi River is so long, deep, and wide
     I done seen my good gal, she moved to the other side
     You got to move to Kansas City
     Yes, you got to move to Kansas City
     Move to Kansas City
     Because everybody's doing the Kansas City Rock

3   I looked down the river, as far as I could see
     The boll weevil had the cotton, the women fighting after me
     They got to move to Kansas City
     Yes, we got to move to Kansas City
     They got to move to Kansas City
     Because everybody's doing the Kansas City Rock

4   If I was a catfish, swimming down in the sea
     I'd have all these pretty-looking women fishing after me
     Because I moved to Kansas City
     You got to move to Kansas City
     Move to Kansas City
     Because everybody's doing the Kansas City Rock

Similar to "How Long, How Long Blues" and "Sitting on Top of the World," "Jim Jackson's Kansas City Blues" was popular enough to lead to "Jim Jackson's Kansas City Blues," Parts Three and Four. Memphis songster Jim Jackson recorded the original two-sided hit in 1927. Since that time it has been a standard, inspiring various other "Kansas Cities." In contrast to "Sitting on Top of the World," Archie has "jumped" this song, creating the "Kansas City Rock."

See: Jim Jackson, "Jim Jackson's Kansas City Blues, Part One and Two," Vocalion 1144, December 8, 1927, reissued on *Jim Jackson's Kansas City Blues*, Agram Blues AB 2004.

Meet Me in the Bottom

I learned that in Franklin County in '34 or '35. I believe it was some-body like Buddy Moss or Blind Boy Fuller who recorded it. But whoever did it, it sounded good to me, so I'm still doing it.

Now Blind Boy Fuller and Buddy Moss were popular around the same time, so it might have been Blind Boy Fuller, but then I would have thought it would have a harmonica in it. But I learned it back when I was a kid and I played it one night over in Rocky Mount. Me and Clayborn Edwards played it over at Grant's Place.

1   Meet me in the bottom, bring me my boots and shoes
      Hey, Lord, meet me in the bottom, bring me my boots and
        shoes
      Gonna leave town early in the morning
      I ain't got no time to lose

2   Now the woman I love, she just gone back home
      Hey, Lord, the woman I love, she just gone back home
      Everytime she leaves me
      Lord, it makes my blood run warm

3   She caught the C & O Limited, left me standing looking down
      Hey, Lord, she caught the C & O Limited, left me standing
        looking down
      I couldn't stand to see
      My little woman leave this town

4   She's little and low, built right down on the ground
      Hey, yeah, she's little and low, built right down on the ground
      Got the kind of loving, make a bulldog love a hound

5 So meet me in the bottom, bring me my boots and shoes
  Hey, Lord, meet me in the bottom, bring me my boots and
  shoes
  Leaving town early in the morning
  I ain't got no time to lose

Still another very popular blues, "Meet Me in the Bottom," also known as "Hey Lawdy Mama" and "Boots and Shoes," has been recorded by various East Coast artists including Blind Boy Fuller, Buddy Moss, and Georgian Amos Easton, who performed as Bumble Bee Slim. The Moss version appears to be the earliest one, but the song should be considered traditional.

See: Harry Oster, 124; Bumble Bee Slim, "Hey Lawdy Mama," Paramount July 8, 1935, reissued on *The Black Country Music of Georgia 1927–1936*, Origin Jazz Library, OJL-25; Blind Boy Fuller, "Boots and Shoes," ARC 7-07-63, February 8, 1937; and Buddy Moss, "Oh Lordy Mama," Banner 33267, August 8, 1934.

Undertaker Blues

The "Undertaker Blues," when they bury them, you play "Taps" over them. That's all, he's gone. There's no more of him now. That's Buddy Moss. I learned that years ago and played it with Clayborn Edwards. But I never did hear much of Buddy Moss's music. That was back in 1934 or so, when I first heard "Undertaker Blues." He came to Washington, but I never saw him. I really wanted to, but I couldn't make it. But John Jackson knew him.

1 You gonna need me, baby
  But it won't do you no good
  Yes, you gonna need me baby
  But it won't do you no good
  When will you stop your low-down ways
  Honey, treat me as you should

2 When the undertaker comes, mama
  Honey, and drives me from my door
  When the undertaker comes, mama
  And drives me from my door
  Take me to some old lonesome cemetery
  Then you won't see my smiling face no more

3   They tell me the cemetery, mama
      Sure, God, is a lonesome place
      Lord, they tell me the cemetery, mama
      Sure, God, is one lonesome place
      They lay you down on your back
      Everybody kicks red mud all in your face

4   Yes, you're gonna need me, mama
      But it won't do you no good
      You're gonna need me, mama
      But it won't do you no good
      You wouldn't stop your low-down ways
      Honey, treat me as you should

Born in Georgia in 1914, Buddy Moss began to make records while still in his teens. Although he made a significant number of records by East Coast standards, he never achieved the status of Blind Boy Fuller. Nevertheless, he left his mark on southeastern musicians. Bruce Bastin noted that "In the years between Blind Blake and Blind Boy Fuller, Buddy Moss was the most influential bluesman."

Archie learned this particular song from the Buddy Moss record. However, Buddy Moss also came to Washington several times, and in 1966 played a festival with local bluesman John Jackson. Buddy Moss died in Atlanta in October 1984.

Opinions vary regarding the role of Buddy Moss within the Piedmont tradition. He was a fine blues artist who seemed to miss being in the right place at the right time.

See Buddy Moss, "Undertaker Blues," ARC, August 23, 1935, reissued on *Buddy Moss 1933–1935*, Document DLP 528.

Everybody Blues

I learned that from a Furry Lewis record back years ago, in the thirties. I've been playing it ever since.

1   I'd rather see my coffin
      Come rolling to my door
      I'd rather see my coffin
      Rolling to my door
      Than to hear my good gal
      Say, "I don't want you no more"

2   Tell me, good gal
    What you gonna do with me
    Hey, hey, baby
    What you gonna do with me
    The way you treat me
    Sometimes, Lord, I just can't see

3   Hey now, baby
    Why don't you treat me right
    Hey, baby
    Why don't you treat me right
    The way you treat me
    Well, it takes away my appetite

4   If you don't want me, good gal
    Won't you tell me so
    Say, if you don't want me
    Won't you tell me so
    You won't be bothered
    With me around your house no more

5   Yes, I'd rather see my coffin
    Come rolling to my door
    I'd rather see my coffin
    Come rolling to my door
    Than to hear my good gal
    Say, "I don't want you no more"

Furry Lewis was a Memphis songster and one of Archie's early favorites. Archie recorded the song at an informal session for Dick Spottswood back in July 1965. His source was Furry Lewis, "Everybody's
Blues," Vocalion 1111, April 20, 1927, reissued on *Furry Lewis in His
Prime: 1927–1928*, Yazoo 1050. Archie's song has been issued on LR
42.042.

Going Up the Country

That's an old legendary song that I picked up at the sawmill. These guys
used to sing it in the woods. That's where I learned some of the verses.
They would sing them, then later I put it together. I kind of quilted it
together, so I guess I could call it mine. I put it together about 1938.
Compiled it, stealing and snatching is what you call it. That's where

some of the verses come from. But I made it up for a girl. She kind of pissed me off, so I decided I would sing it to her rather than tell it to her. But one verse I remember from the sawmills was about:

> I'm going up the country
> But I sure don't want to go
> Gonna leave here running
> Because walking is a little too slow

I don't know who did it, but it's my arrangement. Yeah, I learned it in the sawmills, ballads in the woods.

1   I'm going up the country, sweet mama
    Won't be back before fall
    Lord, I'm going up the country, sweet mama
    Won't be back till fall
    If I find my fair brown
    Lord, I won't be back at all

2   If you don't want me, mama
    You have no right to stall
    If you don't want me, mama
    You have no right to stall
    I can get more women, baby
    Than a passenger train can haul

3   If you don't like my peaches, mama
    Just stop shaking my tree
    If you don't like my peaches, mama
    Just stop shaking my tree
    Get out of my orchard, baby
    Let my peaches be

4   I'm going up the country
    But I sure don't want to go
    Going up the country
    But I sure don't want to go
    Gonna leave here running
    Because walking is most too slow

5   I'm going, I'm going
    Your crying won't make me stay
    I'm going, I'm going

And your crying won't make me stay
The louder you holler, good gal
The further you're gonna drive me away

Archie's term "quilting" vividly describes the process of combining existing traditional verses to make up a new song or expand upon a remembered fragment. Inspired by the need to tell off his girlfriend, Archie came up with a compilation of four traditional verses which hold together quite effectively. Various songs use this common title and begin, "I'm going up the country," followed by, "I won't be back until...," or "Sorry, but I can't take you," or "I sure don't want to go." The second verse can be linked to Jimmie Rodgers, whom Archie admired. The third verse can be found in numerous songs, and the last verse is similar to the first verse of the popular blues "Key to the Highway." All told this is an excellent job of "snatching and stealing and quilting."

See: Sippie Wallace, "Up the Country Blues," Okeh 8106, October 26, 1923; Leola B. Wilson and Blind Blake, "Down the Country Blues," Paramount 4012-2, reissued on *Blind Blake: Ragtime Guitar's Foremost Fingerpicker*, Yazoo 1068; Barbecue Bob, "Going Up the Country," Columbia 41316-D, April 13, 1928; and Turner Foddrell, "Going Up the Country," *Virginia Traditions: Western Piedmont Blues*, BRI 003.

Christmas Blues

Blind Boy Fuller came up with some of those verses, but it's between him and Sleepy John Estes. Sleepy John Estes, he used to be my boy. I listened to him all the time when I was in the service down in Mississippi. Sleepy John Estes and Sonny Boy Williamson on harmonica. Yeah, he was a tough guy.
So I think that song is from Blind Boy Fuller and Sleepy John Estes and then I put in that line about "your husband packs a rod."

1   Just the day before Christmas, little girl
     Let me bring your presents round
     It's the day before Christmas, little girl
     Let me bring your presents round
     I'll be your Santa Claus, little girl
     I'll even let my whiskers hang down

2   Did you get the letter, little girl
     I dropped in your backyard
     Yes, did you get the letter

> That I dropped in your backyard
> I would come to see you
> But your husband packs a rod

3   Tell me, little girl
    What's Christmas gonna mean to me
    Tell me, little girl
    What's Christmas gonna mean to me
    It will be the best Christmas I ever had, little girl
    If I find you under my Christmas tree

Although the first verse is found in Fuller's "Bus Rider Blues," it is also similar to Blind Lemon Jefferson's "Christmas Eve Blues." Archie claims to have "quilted" in the middle verse, drawing on tradition. Usually the couplet ends "But your husband's got me barred." The third verse is similar to Peetie Wheatstraw's "Santa Claus Blues," and as Archie notes, he draws on a Sleepy John Estes song, possibly "Airplane Blues."

For an overview of the theme of Christmas and Santa Claus, see Paul Oliver's essay "The Santa Claus Crave," Oliver 1970, 26–43.

Blind Boy Fuller, "Bus Rider Blues," Okeh 05933, June 19, 1939, reissued on *Blind Boy Fuller with Sonny Terry and Bull City Red*, Blues Classics 11; Blind Lemon Jefferson, "Christmas Eve Blues," Paramount 12869, August 1928; Peetie Wheatstraw, "Santa Claus Blues," Decca 7129, October 31, 1935; and Sleepy John Estes, "Airplane Blues," Decca 7354, August 3, 1935.

New Step It Up and Go

1   Said me and my gal, we had a little fight
    I went out and stayed all night
    She said, "You got to step it up and go, oh yeah
    You can't stay here
    You sure got to step it up and go"

2   Met a little girl walking down the street
    I said, "Baby, you sure look sweet"
    She said, "You got to step it up and go, oh yeah"
    Said, "You can't stay here
    You sure got to step it up and go"

3   I said, "Look here, you listen to me
     Used to be you was as sweet as you could be"
     She got to step it up and go, oh yeah
     Said, "You can't stay here
     You sure got to step it up and go"

Blind Boy Fuller recorded the blues hit "Step It Up and Go" in March, 1940. According to Bruce Bastin, "Fuller's manager, J. B. Long, claimed he wrote it after hearing a Memphis singer do a piece with the words, 'Touch It Up and Go.'"

Archie recorded the song at Dick Spottswood's house during an informal jam session with his friend John Hurt and blues legend Skip James. During the session Archie announced, "I wrote a new 'Step It Up and Go.'" The song is commonly known as "Bottle Up and Go" and was probably traditional before it was recorded by Tommy McClellan.

See Bruce Bastin, 234; and Blind Boy Fuller, "Step It Up and Go," Vocalion 05476, March 5, 1940, reissued *Blind Boy Fuller with Sonny Terry and Bull City Red*, Blues Classics 11.

Baby That Won't Do

I don't know who did that, some guy back in the thirties, Buddy Moss or Blind Blake or somebody. My Uncle Henry had an old record and I went up to his house, down in the country, and I heard a verse about "that won't do," and then I put the rest together. I just picked it up off the old record player and it stuck with me. But I kind of rebuilt it. I built a few verses, "Me and my wife had a little fight," and "I went out and stayed all night." I kind of put that together, but I do that with quite a few songs. But I heard it off my uncle's old 78, way back in '34. I remember it was a man, and he played it like I play it now, in G-major. "Baby That Won't Do." They gave that to me because I was the only one they recognized that could learn to play it, but that was a long time ago.

1   Gonna tell you something, mama
     That you ain't gonna like
     When I quit you this time
     I ain't gonna take you back

She said, "That won't do, no, that won't do
You hear me singing, baby, that won't do"

2   I got a wife
And a sweetheart, too
My wife won't treat me
Like my sweetheart do

She said, "That won't do, no, that won't do
You hear me singing, baby, that won't do"

3   Says me and my wife
Had a little fight
I had gone out
And stayed all night

Now that won't do, no that won't do
You hear me singing, baby, that won't do

4   Gonna tell you something, baby
That you ain't gonna like
When I quit this time
Ain't gonna take you back

Baby, that won't do, no, baby, that won't do
Hear me singing, baby, that won't do, baby, that won't do

I have been unable to locate the song Archie described and on
which he based this piece. The second verse is definitely traditional, the
first verse is common, and Archie claims the third. The song is familiar
but, like other examples of Archie's "quilting," difficult to trace. He uses
verses two and three in his "New Step It Up and Go," which he performed in 1965. Possibly the very popular Fuller tune is a partial source.

See: LR 42.036.

I Had a Little Girl, She Was Sweet as She Could Be

Back in my school days I had a girlfriend. I thought she was the sweet-
est thing in the world. But after she grew up a little, it got to look like
the guys that got to be a little older than we were had gone to West
Virginia and went in the coal mines and came out with a new blue
serge suit of clothes and this new car. I kind of lost the girlfriend. Me
being a little old country boy, you know.

But I said, "I'll get you some day. I'll get this boy in a blue serge suit." So here's the first song I wrote about the girl. Now I took the one line from a guy I met named Noah Davis, called him Noah Lewis. He had a line about "I had a little girl, she was sweet as she could be." But that's all I remember, so the rest of the song I put together. So I call it mine, and all of this is true stuff. So that's the first song I really wrote and pursued to bring it all the way down the line.

1   I had a little girl
     She was sweet as she could be
     Yes, I had a little girl
     She was sweet as she could be
     She went away one day
     And she wouldn't write back to me

2   Little girl, little girl
     You know I love you so
     Yes, little girl, little girl
     You know I love you so
     If you come back to me one time
     I won't treat you wrong no more

3   Little girl, little girl
     Please come on home to me
     Little girl, little girl
     Come on home to me
     'Cause my days are so lonely
     And my nights are filled with misery

4   Little girl, little girl
     Come on and ride downtown with me
     Yes, little girl, little girl
     Come and ride downtown with me
     Because when you're by my side, baby
     I'm as happy as a man can be

Archie often builds his songs around a verse or phrase and this piece definitely illustrates that process. It is the first of three of his early compositions, "I Had a Little Girl," "Pittsburgh Blues," and "Duffel Bag Blues." He now sees them, or at least presents them, as telling an ongoing story.

Pittsburgh Blues

I wrote another song about the same girl later on in life. It's called "Pittsburgh Blues" because after she left home, she finally ended up in Pittsburgh. I thought about going to see her in Pittsburgh but I never did get there. When I left home, after scouting around in New York, New Jersey, and back to Virginia, I finally made it to Columbus, Ohio, and settled down there. But the whole time I was there in Columbus I was thinking about going to Pittsburgh. So I kept saying I was going, but Uncle Sam said, "You got to go in the service first." So I went in the service.

So that's what you call a love story, the real thing. Just like you write your love story and sell it to some magazine. I just make up mine and play it for the public. See, these are things that actually happen. After I went in the service, stayed about five years, came out, went out here to Seat Pleasant, Maryland, and got married. Said, "Uh-oh. I won't go to Pittsburgh now." But I called her long distance on the telephone a couple of times. She said, "I heard about you, the song you wrote about me." I said, "Uh-huh, you make people write songs about you."

1   Said, I'm going to Pittsburgh
       Just to see that little girl friend of mine
       Yes, I'm going to Pittsburgh
       Just to see that little girl friend of mine
       I haven't seen her since I was a little boy
       Lord knows that's been a long, long time

2   She settled down in Pittsburgh
       While I was hanging around in Columbus, O
       She settled down in Pittsburgh
       While I was hanging around in Columbus, O
       Uncle Sam drafted me in the army
       Lord, and to Pittsburgh I never did get a chance to go

3   Yes, I heard from her one time she was in Pittsburgh
       Somebody had told me she was in Buffalo
       Yes, I heard from her one time she was in Pittsburgh
       Somebody had told me she was in Buffalo
       Well, it's one thing that I know
       I'm gonna see her smiling face once more

This was Archie's second composition and a follow-up of his "I Had a Little Girl." These personal-experience songs are sometimes performed as a three-part story.

See: LR 42.036.

Duffel Bag Blues

The reason I wrote the "Duffel Bag Blues" was because when the war ended I was on Okinawa. And they kept on telling us, "Well, you guys are shipping out and going home." Next week they put in this staging area, you're there for two weeks or three weeks. And here come orders from headquarters say, "No, you don't go." You move into another area, you know.

So I got kind of angry with it. So I wrote this song called "Duffel Bag Blues." I was thinking, figuring what I was gonna tell the women folks when I got back home. Isn't that something? That's what you call thinking in advance, way ahead of time. I'm on Okinawa, singing this to some woman when I get out. But it's a good thing I didn't have to sing it to anybody so far.

1   Well I wonder
     Will my duffel bag hold my clothes
     Yes, well I wonder
     Will my duffel bag hold my clothes
     Ain't got so many clothes
     But I got so far to go

2   Going to wash my face
     In the Gulf of Mexico
     Yes, going to wash my face
     In the Gulf of Mexico
     I'm gonna eat my breakfast
     In a town they call Chicago

3   Tell me, baby
     Where'd you stay last night
     Tell me, baby
     Where'd you stay last night
     My duffel bag's all packed
     'Cause you know you don't treat me right

4   Don't need no woman
     I don't need no lady friend
     Yes, don't need no woman
     I don't need no lady friend

I don't need nobody
Saying, "Honey, where have you been"

Archie attributes some of this interesting and aggressive composition to Furry Lewis, although it apparently also connects with Blind Lemon Jefferson's "Matchbox Blues." He did the piece back in 1965, using the same verses in slightly different order.

See: LR 42.036, 1983.

My Little Girl Left Me

"My Little Girl Left Me," that's mine. There was a song back in the 1930s called "My Baby's Gone," but I did a little quilting and put my own song together. That's my title, and the last verse, I put that in. I learned that later on after "I Had a Little Girl," then further on down the line I thought about "My little girl left me, she won't be back no more."

1   Said, my little girl has left me
     Said she won't be back no more
     Said, my little girl has left me
     Said, she won't be back no more
     I ain't had nothing but the blues
     Ever since I saw her go

2   I say, "Hello, people
     I just can't understand myself"
     I said, "Hello, people
     I just can't understand myself"
     My little girl has gone and left me
     And I just can't love nobody else

3   When she left me she bought a ticket
     It looked as long as I am tall
     When she left me she bought a ticket
     It looked as long as I am tall
     When I tried to tell her how much I loved her
     She wouldn't pay me no mind at all

Dick Spottswood and David Evans both think this song connects with Walter Davis's "M & O Blues," but both the title and subject matter are so common to the blues in general that it may relate to many other songs.

See: Walter Davis, "M & O Blues," Victor V38618, June 12, 1930.

I Expect I Better Go

That's an old song I used to do around the sawmill. It's like "Going Up the Country," but I could call it my song because I pieced it together.

1   Said, I packed my suitcase
    Said, I walked slowly out the door
    I hate to leave my old hometown
    But I expect I better go

2   Say you don't want me, mama
    You got no right to stall
    I can get me more women
    Than a passenger train can haul

3   Yes, I'm going, I'm going
    Crying won't make me stay
    Say the more you cry
    The further you gonna drive me away

4   Said I went to the station
    I looked up at the board
    It's good times here
    It's better on up the road

Like the last song, I have been unable to track a single source for this collection of traditional verses. Archie put it together some time ago and recorded it in 1965 during a jam session. It remains unreleased.

The Road Is Rough and Rocky

When I met John Hurt it was just like I'd known him all my life. We sounded so much alike that everybody thought I was his understudy. I never met him in my life until 1964, but, buddy, did we raise some sand from then on. Boy, we had a ball. It was one of the greatest things that happened to me. But here's a song I wrote for him, for the two of us, after we had so much fun together.

See, before he left, he asked me to carry his work on for him. But, by me being a newcomer to the music world, although I did play through life, as far as coming out in the public, I really hadn't done much of that. So I said, "Wait a minute. I got to think real deep." So one mind said, "Just write a song." So John had told me some about his hardship and my life had been up and down, too, so I wrote this song about the road is rough and rocky.

I try to put as many of John Hurt's chords and runs and everything in it as possible, to let the people know that I knew the man. John Hurt had a song called "Avalon Blues," so when I made it, I used some of those chords. So when I went back out in the public, people asked where I'd been. And I said I had been home trying to write a song to justify myself, to face the public and tell them that Mississippi John Hurt asked me to carry on his work.

They said, "What did you write?"

I said, "The Road Is Rough and Rocky."

"Let's hear it."

So I played it to them and they said, "Brother, you're not taking anything from John Hurt, you're adding to the guy."

So I got to feeling pretty good about that.

1   The road is rough and rocky, Lord
    But, it won't be rocky long
    The road is rough and rocky, Lord
    But, it won't be rocky long
    John Hurt was my best friend
    But the poor boy's dead and gone

2   I wonder sometimes
    Lord, why everything seems to happen to me
    I wonder sometimes
    Lord, why everything seems to happen to me
    My mother wanted me to be a good boy
    But they said I turned out to be as bad as a boy could be

3   Well, it takes a worried man
    To sing a worried song
    Well, it takes a worried man
    To sing a worried song
    You got me worried now, good gal
    But I won't be worried long

This is Archie's signature piece. It is the title track on his first album (LR 42.036). Archie also recorded it on a 45 back in 1977 (SRI NR 5328-1). It was also reissued on a sampler album, *American Folk Blues Festival*, 1982, LR 50.001, 1982.

Musically, Archie ties it to John Hurt's "Avalon Blues," Okeh 8759, December 21, 1928.

See also: Newman Ivey White, 264, 293. *Mississippi John Hurt 1928 Sessions*, Yazoo 1065, LR 42.036, LR 50.001.

Three Times Seven

Back during the riots I was trying to make it back home, but they had lots of the roads blocked off. Man, fire trucks and ambulances were running all over with their sirens blowing. So I saw this little boy and somebody had broken into this liquor store. So he had got him a fifth of liquor and he was really drunk, buddy. He was trying to walk forward, but he was going backwards. So I said, "three times seven," because he must have felt that way, like he was twenty-one. Yeah, I wrote it back in 1968.

1 I'm three times seven, I don't take no orders from you
  I'm three times seven, I don't take no orders from you
  I don't do all the things that you think are necessary
  I just do what I want to do

2 Said, I'm going to the whiskey store, get myself another drink
  Said, I'm going to the whiskey store, get myself another drink
  I got so much trouble on my mind
  I'm gonna sit down and sip and think

3 Ambulances coming screaming and hollering, people acting
    like fools
  Ambulances coming screaming and hollering, people acting
    like fools
  Baby, in my long hair and black glasses
  I'm gonna do what I want to do

4 Going back to the whiskey store, gonna buy myself another drink
  Going back to the whiskey store, gonna buy myself another drink
  I got so much trouble on my mind
  I'm gonna sit down and sip and think

5   Look a yonder, good gal, where the train coming down the track
       Look a yonder, good gal, where the train coming down the track
       It's going to take me away one of these days, mama
       Never bring me back

6   Going back to the whiskey store, gonna buy myself another drink
       Going back to the whiskey store, gonna buy myself another drink
       I got so much trouble on my mind
       I'm gonna sit down and sip and think

This unusual historical blues was inspired by a drunken youngster during the riots following the assassination of Dr. Martin Luther King. According to Archie, the young boy must have felt like he was twenty-one. Actually, the verse and image of being three times seven is traditional. It is also interesting to note that in conversation, when discussing the song, Archie strongly condemns the riots, which is certainly consistent with his politics and his job as a police officer. The song itself, however, is musically and lyrically quite aggressive, reminding us that we should be careful when we consider blues lyrics as either sung autobiography or as a literal indication of the author's personal attitudes toward a subject.

    See: LR 42.042.

I Called My Baby Long Distance

I was in New York one morning back in the early seventies. I went up there to see a guy to talk about music, recording or doing some gigs. So when I got there, his secretary told me he was out of town that day up in upstate New York and he wouldn't be back until that evening. So I came down to the lobby of the Rockefeller Plaza to call my wife. When I hung up I thought about a song, "I Called My Baby Long Distance." I thought it through and composed it before I got home. I play it in slide. It's a little bit of Archie Edwards doing Robert Johnson. But it came to me from calling my wife, so I guess I finally came around to writing a song about her. So when I play it, you can just say, "He's talking about Mrs. Edwards." So here's what I wrote that day, before I got back to Washington.

1   I called my baby long distance
       Lord, I want to talk to her real bad
       Yes, I called my baby long distance

Lord, I want to talk to her real bad
When the operator answered the phone
My lord, it took every doggone penny I had

2   I said please, Mister Conductor
Let me ride the blind
I said please, Mister Conductor
Let me ride the blind
I got the blues for my baby
Lord, she's always on my mind

3   I went down to the station
Lord, I didn't see no train
Yes, I went down to the station
Lord, I didn't see no train
I didn't have my pistol with me
Lord, I couldn't shoot the doggone railroad man

This is the only original song Archie plays in slide style in open-D tuning.

See: LR 42.036.

Circle Line Boat

That's the song I wrote when I went to New York and went around the island on the Circle Line Boat. So I wrote that "You can have a lot of fun if you just don't fall overboard and drown." Now, it's my desire to go back to New York someday and contact the man that owns the Circle Line Boat outfit and see if he can put that on the air as a theme song or something, and sell records as a souvenir. Millions of people ride that thing every day. Man, he's got thirteen boats and they go round and round. Soon as one unloads another gets loaded. So I could make a lot of money.

At that particular time I was kind of floating on Chuck Berry's coat-tails for a little while. He was a very impressive man, you know. I really like what Chuck was doing. He was taking the blues and snapping it up a little, putting a beat to it. Most all of Chuck Berry's songs were blues. That's what you call rhythm and blues. I liked what he was doing.

1   It's the Circle Line Boat up in New York City
It just goes round and round

> It's the Circle Line Boat up in New York City
> It just goes round and round
> You can have a lot of fun
> Just don't you fall overboard and drown

2   Well, I'm going back to New York City
>   I might change my mind and stay
>   Yes, I'm going back to New York City
>   I might change my mind and stay
>   And go round and round the bay
>   On the Circle Line Boat each and every day

3   I been to New York City
>   I been to Baltimore
>   Yes, I been to New York
>   And I been to Baltimore
>   But I never had so much fun in my whole life
>   Than I had on the Circle Line Boat before

Back in 1977, Archie put this on the flip side of his 45 RPM release of "The Road Is Rough and Rocky." Of all of his songs, it seems to have the most commercial perspective. He plays it in what he calls his Chuck Berry style and, as he indicated, he hoped to share his experience with other Circle Line Boat riders.

See: "Circle Line Boat," S.R.I. (Sounds Reasonable Incorporated), NR 5328-2, 1977.

Baby, Won't You Please Give Me a Break

I wrote this song in my barbershop one beautiful sunny day. I didn't have nothing to do, so I wrote this song. This little girl walked by the shop and she really put an idea in my mind. And all the other girls that hear me play that song say, "Man, you sure are a begging old boy."

One night I was down in South Carolina and I finished my show about twelve-thirty. So as I finished, they applauded and hollered, "More, more, more." So I said, "I'll do 'Baby, Please Give Me a Break.'" So I did that, and when I finished it all the fellows around there was shaking my hand and congratulating me and telling me how good I sounded and how much they wanted me back there again. So that made me feel pretty good.

But this beautiful little girl got off the stool there, she was sitting up there at the bar drinking a beer. She shook my hand and said, "Archie, you got to come back. Because when you do, I'm gonna give you that break you been sitting there begging for."

I said, "Wait a minute. Am I going back to South Carolina or not?"

1   See the little girl coming down the street
    She's sharper than a tack from her head to her feet
    You got me begging, baby, won't you please give me a break
    Won't you tell me how many things my poor heart can take
    Baby, won't you please give me a break

2   I like the way you walk, baby, I'm crazy about your smile
    The whole world will agree that you're a beautiful child
    But I'm still begging, baby, won't you please give me a break
    Won't you tell me how many things my poor heart can take
    Baby, won't you please give me a break

3   I like the way you walk, baby, crazy about your shape
    When you walk down the street, you put my mind in space
    But I'm still begging, baby, won't you please give me a break
    Won't you tell me how many things my poor heart can take
    Baby, won't you please give me a break

Perhaps Archie's most complex composition, "Baby, Won't You Please Give Me a Break" employs a somewhat unusual chord progression that combines Mississippi John Hurt and jazz. I used the song as an example of blues composition in *"Sounds So Good to Me."* This time around, Archie has tagged a new anecdote onto the piece.

See: LR 42.036.

Down Today But I Won't Be Down Always

John Hurt, he had one little song called "Talk About Trouble I've Had It All My Days," and the chords that I used when I was working with him, I put words to it so I made a double song. So this is the backside of his "Talk About Trouble I've Had It All My Days." He would be leading and I'm backing him, you know, so I used the same chords that I was backing him with, I put the words to it, "I'm Down Today But I Won't Be Down Always." So we call that the double song.

1   I'm down today, but I won't be down always
    I'm down today, but I won't be down always

Well, the sun's gonna shine
Lord, in my back door someday

2   Don't you hear my baby, calling my name
Don't you hear my baby, calling my name
She don't call so loud
She just calls so nice and plain

3   Honey, the sun's gonna shine, in my back door someday
Honey, the sun's gonna shine, in my back door someday
And the winds gonna blow
All my blues away

4   Don't you hear my baby, calling my name
Don't you hear my baby, calling my name
She don't call so loud
She calls so nice and plain

Using chords from John Hurt's song, Archie assembled suitable verses drawn from tradition to develop a nice, workable song. Here we see the process of "quilting" in action.

See: Mississippi John Hurt, "Trouble I've Had It All My Days," Vanguard VRS 9145, July 25, 1964. Dick Spottswood also recalled a similar Carter Family piece, "March Winds Gonna Blow My Blues Away."

Jinky Lou

It was an old song way back about a girl named Jinky Lou, but the Jinky Lou part was all I ever remembered. I took it and put the other words to it. I built this song from just that one word, Jinky Lou. Because I knew some old city girls and I could visualize myself telling somebody a story about these girls.

1   Jinky Lou, Jinky Lou, Jinky Lou, where did you stay last night?
Jinky Lou, Jinky Lou, Jinky Lou, where did you stay last night?
Well, you didn't come home this morning
Until the sun was shining so bright

2   I love you, Jinky Lou, Jinky Lou, tell the whole round world I do
I love Jinky Lou, Jinky Lou, tell the whole round world I do
But the way you mistreat me, gal
Is coming back home to you

3   Jinky Lou, Jinky Lou, Jinky Lou, what are you trying to do?
Jinky Lou, Jinky Lou, Jinky Lou what are you trying to do?
Well you treat me low-down and dirty
When I ain't done nothing to you

4   Jinky Lou, Jinky Lou, Jinky Lou, where did you stay last night?
Jinky Lou, Jinky Lou, Jinky Lou, where did you stay last night?
Well, you didn't come home this morning
Until the sun was shining so bright

Here again Archie builds a song on a remembered phrase, combining traditional images into a cohesive song. Second to "Circle Line Boat," this piece teases the edge of rock and roll.

See: LR 42.036.

Greyhound Bus Blues

My brother Willie gave me some of that. He came up to Washington from Virginia one day and told me he heard somebody singing it. So he knew a couple verses. So I said, "OK, just give me a couple of lines and I will put the rest of it to it." So he gave me a couple of lines and I started thinking about it:

I believe the woman I love has got a black cat bone
She leaves home on Friday night
Monday morning I'm glad to see her bring it back home.

I just started picking up from stuff that I had heard other people do here and there. That's what I call "quilting," take a piece here and put it in there. I have a bunch of songs like that. I just have to sit down and concentrate on it.

1   Went to the Greyhound Bus Station, Greyhound bus had just gone
Went to the Greyhound Bus Station, Greyhound bus had just gone
Say, I want to see my little baby
Lord, and I just went walking on

2   Greyhound, Greyhound, do me a favor, please
Greyhound, Greyhound, do me a favor, please

> Find my little girl, Lord
> And bring her back to me

3   Believe the woman I love, got herself a black cat bone
      Believe the woman I love, got herself a black cat bone
      Yes, she leave home on a Friday night
      Monday morning I'm glad to see her bring it back home

There are a number of blues that employ the image of the Greyhound bus. Leaving or returning by bus or train is one of the more common ideas in blues songs. Piedmont artists Sonny Terry and Brownie McGhee did a song titled "Greyhound Bus Station" in the 1950s, which may be tied to Archie's number. On the other hand, the song may be Willie and Archie Edwards's composition. The black cat bone is a powerful luck charm that gives one power over the opposite sex. According to Archie, the only way to procure it involves boiling a black cat until only the bones are left, then throwing the bones in running water; the bone that travels against the current is the magic black cat bone. References to this bit of African-American magic show up in a number of blues songs.

    See: Sonny Terry and Brownie McGhee, "Greyhound Bus Station," Stinson, LP 55, 1952(?).

My Old Schoolmates

My father was living here in Washington with us and he had to go back to Virginia to finish up a few little odds and ends he had left dangling, you know. So he was living with my brother Wayman, and he wrote all the other kids to ask them to come get him, to bring him back to Washington before the weather got cold. He didn't want to be in Virginia when the weather got cold.

    So one morning, I got up, had nothing to do. It was a beautiful day. So I told my wife, say, "The old man is down in the country, he wants somebody to come get him."

    I said, "You know who has to go get him?"

    She says, "Yeah, you."

    I said, "Let's go."

    She said, "Now?"

    "Yeah, let's go."

    So we just jumped in the car and rode on down there. We got down to my brother's house and everybody was gone from the house but my old man. When I pulled up in the yard he said, "Boy, what are you doing here?"

"You want to go back to Washington, don't you?"

He said, "Yeah."

"Well, I came for you."

He said, "I asked the other kids to come for me."

I said, "I know you did, but they didn't come, did they?"

He said, "Well, you have to give me time to get ready."

I said, "You can take all the time you want."

So, while he was getting his stuff together, I told my wife, "I'm going to walk out to the old schoolhouse there, where I used to go to school when I was a kid."

So I went out there, found the old schoolhouse sitting there, trees, shrubbery growing up around it, briars, everything. I said, "What a change."

So I said to myself, "Wonder where can all my old schoolmates be?" When I said that, it seemed like all of the kids I used to play with—it just went right on back to those days when I was playing, running around and around the old school building, throwing the ball over the house, trying to play "Annie Over." You play you throw the ball over, you catch the ball, you come around, run around the house. If there's anybody standing looking, you hit them then with the ball, they're out of the game.

So it went right back to those days when I was doing that kind of thing, playing "Annie Over." So when that passed I said, "I wonder where can my old schoolmates be?" Then I decided to write the song. I wrote the song about my old schoolmates because everybody thinks about their old schoolmates, somewhere along the line. I said, "I'm standing here wondering, Where can all my old schoolmates be? It makes me sing the blues, because I hope they'll all someday hear from me."

1   Well, says I was standing here wondering
     Wonder where can all my old schoolmates be
     Well, says I was standing here wondering
     Wonder where can all my old schoolmates be
     It makes me sing the blues
     Because I hope they will all hear from me

2   When I was down in my old hometown
     I had to walk out on the old school ground
     When I was down in my old hometown
     I had to walk out on the old school ground

Because that's the last place I saw my schoolmates
One spring day when the school was closing down

3   Said, I went and stood
     I stood on a high old lonesome hill
     Said, I went and stood
     I stood on a high old lonesome hill
     I looked all over the lowland
     Where my schoolmates used to live

4   Say, I walked back to my automobile
     Man, I headed back to town
     Say, I walked back to my automobile
     Man, I headed back to town
     I had two hundred and fifty miles to drive
     I told my baby I'd make it home before the sun goes down

This very personal blues was composed prior to 1965, when Archie
played it for Skip James, John Hurt, and Dick Spottswood. Skip James
asked him to play "School Girl" and Archie responded with "My Old
Schoolmates."

See: LR 42.036.

Some People Call Me Crazy

The last song I wrote was a thing, "Some People Call Me Crazy, But I
Got More Sense Than You Think." I haven't played it all that much yet,
but it's the last song I put together.

1   You may call me crazy, but I got more sense than you think
     Yes, you can call me crazy, but I got more sense than you think
     You may see me staggering and call me a drunk, man
     But I can always stand myself another drink

2   I called myself a black cat and an owl
     Please come and keep me company
     I called myself a black cat and an owl
     Please come and keep me company
     I don't have myself a friend in the world
     Nobody seems to speak to me and give me sympathy

3   I got a date with an angel tonight, man
      Lord, I ain't got me no wings
      Yes, I got a date with an angel tonight, man
      And I ain't got me no wings
      I could hitchhike a ride on the clouds
      'Cause she's such a sweet little thing

This excellent composition is rather idiosyncratic regarding the length of the vocal line. However, Archie plays according to his own rules and is free to change chords when and where it pleases him, so his verses always fit.

Notes to Chapter 3

1. Bruce Bastin came to a similar conclusion regarding Archie's music: "Drawing widely on source material, he remains a fine musician and singer completely in the regional style. Other artists' songs swiftly become his own, but he has an impressive range of his own songs with no obvious recorded source" (*Red River Blues*, p. 317).

2. David Evans notes that the tendency to frame songs with explanatory comments reflects contact with scholars and the folk revival audience. For further discussion see Pearson, *"Sounds So Good to Me,"* pp. 29–45, 122–128.

3. Musicians employ numerous terms to describe their instrumental techniques. Cephas, for example, calls his picking style the Williamsburg Lope. John Hurt's term, originating in deep cotton country, may equate the guitar-picking finger motion to the finger motion needed to pick cotton cleanly from the plant.

4. Other musicians, including Virginian Rabbit Muse, also tell how they slowed the record player down, the better to steal the music. See Lornell, *Western Piedmont Blues*, BRI 003, 1978, p. 2.

5. See Cephas's treatment of Skip James songs.

6. See "I Called My Baby Long Distance," p. 134.

4
John Cephas's Story

The first experience I got at being able to sing was when I was young
... seven or eight years old. My mother taught me and my brother
Ernest how to sing. We were a duet. We sang with no accompaniment.
My mother used to go to church and she would have us up in the
church singing. We'd go there every Sunday and stay there all day.

My mother taught me to sing. She brought us up and would rehearse us during the week, during the daytime. My father was out
working for one of the construction companies, and my mother, she was
very religious and she used to have us practicing. And boy, when I used
to hit them bad notes or didn't sing in tune, my mother used to whap us
until I kind of got it. My mother ... she really taught me how to sing,
how to use your voice.

So we sang in the church under the direction of my mother for
years, until I got up to about ten or twelve years old. So that's really
where I got my start. That was the cutting of the teeth of how to do it.
My brother and I would sing in church, but I never got any money for
that.

At that time we didn't even know gospel music. We used to sing
those straight songs, spirituals. The first song that I remember that she
taught us was "Daniel Was a Good Man":

> Daniel was a good man,
> Lord, he prayed three times a day
> And the angels hoist the window
> Just to hear what Daniel say, say say

I had a little high tenor, and I would sing, "Daniel was a good
man." And my brother would sing, "Lord, he prayed three times a day."

And we'd harmonize, "Well, the angels hoist the window, just to hear what Daniel say, say say." And I'd sing, "I do thank God, I'm in his care, I'm in his care."

These were the first songs I learned from my mother, "Daniel Was a Good Man," "Amazing Grace," "Help Me, Dear Saviour, I Pray." My mother used to have us right up there when I was that tall, singing those church songs, but I've forgot them. I would know them if I heard them, though. "Didn't It Rain, Children," we used to sing that. Lord, it's been so long ago.

But I think more than that, when we weren't singing, I would see my mother, how she was praising the Lord. She was singing and moaning and praising God. She used to have such a soulful voice that I can remember that I used to hear it in my sleep. You know how she was humming and she used to sing words like "I love the Lord" as she was doing her work during the day. "I heard Jesus cry and I pitied every groan," and I think you can hear that reflected in a lot of things that I do, in songs that I sing. You can hear that reflected. That's how I learned it.

I wasn't playing guitar in church, just singing. I guess that was when I was having instilled in me that black person's way of singing with soul, you know. Of course, the blues and spirituals, if you listened to them, are so closely related. Well, automatic you could sing the blues and the only other thing you needed was to learn to play the guitar to accompany yourself.

Early Days in Washington

I was born in Washington, D.C., back in 1930. My past is here. I was raised in what is known as Foggy Bottom, that was supposed to be a bad part of town at that time.[1] But growing up in Foggy Bottom, now that was a real good experience for me. During that period of time I think that families were much closer together and you lived in neighborhoods where everybody knew everybody. There was something kind of genuine about having a home or family life, or an environment that you really felt like you were a part of.

In contrast today, it's very difficult, because I don't care where you live, everybody's strangers. But we were all one big happy family. A lot of my relatives lived nearby in the same neighborhood and they visited each other's houses. We shared music together. There was so much that we shared together. I knew everybody living in Foggy Bottom, all the people in the neighborhood. We all went to school together, we went to church together, we played together, and we grew up together. We shared almost everything that we did together. It was such a wonderful experience. It was really like a person would think of as a home or a type of environment that was generally good for you.

Most of my family though, they're from Virginia. That's where they migrated from, from Virginia here to Washington. So I've lived in Washington and Virginia, off and on, all my life. I was raised here and there. I'm presently living in Virginia, near Woodford, which is very close to Bowling Green, Virginia, our county seat in Caroline County. Most all of my people are from that area and I still have a lot of kinfolk there. That's really where my roots are and that's where I settled, too. That's where my home really was. That's where I live now.

I went to elementary school, junior high school, and senior high school in Washington. In elementary school and junior high school, everybody was from the same neighborhood. I went to Francis Junior High School over in Foggy Bottom. Everybody in Foggy Bottom or Georgetown, that's where they went to school. That was the only junior high school over there in that neighborhood. Then I went to Cardoza High School, which was in the center of town, around Eighth and Rhode Island Avenue. They've since moved to Eleventh and Florida Avenue.

In senior high school I was thrown in with people from all parts of town. Then it started getting to where you had to pick friends, whereas in your own environment, in elementary and junior high, you really didn't have to pick friends. You knew the guy because he was always there. He was your friend because his mother knew your mother, his father knew your father, and everybody went to church together. My brother and I and just about everybody in my family belonged to the same church, were baptized in the same church. And it was a really good home and family environment.

I was kind of mischievous in school. Like with book learning, mathematics, English, and geography. I wasn't too good at that, or I wasn't too interested in it. I didn't apply myself. I managed to get passing grades, but I was not really interested. I think I didn't start to get good grades until I started taking some of the trade courses in junior high school—carpentry, woodshop, and electric shop. Then I started excelling in all my classes because I was interested in going to school then. I guess I was the kind of guy that was prone to work with his hands. That really fascinated me, doing something with my hands, creating, making something.

But as far as the mathematics, geography, history, and English, in the early days that didn't interest me, but I managed to get passing grades. Of course, I did stay back a couple of times. Yeah, they kept me back a couple of times. But I really started excelling when I started doing things that I was interested in, like in the woodshops. I'm a carpenter today. That's what I applied myself to, and I really did good then. So I guess I was a fair student.

Even at that age I was kind of interested in the stage, in the theater. I used to sing a lot in programs. They used to have these presentations and I was really active in that. I was on I don't know how many programs where I had singing parts. And I also did some athletics. Gymnastics, I did some of that. And I was really good at anything pertaining to the stage.

The very first blues music I heard and the first time I picked up a guitar, I was young, maybe eight or nine years old. I can remember when I was a kid, my aunt Lillian, she really introduced me to the blues. She had a boyfriend and his name was Haley Dorsey. He used to go around from house to house and he was very good at playing the guitar. He used to come to the house on a regular basis and spend time with my aunt and every time he would come around he would bring his guitar.

I was just a little tot, but I remember he would come around and play the guitar and I loved the sound of what he was doing. That just captured all my attention. He was living in Washington at that time and he was a real good blues guitar player. I was just attracted to that sound, that blues, you know, when I was young. I just loved to hear him play and it seemed like he and my aunt were so gay and happy. He would come and play the guitar and they would have drinks sometimes, and it was almost like a party.

And my aunt Lillian, she was a guitar player herself. She also had a guitar. So I used to listen to her and Haley play the blues. Sometimes she would play the guitar and I would stand there, so young I wasn't even realizing what I was hearing, but I was so fascinated with it. And my aunt knew that I was interested in it. So even at that early age she would give me that guitar and in her spare time she would try to show me how to play a few chords.

And when I got old enough, I would ask her, "Will you show me a little bit?" And boy, she kind of struck a spark in my heart, in my life. I was always asking her, "Will you show me how to do this?" And she would show me different chords on the guitar. And I did learn a few chords and it kind of just always stuck with me. I was always trying to pick out something on the guitar. So I guess that's when I started off. That's about the earliest I got exposed to the guitar. I guess it was kind of instilled in me. But she's still like that, even today she'll tell me, "Play it right, baby, play it right."

This was mainly in D.C., but they used to take us back and forth to Virginia. We had a family home down there. We'd go back and forth between there and Washington, D.C., all the time. I went to school in D.C., but my roots were in Virginia.

Down in the Country

I'm going to tell you the truth. My real inspiration in life, believe me, was my grandfather. When you talk about roots, I think I was mainly influenced by him. It seemed to me that he was everything that I ever wanted to be in life. He was a guitar player, a gambler, a ladies' man. My grandfather was just about everything that appealed to my interests. And sometimes I've been associated with being the sole heir of John Dudley. That was his name, John Dudley.

When I was young, he used to come around to the house in Foggy Bottom and say, "Hey, boy, come on. I'm going down the road. I want to take you with me." So my mother kind of agreed, and we used to go down in Virginia. I can remember I had a cousin named Wallace, and he was such a fine young guy. My grandfather used to get us and take us down to the country together and show me all about where my roots were. Show me my cousins and our home place and where he was born. And I was really impressed by that. That impressed me more than anything in my life. That lifestyle—frolicking, good times. That was where it was at. That was the real thing.

Yeah, I was really inspired by my grandfather. He was a fighter and a ladies' man, and kind of instilled in me that you got to be a ladies' man, too.

Now, he loved those country breakdowns and he used to have them at his house. On every Friday or Saturday somebody would say, "You-all going over to John's house tonight?" He used to have those selling parties where he sold corn liquor on the weekend. And almost everybody in the country, or even D.C., would know that wherever John Dudley was on the weekend there was going to be a party. They knew that they were going to John Dudley's house because he would have plenty of corn liquor, you know.

As a matter of fact, I had a cousin named Jim Henry Coleman from down in Virginia used to make liquor. So my grandfather used to sell liquor and used to drink it, too. I think the very first drink of liquor that I took in my life my grandfather kind of oversaw that. I was with him at my cousin Jim Henry's house, and he had some of that still liquor. I was just a young fellow, but I remember he and my brother and all of us were together. My grandfather told me, he would say, "Boy, you got to start. You got to cut your teeth, boy, and be a man." He would say, "You won't be a man until you can drink this. You got to stand up and drink it, like a man." So he gave me some of that stuff and that stuff liked to kill me.

He also showed me about music and taught me a lot of songs that were really influential as far as getting the party going. Even though my aunt Lillian had introduced me to the blues, I hadn't really got the true essence of it until my grandfather started taking me around with him. He used to play guitar and he played the piano. But he played left-handed guitar so it was kind of hard to learn anything on the guitar from him. But I can still remember some of the tunes he used to play and I play some of them still.

He used to sing "Railroad Bill" and "Careless Love."[2] Those were a couple of his favorite songs. "Black Rat Swing," I think that was the first time I heard that. Then he used to sing a lot of songs like Blind Blake used to do. He was very good at ragtime and also religious music.

My grandfather was very smart. He knew a lot about the Bible and could debate it with anyone. But he wasn't so religious; he was not a staunch, churchgoing person. But he was religious in the fact that I think he understood more about religion than most of the people down there in the church, jumping up and shouting and carrying on and acting like damn fools. Jumping up and talking about some religion with no sense of understanding or true knowledge of what religion is all about. He was the kind of guy that would say, "Why in the hell are they jumping up and down and acting like damn fools?"

He felt that people in the church were under the influence of the people that really weren't teaching them the true way of the Lord. And even today, I agree with him one-hundred percent. And, like him, I don't attend church too much myself. But my grandfather was a Christian even though he wasn't a regular churchgoer. He was an individualist, and he studied the Bible on his own.

He also knew a lot about nature and things of nature. And he learned a lot of that from his parents. Like when a person got sick, they could go out into the forest and find roots and herbs which had healing powers. He used to take me out there and show me a lot of those things. Like you take mullein or sassafras, I know how to go out there and find it. Take the bark off cherry trees and boil it and mix up a little concoction. If you got sick with the mumps, they'd take camphor and the fat from hogs and they mix it together and rub you down with it.

Now, my mother, she used to use some of those old home remedies. Like poke salad if your system needs to be purged, and mullein for arthritis. You boil the leaves and put them on your joints. I used to see old people do stuff like that. My grandfather, he knew quite a bit about that. They used to call him, they said he was a root doctor because he used to carry a little bag with him all the time and wouldn't never let nobody see nothing in the bag. They say he had his herbs in the bag, say he had all this old conjure in the bag.[3] But he wasn't no conjure man. He knew about things that would preserve you, and he used to tell me about things like that.

You know, he lived to be one hundred and two years old. And I don't think God would have elected him to be a hundred and two if he didn't have something going for him.

Even back then he used to love the blues and those house parties. But he also loved singing religious music. It wasn't any problem for him to do that because at that time he was like an elder statesman, and almost anything he did, it was OK. He was such a likable person that people on the religious side and people on the blues side, they respected him in every way. Yeah, he was the kind of guy that introduced me to all those things: corn liquor, music, country parties, and all those good times.

I can remember they would have house parties and they would send us upstairs to bed. And all the kids would be upstairs and they would be partying downstairs. We couldn't help but hear all that music and stomping and frolicking that was going on downstairs. We could hear it. A lot of times you couldn't go to sleep for all of the music and frolicking that was going on. But we weren't participants. That didn't come until later years when they kind of loosened the reins on you. You know, the older people used to have the reins on you. They wouldn't expose you to too much of what they were doing during that time.

And I would hear the sound in my ear, you know. The words that they was singing and how they would be affected by it. And it kind of affected me in the same way. But even though I was going to church I always had that aspiration to be with that other crowd. You know, of course, the people in the church, especially my mother and family, they frowned upon that. Even though they were doing the same thing. They would go to church on Sunday and they want us to go to church on Sunday.

But on those Friday and Saturday nights, they would gather at each other's houses for those country breakdowns and hoedowns where they dance and drink corn liquor and just have a good time. And that sound kind of appealed to me. Even though I was going to church I always wanted to be where they were playing the blues. At that time, just being involved in that environment, I got where I didn't really want to go to church. I'd rather go to the places they were playing blues.

Learning the Blues

I was attracted to string music at an early age. Down in the country they used to have quite a few old-time blues guitar players that would come around for those weekend parties, or come to visit you in your home. And they would bring their guitars and play music. I was more or less attracted to the blues because if you could play guitar, well, that's what most everybody was playing. There were a lot of guitar players that could play blues and spirituals, but it was mainly the blues that got to me, and I was interested in learning how to play it.

But my father was a Baptist minister, and my whole family was active in the church. So I had to keep the type of music I wanted to play kind of secret. Like I said, my mother had us in the church just about all the time so I had to keep my leanings toward the blues hid for a long time. See, they didn't want the young people playing the blues because blues were around houses where people were drinking, or where they had these fly women or places like that. They'd try to lead us away from that, and lean us more toward religion. They used to say it was the "Devil's music." And even later in life my mother would ask me to give more time to the church and stop singing the blues.

When I was younger, I used to try to make something like a guitar, take strings and string it up on the side of the barn. Or make a little box, take a cigar box and put a neck on that thing and string a string through it and try to play it. But it wasn't nothing but running a slide up and down the string. We used to break the neck off of a bottle and run it up and down. We used to do that.[4]

But my first real guitar . . . you know, this is the kind of story that I tell a lot. This is a very true story. When my father first bought a guitar he was an adult man and he was kind of fascinated with a guitar. And he had aspirations of playing, of being a musician. So at that time I had already been exposed to the blues. I was actually playing a little bit of open-key stuff and slide that he didn't know anything about. So he went out and bought himself a guitar and he used to hide it in the closet and he would not allow me to play it, wouldn't allow me to touch it. He forbade me to play his guitar because he feared that I would break it up.

But every time that he would leave, I'd go to the closet and get his guitar and take it out and I'd play it. And—I've told this many times—I got many lickings over that guitar. Almost every time he would inevitably catch me, or know that I had been fooling with it and give me a licking over it. One way he used to catch me, a couple of times I'd break a string. And I got where I could tie them back up and tighten it back up. And he'd go and look, see the string tied up and say, "Oh, you've had the guitar." So I got many a thrashing over the guitar. He had ambitions of playing himself, but he was kind of unsuccessful at it. He never did learn to play.

So, one day I had been after his guitar again and he just told me,

"Well, I can't stop you and I'm getting tired of whipping you. It don't look like I'm ever going to be able to play it, so I'm going to give it to you. Here's the guitar if you want to play it. Here it is. You can have it. You can play it. It's your guitar."

So then I was kind of home free. That gave me a chance to play it as much as I wanted, after he almost killed me trying to keep me from playing it. And I really went for broke then, because I didn't have to be ashamed of it or try to hide it. I used to play around the house just for myself or my friends. I had a lot of kinfolks around that had guitars, so I might go to somebody's house and play one there. Or take my father's and play that.

All that time I was practicing and kind of getting pretty good with the guitar, but they didn't know it. And then, just by coincidence, they found out that I could play it. I used to play in open tuning then because I didn't know too much about how to tune it up. But I could tune open tunings, or I'd get somebody to tune it up for me to play in standard tuning. Sometimes they would have company come over to the house and they'd all be sitting around, you know, and they'd be having a lot of fun playing records. And if they had guitar players there, they'd play music. And then they found out I could play and they'd ask me, "Come on, play a tune." Ask me to play a tune for such and such a person. I used to be real bashful and not really wanting to do it, but they would insist. So then I did it.

I don't think they had any bad feelings about me playing the blues or wanting to play the blues. I don't feel they were against that. But going into places like speakeasies, bars, and restaurants and houses of ill repute, you know, I was always warned about places like that.

But it's funny, you know. Like I was saying before how the older folks didn't want the young ones to fool around where the people was playing the blues. They wanted you in church and not to play the blues at all. But when they would have company come to the house, like on Friday or Saturday night, and they know that you had been fooling with the guitar, the first thing that they say, "Hey, come here, boy. I want you to play so and so a tune." You know, play the blues for them. And if you didn't play the blues right then, you're liable to get a licking. They tell you on one hand, "Don't do that." Then they would encourage you the other way.

When I was a teenager, we would get together with my cousins and all of us kids would gather together and I would play for them or we would play together. I didn't start really participating at those house parties until I was a teenager. At least I didn't start drinking corn liquor until I was about fourteen years old. Then I kind of got more exposed to the intricacies of it, the real low-down blues. Oh, I used to play spirituals and slide stuff in open tunings, but as far as getting down to the real picking stuff, hey, look, they wasn't playing that in church.

So every chance I would get I would try to go down where they were playing the blues and dancing. It just came naturally to me. Even when I wasn't with my grandfather, I knew where I wanted to be. I wanted to be wherever they were playing blues. It was soulful, like a magnet. It drew me like a magnet. It was part of me, part of my heritage, part of my soul. If I heard it, I didn't have to be playing it, and if I could hear it down the road I would be drawn to that place. Walking on them country roads, seems like you could hear the music coming from that house, look like a mile away. And if you was walking, as soon as you hear that sound you start walking a little faster. We stand around the outside of the house and listen to that noise going on inside there. Boy, it sounded some kind of good.

Out in the country when I was coming up and playing, it was more like a home type of thing. Everybody, they would gather around different family member's or friend's house, and we would play guitars or whatever other instruments we had. Some nights we go to one person's house, and the next night we go to some other person's house. We wouldn't play in clubs or places like that. It was never nothing formal, like stage playing. We would just go from house to house and all get together, drink corn liquor and play guitars and have a good time. What we used to call a "country breakdown."

We really didn't have nothing much else to do on the weekends, especially after a hard week's work. We didn't have no place to go because there was segregation then. So, weekends we would entertain each other at home by having music. It was like a community type of thing. You know, if somebody be having a party or you would just sit around and have a few drinks. You have to understand, music was a kind of outlet for black folk. A lot of people couldn't play, but they enjoyed the music. And weekends, well, during those early days we didn't have no place else to go. We were mostly poor. We didn't have any money to really go anyplace, and a lot of places we couldn't go at all because we were black. So this was an outlet for us. This was something enjoyable that we used to do and we really had a good time.

They would play all kinds of songs, mostly blues. But when I was a youngster, some songs like "Frankie and Johnny," "Staggerlee,"[5] and "Railroad Bill" were real popular. I used to do "Railroad Bill." That's one of the first songs I learned to play on the guitar and sing. I also played "Casey Jones," but I never did sing it. Those type songs were popular. I remember they would sing "Little Liza Jane," and then songs like "Careless Love." It seems like those old songs kind of died out. But during the time that we were young and coming up, the older people playing them were in the prime of their lives. Then after they died out the younger people departed from those kind of songs and got interested in newer types of songs.

As I grew older I picked up a little here, a little there. Mostly blues, because back in my younger days blues was synonymous with black folks out in the country. That's what black folks was playing. Just about all the guys had leanings towards the blues. Some wasn't as good at it as others, but as you came along you'd learn.

So on weekends we'd gather together at somebody's house. Sometimes here, the next time there, and play guitars. Or some guys maybe banjos, or violins, the spoons, the bones. People playing washtubs, you know. Take a stick and put it on a washtub to make a bass. So if somebody had a party they would invite me, say, "Bring your guitar." Well, at first I was kind of shy but they would always say, "Here's John. He'll be wanting to play a tune." So that's what I did. It was always my aspiration to try to learn and I guess I never lost the desire to play.

My music coincided with where I was. I had two homes, one in Virginia and the other in D.C. I went to school in Washington, and even as a youngster I was into the music scene here in Washington.

We used to have those corner groups with my brother and some of the guys in the community. We would do quartet stuff with my brother and a couple of other guys, Mason Thomas and a guy named Dowden. My brother married one of their sisters. We used to sing pop stuff, a lot of things I used to hear my aunt sing.

I told you before how my aunt and Haley Dorsey influenced me. He used to play some of those old torch songs like "When You Find Your Sweetheart in the Arms of Your Best Friend" and "That's When Your Heartaches Begin." Then he used to sing songs like "Please Don't Talk About Me When I'm Gone." Songs in that vein. A lot of them were quartet songs, but they were those kind of torch songs. Songs like Lil Green would sing, Billie Holiday, Bessie Smith, and songs like "C.C. Rider." A lot of really complicated progressions, too. And then some ragtime numbers, where they used to have those old tinkly pianos and the guitar and whole house would be jumping.

But those songs influenced me. I guess that's where I learned a lot of progressions, because my aunt used to teach me how to do those progressions on those songs. Like "When There's Darkness on the Delta," and "Times My Heart Is Light," and "Just an Old Shanty in Old Shanty Town." All those progressions, I learned them from my aunt. She used to teach me how to do them. All those minor chords. Oh, man, it was beautiful.

But anyway, we had one of those corner groups back in the late forties and we would sing together... pop songs, rhythm and blues, and doo-wop stuff. It was popular then. We had a group, four of us, but I don't even know that we had a name. As a matter of fact, we even did a couple of gigs doing pop stuff. We used to sing at Turner's Arena and places like that. It was a corner group, like the boys harmonizing together. So you could say I got some background in doing pop stuff, rhythm and blues, and doo-wop. There was a time, even after I started playing the guitar pretty good, that I used to do pop stuff and rhythm and blues in my repertoire. And I still play some of it today.[6]

Gospel Days

You know, before I was a bluesman I was a gospel singer, but I don't ever speak about that. I haven't told anybody about my religious life. I don't talk about that. But there was a time in my life when I traveled throughout the South with a religious quartet, a group called The Capitol Harmonizers. This was when I had become disgusted with the blues. I laid off playing blues for a long time and worked with The Capitol Harmonizers, and we were one of the top religious groups on the East Coast at the time.

Of course I had a lot of experience with religious music before that. You know, my earliest beginnings were in the church. We used to sing family religious music, where all the family got together, mother, father, all the cousins and uncles and grandfather, got together and sang religious music, which was traditional music.

My grandfather, he really loved to do that. I can remember that when we used to go over to his house that inevitably we would wind up in quartet singing.[7] That's how I really got fine tuned on how to use my voice, you know, when we used to have those spiritual sings. He used to love for all of us to get together and harmonize together. My mother, my father, my brother, and my cousin, like a family thing. It was like we would look forward to these times when we all get together and we would have a church sing. I mean it was a wonderful thing. It kind of kept the family together, and gave us a sense of dedication to the family. And my grandfather inspired all of this.

As far as religious singing goes, that was before the Capitol Harmonizers. I got into gospel before I went in the service. I really don't like to recall those days because I think sometimes, maybe they would have been my best days had I stuck with them.

But when I came of age, when I was in young adulthood, well, I tell you, this is hard and kind of strange. When I was able to leave home this was the time when I met my first wife. There was a girl that I, well, we used to call that "potting around" with. I wasn't hardly able to come home at the time when my mother and father would tell me. This was during the time when I reached puberty, at the stage where I still had respect for mother and father and home. But you know how young boys are. They want to step out on their own and be free from family authority.

So I met this girl and was hanging out with her and many nights I used to come home in the morning. My old man used to tell me, "Look boy, where you been?" I used to tell him, "I've been out with the boys." I was just a young guy. I said, "I was out with the boys. We laid out in the park last night."

Well, my old man, he knew what was going on, and he told me, "Well, look, you be in here by twelve o'clock," you know, extended from ten to twelve. And I couldn't conform with that because I was going out with this girl. And, shucks, she was like an all-night thing. I'd go to sleep and I couldn't get up and go home. So my father, he told me, he say, "Boy, if you don't be in here by a certain time, ain't no sense in you even coming here no more."

So I started hanging out with the girl, staying with her. She was from South Carolina and her whole family was into that scene and were influenced by the Baptist preachers and gospel music. They were into the gospel music out of South Carolina and down south there.

Now there was a woman named Edna Gallmon Cooke, who was a prominent Negro singer here in D.C.[8] Her father used to be the pastor of the Springfield Baptist Church over at Sixth and P Street, Northwest. At the beginning of her spiritual career she was looking for a group to back her up on some of her spiritual things and was taking interviews with different groups. She came over to Foggy Bottom, that's where we were quartered at, and she had a friend, Mason Thomas or one of the Thomas boys. So she came over and did an interview with us and we did some singing with her. But I was so young then that I really don't know what happened with that.

But, anyway, we used to go to Springfield Baptist Church and hear groups like the Dixie Hummingbirds, Fairfield Four, the Flying Clouds, and the Blind Boys. Some of these was raw boys right out of the country. Anyway, we used to go up there and that's where I met Cliff Tyler, who was the founder of the Capitol Harmonizers. And you know how you used to get around and sing, well, they heard me singing. They heard me singing lead and singing baritone, and one thing led to another. So Cliff wanted to know if I could sing bass for the group. Well, at that time I could sing bass, baritone, lead, and tenor. I had that type of voice, and I've always had the God-given talent to harmonize. So that was the group. Reverend Cliff Tyler, he was the founder and the leader;

Harvey Tyler, who was formerly the bass; and Wilbur. It was sort of like a family thing.

I did a whole stint with the Capitol Harmonizers, and we used to travel quite a bit throughout the East Coast. And, believe it or not, I was singing bass. It was a professional group and we were very popular throughout the spiritual world all over the country. We were like equivalent to the major groups. You know, at that time they had a bunch of groups. The Pilgrim Travellers, we did gigs with them. We were in that category. We had our big anniversary, and I think after the anniversary that was the time I kind of got back into the blues. But we had our anniversary here in Washington. Man, placards were plastered all over about the Capitol Harmonizers and our anniversary.

There were some great groups and I knew a lot of them personally. There was the Flying Clouds, the Singing Crusaders, the Fairfield Four, the Five Blind Boys. Well, there was two Blind Boy groups, one from Birmingham and one from Jackson, Mississippi. And about the most famous of all was the Dixie Hummingbirds. That Ira Tucker, he was a bad motorcycle. Man, they were professionals.

And the Blind Boys, they would have the whole place like it's shaking and trembling. And then they'd go into a tremble and all them voices laying back, and old Archie Brownlee, he'd—oh, man—he'd come in with a high voice like that. And, man, they used to carry people out. They were so emotionally disturbed that they had to carry them out bodily on stretchers. I know all about that. That's a timing thing. You got to know when to do it. The softness . . . then out of the softness comes the yell. Yeah, I know how to do it. I knew them and worked with them.

I've done gigs with the Dixie Hummingbirds and the Flying Clouds. I've even done some singing with them. At that time I had ambitions that I could join one of those groups because that was kind of the thing then. I interviewed with the Dixie Hummingbirds when they were doing some shows up there at Turner's Arena back when they had big shows there. And I talked with Ira Tucker, and we did a few numbers together. He said, "Hey, maybe you can come up to Philadelphia and we'll audition you." They said they needed another second singer and they thought that I could do the job. Ira Tucker, he told me, "If you come to Philadelphia, we'll do some recordings and get you in the group." Well, I was a young man and I really didn't think I could do the job. I didn't have confidence in myself and my voice and I didn't go.

Now, we might not have been quite as great as them, but I mimicked them and that's where I got my experience at. Now them dudes knew where it was at, and that's the way I was brought up. I do know a lot of gospel tunes, but I don't normally perform them. See, there were church numbers and there was gospel. That's what the Dixie Humming-birds, Fairfield Four, and the Blind Boys brought out. But, if I do a gig where it is in a church and I am expected to do gospel numbers, I could do a whole show of nothing but gospel music. But it's normally not required. Most audiences come to hear me play the blues.

After that, for some reason or another, I kind of got disenchanted with the travel, with the stringency of being associated with that type of thing. I'm convinced that this was a pedestal, or a mode to achieve some personal gain rather than a message.

Hey, man, we used to get just about any woman. If I wanted a woman, hey, all I got to do is get up there and sing good one night and kind of look at this woman and that's my woman, you understand what I mean? It was so emotional, emotional attractions, not in-depth true-ness of the whole matter. It was only a method just to achieve personal gains. So I kind of got disenchanted with that. Why should I get out there because I can sing good just to use somebody for my advantage?

Well, I think that's been documented, that that's been a detriment to the black people for years. That the people who have the most influ-ence over them, like the spiritual leaders, they exploit the black people for money or personal gain. Like the preacher. He run with everybody in the church, all the big sisters there. They got husbands at home, chil-dren at home, and could be half the children at home belong to the preacher.

I am a Christian. I profess to be a Christian, even though I'm not a regular churchgoer. But I don't believe in a lot of religious influence as far as being in the church, because I don't think the ministers are al-ways teaching the true ways. From my experiences in the gospel field, my personal feeling is that there are too many black people that are in-fluenced by emotional rather than factual things. I think in some re-spects we are being deceived by ministers and preachers that are in the church, but don't teach us truthful things about religion.

I think I am an individualist like my grandfather as far as my un-derstanding of religion. I do a lot of study myself and I do a lot of listen-ing. I read the Bible and I am a Christian. I believe in God and I believe in Jesus Christ. I have delved and I have searched for the true Word. I have got the Book and I have read it and searched for it. I have not accepted anything in an emotional fashion or at face value. I have ac-cepted it from what I have deciphered with a calm, intelligent approach. And I think the Holy Spirit has revealed it to me.

All you have to do is ask the Holy Spirit to give you guidance and listen to the Word. Read the Word. Explore the Word. But there are so many people that are going down this way of life who have been influenced by emotional things. Listen, I ain't knocking nobody, but you take people that are influenced by people like Tammy Bakker and Jim Bakker, Oral Roberts, Jerry Falwell, and, believe me, I am no judge and I should not judge, that's not my thing. All those people that they're preaching to, they don't preach to them that they themselves can come to God and ask God through Jesus Christ for the guidance of the Holy Spirit. They don't need those people that they give all their money to in order to have a go-between. I can go to the Savior. I can go to God through Jesus Christ. I don't have to go through those people. All they are thinking about is themselves and their empires. But that necessarily wasn't my thing. I mean, I couldn't be a part of that. Spiritualism that was not real.

Yeah, I had a good voice for gospel, but at that time I had other influences dragging me back to the blues.

House-Party Days

I had a cousin who was a great influence on me named David Talliaferro. David was six or seven years older than me and he was one hell of a guitar player. I'll tell you the truth, David was the best guitar player around. He was the best in Caroline County, Virginia, maybe all of Virginia. Didn't nobody fool around with David Talliaferro.

But he was just a country boy and never got exposure. Now he's deceased, he died about fifteen or twenty years ago. But he really taught me a lot, I'd say eighty percent of what I know on the guitar. He taught me most of the chords I know. He just played those raw blues, like "Richmond Blues."[9] He was the first to show me that.

He also taught me to play the thumb and finger style, like the other Piedmont guitar players do. Well, we called that style the Williamsburg Lope. You know, trying to get the guitar to say what you want it to say while keeping the rhythm behind it. I used to sit for hours on end just playing and singing to myself, trying to get that three-finger style of picking. When I first discovered I had it, that style, I want to tell you it was the best thing that happened to me in my life. Man, that was an experience. I think I went out and got plastered. Once I got that, I started feeling comfortable with the guitar. I could sit down and play what I wanted to play and it sounded like I wanted it to sound.

But David was the first to show me and that's been some years back. He and I kind of teamed up and we would go around together on the weekends and play at parties or just about any affair on that house-to-house circuit. It was mostly just two guitars and he sang and I sang.

We did that for quite a while, almost every weekend. And the more I played, the better I got.

David was the best I worked with back then . . . if he would play. But he got to be some kind of trifling and he would drink a lot. He wouldn't play unless you gave him something to drink. Then, in order to keep playing, he'd have to have something more to drink, and then soon he'd get drunk and then he couldn't play anymore. Well, I guess that's characteristic of a lot of other blues players.

Of course, back then, I had quite a tolerance for alcohol. I could drink David under the table and still be going strong. So I guess some people can stand more than others. Of course, I'm paying for it now. I got all kinds of things wrong with me . . . an ulcerated stomach, diabetes, arthritis, I'm telling you. But back then we would just play music and drink corn liquor. Man, I've drunk so much of it, I'm going to tell you the truth. It used to run out of my ears.

Then I had another cousin, John Woolfork,[10] and sometimes he would go around and play with us. He could play pretty good. He's still living down in Virginia, but I think he's lost interest in playing and doesn't play anymore.

As I grew older I played more and learned more songs. Even back when I was a kid we used to have these old wind-up Victrolas and we'd have records we listened to, mostly blues and spirituals. There was Rosetta Tharpe, Reverend Gary Davis, Blind Boy Fuller. I was attracted mostly to the old country blues, especially Gary Davis and Blind Boy Fuller. They were my main inspirations and they still are.

So, that's the way I learned to play. Playing for house parties or maybe somebody out in the country would have a wedding. Even here in D.C. they would have rent parties and have entertainers, somebody playing the guitar. That would draw a lot of people. But we never made any money, just all we could eat and drink.

Even when I got older and started working, I still preferred to be down in the country, even though it's a long drive back and forth to Washington. I must have driven that 301 highway a million times, because even years ago, I would head for the country on the weekends. I don't think I can remember a weekend when I got off work on Friday evening that I didn't have somewhere to go. See, everything started on Friday and kept on just the whole weekend. Man, I couldn't wait to get out of town.

After work you come home, change your clothes, take a nice, hot bath, and put on your weekend best clothes. And you'd get your instrument, and you'd always know there would be some central place, somebody's house where everybody would kind of meet up. It may be a family member, or it may be a friend, but almost invariably there would be a place where everybody would know that there's something that was going on.

So I'd go in Virginia and stay all the weekend. We'd play music and sometimes we'd go to different places, go to some other counties all up in West Virginia, Virginia, North Carolina. All around different places...Philadelphia, New York City. You know, we'd travel around where there were parties at. And there were parties going on just about everywhere. And being able to play the guitar, a lot of people, they would seek you out. But mainly, I would go down in Bowling Green, Virginia.

Someone who was a friend would take me to someplace that belonged to a friend of his. And I'd meet a lot of people like that, and then we'd all become friends. But it's usually like someone would know somebody that's having an affair. It wouldn't be like somebody would call you on the phone and say "come over" and not know you. This was just like a network within the black community in Washington, D.C., and in other cities out in the country. It's just like a network.

We mostly played for drinks and food. We never thought about money. It was just fun to play the guitar and everybody have a good time. We used to drink a lot of corn liquor, home brew and, of course, they would feed you. That's mainly what it was.

And sometimes they would have house parties specifically to sell dinners, to raise funds for themselves, kind of like the rent parties in the city. When I was younger, a lot of people living in the black community ...they were poor and some didn't have any particular skills or no particular work, especially in the wintertime. They couldn't go out and work in the winter, so on the weekends they would sell dinners and liquor and have a party.

You go in there, first place somebody's always selling something to drink. Second place, somebody's maybe selling something to eat. Well, at that time, they used to make home brew. They would make beer at home and have either homemade beer or store-bought beer. They'd have that and corn liquor, bootleg liquor, not no liquor out of a store. They'd have white lightning and rye whiskey that somebody had distilled.

You could get a meal for a dollar, dollar and a half. You could get a nice big plate of black-eyed peas, cabbage, some kind of greens. Pig feet was very popular, hot chitterlings was very popular, and chicken. That would be the basic menu. And they would have all different kinds of greens that they would serve you. I'll never forget it, it was almost like going into a restaurant because you knew that when you got there the pot would be on and the food would be ready. Pig feet, chitterlings, potato salad, and greens.

They'd sell dinners and sell liquor too, but that wasn't all the time.

Other times you would go to people's houses and they'd have a big weekend breakdown, and you could get all the free food you could eat. They'd beg you to eat. The only thing they would sell at a place like that would be the liquor and beer. Or if they had wine they might charge you for a glass of that.

But other than that everybody comes to the party could eat for free. In those times most everybody had their own garden and they had plenty of food because they were growing it right outside their houses. So there was no problem to feed a whole houseful of people. Like for the meat; they raised hogs, they kill a hog. I can remember sometimes, when people used to kill hogs, they'd have a special to-do. You come over to the house because they were going to cook hogs that night or something like that. They want you to come by and celebrate for the party. Yeah, especially during hog-killing time. In the fall of the year it was cold and people didn't have much else to do so they'd gather at each other's houses, drink plenty liquor, and eat plenty home-cooked food and have a real good time.

And the music! Man, it could really get hot. They would play swinging numbers like "Black Rat Swing" or "Richmond Blues." Then they would sing songs like them old, way-down dirty blues, like Lightning Hopkins used to sing.

And they would dance. They'd buckdance, depending on the tempo. The fast songs, they would dance. The house would be rocking and rolling. If it was slower, they'd slow drag or if it was really slow and sad, they'd just sit and listen. And they had "kicking the mule," that style of music where they jumped it. Call that "kicking the mule."

And they used to have contests. People come from miles around to see who was the best dancer or who was the best guitar player. They used to bring them old guitar players around, especially if they came from way off somewhere. Like they used to get some good guitar players from some other county.

You know, like a guy would tell you, "I got a man that can wear you out with the guitar." He's bragging, so I might say, "OK, well, go get him. Bring him on down and we'll see can he play," or something like that. And some of them old boys would have different reputations, especially like the boys from North Carolina come up here to Virginia. Then the boys say, "Man, don't mess with that boy, he's from North Carolina."

Well, you got to be a little nervous about that. So you sit back waiting, or tell him, "No, no. I can't do nothing." Got to see what he can do first. And after you see what he can do, you either jump on him or turn him loose. And sure enough, every now and then they'd bring one of them guitar players in there and you all would go at it. And sometimes you would get beat. That boy would wear you out. But then you lay back, and see what he was doing on that guitar so you could get that thing together and next time you see him, it might be right.

I mean those parties last all the weekend. Like they start on Friday night and last Saturday on into Sunday. Just as long as it's good and folks enjoy it. Well, I've been to parties where some of them would go to sleep and wake right back up, right in the same place and start playing again, all over again. People would come and go. They'd be coming in and out all the time, fifty or sixty people. And then some would come and stay the whole time. They'd come in on Friday, then they'd be sitting on the couch asleep until they get a little rest. Then, like I said, wake up and continue on with the party.

If you wanted to leave that particular party and go to another one, there was always plenty of musicians. Somebody would still be here, or the whole party might just pick up and everybody go to another place. Just pick up everything and go to another place. And that would go on all night long, or all the weekend.

We're talking about every weekend. Like Friday and Saturdays was the time when most parties was going on. Sunday's the time you go to church. Yeah, you go home and clean yourself up and you go there with your bloodshot eyes, and sit up in the church.

In this part of Virginia certain people were noted for having gatherings at their houses. They would pitch a party almost every weekend. One place in particular was my cousin, named Christine Woolfork, and she used to have something almost every weekend. That was one place where people knew that's where the music was going to be, because we used to play there all the time. It was just like going to a juke joint.

Now there were some juke joints, too. I know one up on Number One Highway, the Red Robin. It was nice. You could go there. That was a juke joint really, because it was like a restaurant or bar, but they didn't sell all that much food. They used to sell drinks and have dances and we used to play there. Then there used to be another place over by the school where they put on shows, like if someone who was on the road came through there.

But mainly it was at someone's house in this area. And over in Richmond it was the same scene. Somebody would have a party and that's where the music was played. Sell liquor and food, and people come from all around. But in the city, in places like Richmond, you're liable to meet strangers. People would come in that you weren't familiar with. You'd meet some new person and you might meet someone that was really hostile. And since you're not knowing who this person might be with, I mean these girls, it was possible to get into an altercation with somebody because you didn't know exactly what was going on. But here in the country everybody knew everybody, so you knew what you could do and what you couldn't do. So it wasn't much of a problem.

Of course, there used to be a fight every now and then. Like if somebody gets jealous because he thinks somebody else is shooting at his woman. I tell you, them guys used to be aggressive, particularly about the girls. Yeah, that's what most of them get to fighting about, them girls. Especially after you get a little high, you know, and the music gets jumping and you're dancing on the floor. You better not dance with somebody else's woman too long. And not too many times. And maybe one of those women was cheating on somebody. Well, they used to fight and cut, and shoot each other over that.

And sometimes the parties used to get turned out. If you weren't involved in it, you just pick up your stuff and go over to somebody else's place. It's usually men start when they get to drinking. I mean, some guy might get jealous or some women might get jealous. The women used to fight just as bad as the men did. And they believe in cutting and shooting, too.

A lot of times I have almost gotten in fights over women. You know, somebody else's woman. Well, you get a reputation, you don't really have to do anything at all. But especially if you're an entertainer or if you're in the limelight for doing something that draws attention. People are envious and jealous of that. But that's the way people are. That's what comes with being in the limelight, brother, I'm telling you. Somebody cut your head off for nothing, just because they don't like you.

I've had many experiences at house parties being a guitar player and the center of attraction. You take some of those rough guys that come into places like that. He may have an attitude with his old lady, or he might have an attitude toward somebody else in the place. And a lot of them look for scapegoats, somebody to attack. And a lot of those guys, as soon as they get drunk, then they want to start something with you. They'll come in there and pick at you. "You ain't doing this," or "You ain't doing that," or "Why you looking at my woman?" Or something like that.

So then you got to get yourself together and either get ready to get out of there or get prepared to fight. Now, if you're there with somebody that's friends of yours, the more friends you got there, you just tell them, "Hey, look. This guy over here is getting ready to start something. And if anything breaks out, man, we gonna try to clean this place out. And then we gonna get our hats and get out of here."

Now if you're outnumbered, the best thing for you to do is to try to ease on out of there. Maybe talk to somebody, tell them, "Hey, look. I'm gonna have to get on down the road." And you have to be able to recognize that because once you get in one of those fights, like I said, a guy would cut you and shoot you just like that! Snap! And you would be gone. For no reason. It's just something that he done got an attitude about. He'd get drunk, you know.

I remember one time I went to a gig right down here in Caroline County, and this guy was a friend of mine. He was a blues player and he had a guitar so I asked him could I play his guitar some. So, I played his guitar and I think I bumped it and put a scratch on it. And, not him, but his brother, who had an attitude against me, thought that maybe I was shooting at his old lady. And he used that as an excuse to want to jump on me. Because I scratched his brother's guitar.

So I saw where he was coming from because he was talking real quick and irrational. So I said, "Uh-oh. Now he's getting ready to start something in here." And I had been drinking, and I was getting a little woozy from the drink. So what I did was, while he was standing up in the middle of the floor arguing and carrying on like that, I called one of my cousins over. And I said, "Hey look. Come here in the room. I want to talk to you."

I guess he thought we were going back there to get our heads together, and then he's going to get his head together and get his group and they were gonna start a big fight. So what I told my cousin, I said, "Look, where's your car?"

He said, "It's out in the yard."

I said, "I'm going out there and get in the back of your car. See if you can lock them doors, lock me in the car. I'm gonna take me a nap. I see that guy wants to start something, and I don't want to get involved with this." So he did. I went on out there and I went and I slept in the car. Until the next morning, as a matter of fact. I been at parties like that when people got shot. Not necessarily people after me, but I've had a lot of narrow escapes.

And then I've been to parties where I've been involved in actually fighting. We started fighting maybe one or two o'clock. If somebody that's a friend of mine gets in a fight, we fight all night long or fight until everybody gets too tired and go home. Yeah, get black and blue and bloody if one of those free-for-alls start. Boy, I'll tell you, back in the country things could get rough. Everybody gets steamed up drinking that corn liquor and someone starts fighting. I've been in free-for-alls where everybody would be fighting and nobody knows who's fighting who. Breaking all the windows out, tearing the doors down. I've been to quite a few of those.

Police wouldn't come to them. I mean, the ones in the country. Now some of them they'd come to in the city. But then, the police didn't have good communication like they got now. And the people used to start up fighting and by the time police get there, the thing was all over with. They'd come and investigate who got cut or who got shot the next day, because they didn't necessarily want to come in there because they might get beat up.

But down in the country, shucks, they used to start a fight and who's going to call the police? Nobody had no phone. So they just fight until everybody gets straightened out and then they go on home. The only time the police would ever come was like if somebody would get seriously hurt. And then they'd come the next day. Somebody would go there and report that somebody had been shot or somebody cut somebody. Nine times out of ten the police were scared to come in the black community then anyway, when all this stuff was going on.

Yeah, they were hard times, but they were good times. Yeah, looking back, it was a lot of fun. The fighting wasn't no fun. But just the atmosphere. You know, families were closer together then. And you could just look for a place to go on the weekend. There's nothing that really replaced that. See, this was the kind of thing where everybody could participate, and everybody that was there was participating in it. But you don't have anything like that now, where you go and everybody is participating. Talking, dancing, drinking, playing the music. Everybody used to partake of this, you know.

But house parties are more or less a thing of the past. It doesn't seem like black people are involved in these things anymore. But during those times it just seemed natural. It was just something for them to do. I think people in the black community were more closely knit together. They kind of needed each other then. But that's faded out. Mainly, I guess, because black people have become more affluent now and they're involved in so many other things. They're free to travel and to go where they want to. They have a little bit of money now and there's no need for a house party, because their lifestyle has absolutely just changed. But, that's not the way it was back then.

Down-Home Life

Things were different back then. It always seemed that everybody was more loose down in the country. They weren't so reserved and when they had a party, they would really let their hair down. Mostly everybody knew each other and knew or suspected what you were up to.

Back then, in the country, they used to have those little stores where you would buy on credit. It was almost like those store people used to own you if you didn't have enough money to pay outright for your food. And on the weekend, when it was time that your old man got paid, he had to go there and settle up with the bills. You'd go in the store and he had a book. They used to have a book with your name in it and every time you came in there the guy used to let you have what you wanted. He'd let you have anything in that store that you wanted, any food. You didn't have no problem. But on payday, you had to go there and settle that bill.

It was a good thing and it was a bad thing to buy on credit, because you're always in debt, always in hock for something. Then it allows the people in the community to kind of control you. You can't speak out. You have to more or less conform to whatever public opinion is or whatever they want you to voice your opinion about. You can't really speak out because you're always in debt and owing people. That's the bad aspect of it.

But at that time the people that couldn't establish credit, didn't have credit, they were the people that were really poor, or poorer than we were. And they were the people that were hungry because they couldn't get nothing on time. So if somebody didn't give it to them, then they had to go without. But that thing of buying on credit, that was bad for the black people always. But then if they didn't make any money, what else were they going to do?

I've always been the kind of person where it troubled me to be in hock to anybody for anything because this restricted my freedom. This is something I've lived with all my life; that if I didn't have the means to acquire what I wanted outright, without ties, then I'd do without. It was always something deep down inside of me, that I wanted to be independent, free from owing anybody. Because when I owed somebody, it worried me. First place, it worried me because I owed them, and then it worried me because I wasn't really free. You owe yourself to them.

Another thing back in the country, there used to be conjure women. There were some even in the city, but most of those people came there from South Carolina. In my early days, I remember those people came from South Carolina. They believed in all kind of old conjure stuff, like with roots. And Haitians, there were a lot of Haitians. They used to say they came from the West Indies. If you ask them, they wouldn't say, "Well, yeah, I come from Haiti." But it was always they come from the West Indies. And that sounded kind of proper and made it sound like they were an Indian and had special powers.[11]

They had a whole lot of people that called themselves "working roots" down the country. I know a few of them. They would give you stuff like herbs to heal you or herbs for good luck. Or, if you're having some kind of marital problems, they would give you some kind of powder or something that you could use when they'd tell you—give you instructions on how to use it or what to do. And it was supposed to have the power that you need, you know. But actually, they were in business to make money.

Of course, I didn't really believe in that. But I wouldn't fool with those people, though, because I didn't really know for sure whether what they were doing was real or not. But I kind of stayed away from them. Of course, I believe that somebody could give you something to hurt you. Now, a lot of people got poisoned, especially around some of those old juke joints where they were drinking. If they didn't like you they put something in your drink that would make you sick or could kill you. There was people around there like that. Yeah, I know some of them.

Now this woman, don't use her name, I went to her place down in the country. Me and my cousin, we went there and this lady had some wine. And she gave me some wine and gave my cousin some wine and the wine tasted like rubber. And I was like in a trance for a whole week after I drank that wine.

Later on, one of my cousins told me that somebody had told this woman about me and that they wanted to try and fix me. Now, I don't know whether that was true or not, but that's what she said. And she said that when I went over to her house, said when the woman gave me the wine, she gave me something in the wine. But I know one thing. I stayed in a trance. I couldn't get myself together. I was like walking around in a daze for about a whole week like that. And that was the worst-tasting wine I ever had.

So maybe she did put something in there. But I could imagine that somebody might have wanted her to put something on me, because during that time I was running around with a whole bunch of girls. And some of them were married, too. And some of them dudes, they couldn't catch up to me. They knew that I was one of those fast dudes, and I was taking care of business. So they might have wanted to do something like that.

Work

I was inducted into the army around 1951 when I was twenty-one years old. We left from Washington, D.C., and they sent me off to Fort Meade, Maryland, induction center. And I was there for about three or four days and then they sent me out to California for basic training at Camp Roberts National Guard Training Camp out in San Miguel, California, which is right close to San Luis Obispo. When we were out there, remember I told you we were going right by the army camp when we went down 101, we went right by the entrance to the camp. Boy, that sure brought back a lot of memories to me.[12]

I took sixteen weeks of infantry training there. After training was over, I got like a ten-day delay en route to Pittsburgh to Camp Stoneman for embarkation for the Far East. I went home for a very brief time, and then I came back and got on the ship and went over. They sent me to Japan first and then on to Korea, where the conflict was going on at that time.

I was in Korea with the Third Infantry Division for about fourteen months, and I was fortunate enough to be one of the ones that came back home. After I came home, about a month or so after Korea, they discharged me, or separated me from the army.

I wasn't too military-minded. I didn't care much for the military service, but made the best of it. But I would have much preferred not to have gone, or not to be involved in any of the conflict part of that Korean War. Of course, like I said, I made the best of it.

The Korean War seemed to be more of a legitimate type of conflict because they had the whole United Nations in support of it, whereas in Vietnam, it was mostly Americans fighting a battle that the whole world seemed to be against. But we fought under the United Nations flag in Korea.

Several times we got into some action, but not hand-to-hand combat or nothing like that. We got shelled several times. I was in a quartermaster company, and we were responsible for moving troops and stuff like that. Well, couple of times we had to go out up into the combat zone to move troops from off the front line and were under fire. I was fortunate. I got hurt a couple of times, but nothing really serious while I was over there. But I didn't particularly like it. I just couldn't wait to get my ticket back home so I could put my name on the dotted line to separate from the army.

I think had I joined the navy, which I was really interested in, I possibly would have made a career out of it. But I just didn't like army and army life. I think I would have enjoyed the navy much more, and I'm sorry I didn't enlist in the navy right today.

In the position where we were, I made a lot of friends with the ROK soldiers, and I had an awful lot of Korean friends. I visited their villages and I had some real personal friendly relationships with quite a few of the guys that I met there. And they taught me how to speak a bit of their native language. I went to their homes and I ate with them. I ate their food. We shared quite a bit together. I didn't think of them as being foreigners. I just thought of them as people that I made friends with. As a matter of fact, I used to write to several of the guys even after I came home. I used to correspond with them for a period of time, but then you get involved with other things and you stop writing, you know.

But it was a good experience. I think that was the first time I ever traveled a long distance from home. It was really a wonderful experience as far as the traveling was concerned. I know under different circumstances it would have probably been even greater had it not been during the time of conflict.

When I got out in fifty-three, I went back to a job that I had before I went in the army, working for a janitorial supply company, a place called D-Con Products in Washington, D.C. But I didn't stay there too long. Before I went in the service I was a warehouse man, and that's what I enjoyed doing. But when I came back, they had placed someone else in my job as a warehouse man and they wanted me to drive a truck. I wasn't interested in driving a truck. I didn't want to do that for a living. So I quit the job.

Right after that, for another year or so, I kind of just walked around looking for some job that I would be interested in. That was hard. I took all my credentials and things to just about every place that I could think of, but I just couldn't find a decent job. Nobody wanted to hire me.

I tried just about everything. I got a job working for a magazine company, *Atlantic Monthly* magazine. I delivered magazines to stores all around the area, in Washington, Maryland, and Virginia. I wasn't really satisfied with that, but I did it for about two years. Then a friend of my father's helped me get a job with the Potomac Electric Power Company in Washington. I worked there for quite a few years, even though I didn't like that type of work.

Then, on the weekends, I worked in Lewes, Delaware. You know my friends know me to be a great fisherman. Well, when I was younger, I used to go over to Delaware and go fishing there. I did that for maybe five, six, or seven years or so, and then I just got to be kind of known to the people up there. They could almost count on me being there on the boat. It was a head boat I was working on. And one time the boat went out, and the mate, Harry Holland, an older guy, was sick for some reason or another, and the captain asked me would I be his first mate on the boat.

So I told him, "Yeah," you know. And that involved assisting the captain and the others on the boat, whatever their needs might be. Like shucking the clams and oysters, and cutting up the bait, taking the bad fish off the lines, baiting hooks and all kind of stuff like that. So my first trip out, he was kind of impressed with me, so he asked me, "Would you like the job of being the first mate?"

So, he said he would talk to Harry and ask Harry, could I be his assistant if he came back. So I agreed to it. I said, "Yeah, OK, I'll do it." From that time on I used to be there. Now the weekends was the most busy time, when they really needed a first mate. During the week it wasn't a lot of people. But the weekends, on Friday when I got off of work I knew that's where I was supposed to be going. I'd drive up to Lewes, Delaware, and that was my job. I did that for maybe three or four years or so, working on the water there.

I worked with Harry Parsons, then his son, Dale Parsons, on the boat.[13] Then I also worked with Slim Rudolph, who was a black captain. As a matter of fact, he was the only black captain in Lewes, Delaware, at that time. He was a native of Washington. He went to the ocean and he loved it so he stayed there. He was running a boat up there, and I worked for him for about a year or so. This was after I came out of the service. This was probably in the early sixties when I did that about four or five years.

They used to have a club up there in Lewes, Slim Rudolph carried me to this club and it was like a juke joint where they sold beer and they sold food in there, too. And they played music. And not only did they have out-of-town people coming in playing music, but they had people that lived in the community that would come in there on the weekends, bring their guitars in there and play. It was sort of like a juke joint, but a little more professional than around Bowling Green.

I went to some of them gigs in there, but not to play or to be recognized as a power in guitar playing. I was mostly too drunk then. After going out fishing all day and coming in there, boy, shucks, only thing I could think about was getting a drink. If I wasn't already drunk. That was them days when mainly I was plying my trade as being an alcoholic.

In the sixties I really went through some pretty hard times. I used to be a wino. I was a wino for years where that's about all I did. Drink wine. Couldn't work. Couldn't do nothing but drink wine, hang out on the corner, sleep in old cars. Man, I used to stand outside the liquor store and hustle nickels and dimes to get wine with. Those were really tough times. I've been down in my life, I've had experiences with drugs and alcohol. I even was committed to the insane asylum. See, my mother knew I needed help. She looked for me and found me asleep in a car. So I had to go into St. Elizabeth's and also the Washington Hospital Center. I spent time there.

But I was saved at that time by my mother, or rather, loving God delivered me from that through Jesus Christ and the prayers of my mother.

But finally through all that another friend told me about a job that

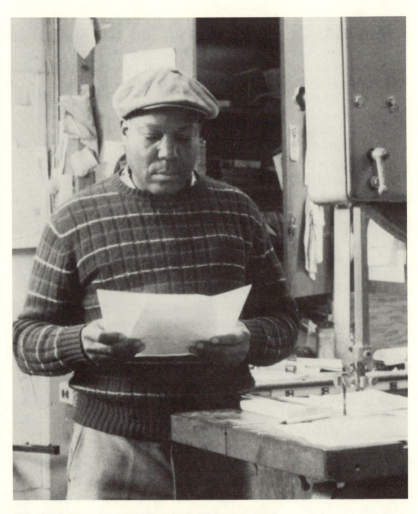

John Cephas at work in Washington, D.C.
John Cephas's private collection.

was open for a carpenter at the Army National Guard in Washington, D.C. That sounded good to me because, you know, I felt qualified. I had been in the service and I had basic carpentry courses in school. That's where I got my first beginning knowledge of carpentry. And I had also done some moonlighting and took a training apprenticeship with William H. Pierce and Sons in Washington, D.C., who had a construction company. I worked as an apprentice for about eight or nine years. But that was besides the job I was working. I used to work Saturdays, Sunday evenings, moonlighting and stuff like that.

But I went over and the general interviewed me and they hired me for the job. I came here under General Bryant, he's retired now. But the years that I was here he kept my nose and everything to the grindstone. But, I'll tell you the truth, he was a real man and a real friend of mine. And I've been working for them ever since. That was a very good job for me.

Making a Comeback

I guess I had played around throughout the country on the weekends, Friday, Saturday, and Sunday, drinking and staying up all night long. And that kind of got to me after a while. We would play those old juke joints and be on the road all the weekend, going from place to place, and I got a little tired of that. I never really got any recognition and it didn't seem to profit me much. And then there was the headaches from some of those bad weekends when you drink too much. I wasn't getting paid for it, and I think I kind of got frustrated and disgusted with the music scene.

So I just gave up playing the guitar altogether. I didn't want to play any more music. I didn't want to play guitar for about five or six years. As a matter of fact, I played at a party one night and left my guitar and I didn't go back to get it, you know. That was in the late sixties. I just decided I didn't want to play no more. I wanted a more settled life. I was getting older and was trying to raise a family, and didn't have time to spend playing a guitar. So the guitars I had, I gave away. Except for a small electric. But I didn't pick that guitar up because I just didn't want to get involved with it. I just got tired of it.

Then one night I went out to a birthday party. A girlfriend, she invited me to this party and she knew that I played the guitar. She asked me would I bring my guitar along with me, but I wasn't really into it because I was kind of rusty. I hadn't played for a long time. So I went there, but I didn't take a guitar. I didn't have any idea about playing guitar.

So there was a guy there she introduced me to. His name was Big Chief Ellis.[14] She introduced us and told me that he was a well-known blues piano player. And she told him, "Chief, John plays the guitar."

So we started talking. I said, "What kind of music you play?" He said, "I play the blues." I said, "I play the blues, too." So he and I just started talking and what have you. He asked would I like to play with him sometime, and I told him I didn't mind and we exchanged phone numbers.

Well, that same evening the hostess of the party said, "Say John. Why don't you get your guitar so Chief can hear you play?" So I said, "Oh, shucks, I don't feel like fooling with no guitar." I just said, "No, I don't want to play." So she just kept on insisting and I kept saying no. I said, "No, I'm not going to get the guitar. I don't even want to play the guitar no more."

But then Chief said, "Man, why don't you go on and get your guitar. I'd like to hear you play." So then I said OK. And I went on home and got my guitar and brought it back. All the people were sitting around in there and they wanted to hear blues. So I struck up a few tunes.

So Chief, he said, "Man, you play a mean guitar. Boy, you can really play that thing." I said, "Well, I'd like to hear you play sometime." So then the girl that had the party said, "You know, I've got a piano downstairs in the basement. Why don't you guys go down there and hook up a little bit. Maybe you'd like to play a little together."

So Chief and I agreed and went downstairs. And boy, when he started playing the piano, it just captured me. I said, "Man, this guy is ready!" He was playing the blues. Stuff that I love, like Walter Davis.[15] And believe me, when I heard them, it was real. It was rebirth.

So we played and all the people that was upstairs came downstairs. I guess it was about ten o'clock when we hooked up and we played until the next morning at daybreak. Straight through. We was drinking and having a heck of a time. They had a house party like you've never seen before.

So after that Chief told me, "Man, I've been looking for a guitar player like you." He started telling me about some of the things he was doing, playing festivals and all, and asked if I would come and play with him. At first I told him I wasn't interested. But he would call me every day to ask me to come over to his house and play. I can never forget I used to try to duck Chief sometimes. I wouldn't answer the phone because I thought it was Chief telling me to come and play and I didn't want to get involved with the playing. But that was almost impossible.

So finally I started going over to his house in the evenings and me

Wilbur "Big Chief" Ellis, circa 1975.
From the National Council for the Traditional Arts.

Left to right: John Cephas, Phil Wiggins, Chief Ellis, James Bellamy. *Library of Congress, 1976. Courtesy of the Folklife Center.*

and him would play. I was really catching on to what he was doing and we got it together and made a good connection. Then I went out and played a few festivals with Chief and then people started to hearing me and Chief playing. And then we started getting gigs and more gigs. And I was almost just eased back in to it, you know.

But really, he brought me out of retirement. I think right from the first time we played together, it was so vivid, so good. It sounded so good to me. And man, like I said, we played all night long, like in them old parties I used to play. When the sun came up the next morning, we were still there playing music.

Then we started going out on shows together, just he and I. Right from then things started to happen for me. We got a lot of calls and started playing at universities. Course, I'd never played really for money until I had met Big Chief Ellis, you know. And really, I was unaware that people were interested in that blues type of music I was playing, that black man's country folks music.

That was the first time I was exposed to the festival circuit. I was unaware that they were interested in the type of music we were playing. But it's funny how things come around. You know, when I first started playing, blues was very popular, but mostly with black folk. But then for a time the type of blues I play, the old-fashioned blues, kind of died out among the black people. And the young people coming up were playing more hip songs, so to speak, more jumping songs, upbeat stuff and rock and roll. And it seemed like the real raw blues just about died out. As a lot of the older guitar players were passing away, it became harder and harder to find anybody that could play them.

A lot of black people during that time, if you came in and you were going to play the raw blues, they don't want to hear that. They all say, "We don't want to hear that, man. Put something on that's swinging. We don't want to hear no blues."

The younger people growing up, they didn't want to hear that old hick stuff. They wanted something different and got kind of out of touch with that type of playing. And they were prejudiced against the older raw blues. Possibly, back when segregation was more apparent in this country, it was like anything that a black man did or created really wasn't worthwhile. There was an attitude that if a black man was doing it, it can't be all that good. And I think some people back then might have thought that, "Well, maybe we don't have nothing of value."

But over time that attitude changed as people became more educated to the importance of the blues as the roots of these other types of music they were listening to. Then fifteen years ago or so, folk festivals and other events like that became more popular and people had a chance to be exposed to different types of music. And the guys that were still around that could play the blues started getting more jobs and playing publicly. People seemed more interested in how the music used to be and they began to appreciate the blues more so. And the more people had a chance to hear it, the more they got interested in it.

So Chief and I, we played together for about five or six years, traveling around to different places. It was really great. Big Chief played that old barrel house piano, which was unique because very few people can make the piano roll the way he could. And I'll tell you, it really went good with the type of blues guitar that I played. We really had good times and a good sound.

And we were getting a lot of gigs. In 1976 we were playing at the American Folklife Festival in D.C., down on the Mall. That's where we met Phil Wiggins, who was playing with Flora Molton, a gospel singer out of Washington, D.C. I was playing with Big Chief. We had Johnny Shines, Sonny Rhodes, and other blues musicians there. So, in-between one of our breaks, we were planning on having a jam session after we were offstage. And we heard Phil playing that harp, Chief and I. So we

John Cephas and Phil Wiggins. *Photo by Dexter Hodges.*

kind of conspired. I was telling Chief, "Man, the way that guy plays that harp, we ought to try to talk that guy into coming and joining with us." So Chief say, "Yeah, we ought to do it."

In the meantime we had a gig in Washington up at the Childe Harold, Johnny Shines, Big Chief, me, and Phil, all of us. We converged there and we all jammed, and it was a real good sound. So we asked Phil, would he join in with us and play with us? So Phil agreed.

Then we started off with a group called the Barrelhouse Rockers. It was four of us: Chief, James Bellamy on bass, Phil on harmonica, and me on the guitar. I guess we played together until, I think it was 1977. Chief had a heart attack down in Birmingham, down in his home. He went home, I guess for his final rest, and he only came back to Washington one time for a big gig at the Smithsonian. Then he went back home and he died.

I would still get a lot of calls from people to come and do a gig just by myself. So I did a couple of gigs, but I kind of felt uneasy. I just wasn't really into it. So I asked Phil, say, "Hey, Phil, why don't you come and we do a couple gigs together?" So Phil agreed and we really had a good, tight sound together. So then we started getting a little notoriety as a duo and we just progressed until this present day.

But meeting Chief was a turning point in my life. He just kept after me, "Come on, boy, come on back and start playing this music." He kept that up until I came back and started playing. Otherwise, I probably would have still been obscure and would have been unknown. And also there was Dick Spottswood who came along about this time. In the beginning, Dick Spottswood was a very good friend of Chief's. Then Dick introduced me to a lot of different people and got a lot of gigs for me.

I made a record with Chief for Trix label. It also had some guitar work by Brownie McGhee and Tarheel Slim. Now, I've met Brownie McGhee several times, but I never did meet Tarheel Slim, though I was supposed to be on a festival with him and Chief. But every time Chief went to play with him, for some reason or other I didn't go. I think I was running around with some girl, and when it came time to go I didn't go.

But I did meet some other great Piedmont musicians, like Sonny Terry, Brownie McGhee, Buddy Moss, the Foddrell Brothers, Frank Hovington, and Carl Martin. I met Buddy Moss at a festival when they brought him up here and I spent the better part of a weekend with him. And he and I were jamming and playing the whole time he was here. We had like a workshop, and we just played the whole time he was here. And I went down to Atlanta, to his home where he lives. Matter of fact, I went there several times to locate him so me and him could get together and play some, but I couldn't find him. And the third time I went down there I was going to look him up and that day I was there, he died. That day, Buddy Moss died.

We played with the Foddrell brothers quite a few times down where they were from. We were down there several times for festivals and I was really impressed by them. We've been on a number of gigs together, so we all know each other and it's a pleasure to play with them. If we know they are going to be on a gig, boy, we're happy to see them. They were at the National Folk Festival with us once, too. Marvin Foddrell, he and I have a similar sound, and I learned "Reno Factory" from them.

Frank Hovington, he was a Piedmont-style guitar player that I met through Dick Spottswood.[16] I had heard about Frank Hovington for quite a while and I heard some of his recordings. His style of music coincided very much with the style that I play. Dick Spottswood introduced me to him when he was living near Rehoboth Beach, Delaware. We went up one Sunday because Frank had been ill. We went up and visited him in his home and we stayed a whole day up there and had a lot of exchanges and talked and played music together. And we played with him at a house party on another occasion. We came to be really good friends until his death. He was a good guy. But I'll tell you, his style of playing is so similar to my playing that when we first met and started playing everything melded right together and it was just like we had been playing together for years.

And Carl Martin, we did some gigs with him; Martin, Bogan, and Armstrong. We were on the festival circuit together, go around to colleges and universities. Really, we've met so many musicians over the years, but those are a few of the East Coast players, like myself and Phil, John Jackson, Archie Edwards. We all play the Piedmont style.

On the Road

Over the last ten years we've played just about any place you could imagine. We've been all over the country, the East Coast, the West Coast, Washington state, California and Texas, the Midwest, Chicago, Detroit, Ohio, and all over the South. So you could say we've covered the country and Canada, too. We've played about all the major festivals; the National Folk Festival, the Smithsonian Folklife Festival, and the Atlanta Downhome Blues Festival, which was made into a television show.

We played at the Chicago Blues Festival twice and the San Francisco Blues Festival and the Long Beach Blues Festival. And we did a long tour with Joe Wilson and the National Council for the Traditional Arts on a program called "Saturday Night and Sunday Morning" that played in ten states down South and in the Midwest. We even played in a women's prison down South.[17]

Then back in 1981 and 1982 we went to Europe with the American Folk Blues Tour. So we've been all over the European community, too. Scandinavia, Germany, France, you name it, we've been there.

We were also fortunate enough to audition for the Arts America Program with the United States Information Agency, and were selected as a team to go over into some foreign countries. First they sent us to Africa and we played in Botswana, Zimbabwe, Mauritius, Madagascar, Ghana, and Mali. Usually we had a pretty full schedule doing two or three gigs a day. I mean, not all playing but concerts, workshops, radio or television shows, parties or meeting different representatives of music associations or cultural groups. We also had stopovers in Nairobi and Abidjan, but those were long travel days. I don't know how many times we seemed to spend the day or evening hanging around airports waiting for a plane. I got to where I didn't care if I ever saw another airport in my life.

It's funny, we toured as the Bowling Green Blues Trio, that was Phil and I and Barry Lee Pearson. Two guitars and a harmonica. But, you know, we didn't start out with that name. It was just American Country Blues, but one day we showed up at a gig and there was the poster with the "Bowling Green Blues Trio" on it. So that kind of stuck with us.

Each place we would go we would always do a big public concert. Then we would do some type of workshop explaining and demonstrating different blues styles and meeting with local musicians. And we would usually give a performance at the ambassador's house or someone else's house for invited guests, ministers of culture, or ambassadors from other countries. And we met lots of musicians from these countries and played music with them in workshops or worked together in concerts. When we got time off, though, we would go to the markets and shop for souvenirs. And we collected quite a load. I don't see how we got on some of those airplanes with all the stuff we had.

In Africa I was really impressed with how their music was associated with what we were doing. Sometimes the musicians could play their traditional styles and play our western music, too. And in Botswana, that Botswana Defense Force Band, they really impressed me. In fact, they kind of took us by surprise because they played traditional music at the workshop, but then when we did our show at their officers club, they came on with a pretty hot dance band. They played American music, soul music, and you could say that they bushwhacked us because we were surprised. But we all wound up on stage playing the blues together and the audience loved it. Then later, we all went out for a drink together and, man, they kept us up almost all the night.

But that happened quite often. I had kind of figured that the people might be a little standoffish, or not used to our music, but they really showed a lot of enthusiasm. It seemed like they were starved for some face-to-face performances of blues musicians. I was really impressed

Bowling Green Blues Trio. Left to right: Barry Lee Pearson,
Phil Wiggins, and John Cephas. *Photo by Mike Joyce.*

with the response, especially in places like Zimbabwe and Mali. But the best part was always the workshops where we could meet with the local musicians. Then it was more of a cultural exchange because we could share our music and they could share their music. I was always interested in hearing how they played. But the funny part, almost every workshop, somebody would come up and play the blues for us. So we

John Cephas in Accra, Ghana, 1982, with Ko Nimo Group.
Photo courtesy of The American Center, Accra, Ghana.

heard a lot of blues all over Africa. Sometimes in sounded like we were in Chicago.

Then in 1984 we toured South America, Central America, and the Caribbean. We went to three cities in Colombia: Barranquilla, Medellin, and Bogotá, and of all the places we have gone, that was about the most dangerous. In fact, they set off a bomb near the embassy in Bogotá. But beyond a doubt Barranquilla was the most dangerous place we toured. Of course, in Ghana, there was a coup attempt and a curfew, but in Colombia . . . I might not have showed it, but I really felt shook up. It seemed like everything was so unstable and out of touch with basic law principles. The whole situation in Barranquilla was scary. You ride down the street and you say, "Wow." Like, almost any minute something could happen. And with us, it did.

First we got caught in a flood. Then somebody tried to run us down in a truck. Then turn around and here come the police and jacked us up against the car with our hands up. One had a machine gun on us and he stood back while the other guy searched us and searched the car. We showed them our picture in the paper and they just smiled and made us put our hands back up. That was a hair-raising experience!

And in Peru, we went through a security check to get on the plane.

We had been in there doing some shopping in the airport in Lima, and when I went before the guy to get on the plane they took that magnetic thing and checked you all down. Then they told me to take off my hat. Well, I had two hats on. So I reached up and I took one hat off and the guy looked like—his eyes bucked open, you know. Then I reached up and took the other one off, and, boy, when I took that one off, he got a real big kick out of that. And actually the people in the line got a big kick out of it. Because everybody was laughing. Yeah, that was real funny. He never expected that.

We spent time in Guyana and the people there were just so receptive. I remember we did a show out in a little mining town called Linden. When the show was over the mayor invited the whole show, audience and everyone, over to her office for a drink.

Then we went all over Central America, like Belize, Panama, Guatemala, and Honduras. We were in Belize playing at this little outdoor thing and when we first started there wasn't a mosquito in sight. Nowhere. And we played right on up into the dusk hours and just about dusk, in between dusk and dark, the mosquitoes came out and it was like pestilence had hit all at one time. I mean, they came in droves! And they were sucking blood out of everything that was in sight that had blood in it. I think they was even sucking each other's blood. So that lasted for about, if I can remember, about an hour and a half and then they were all gone. But by then we were all ate up. Phil had knots on his head and everywhere. I'm telling you, that was terrible.

And I'll never forget that woman. She said, "Oh, yes, yeah, we got them pretty bad, but they're only out for an hour." I said to myself, "Well, hell, they don't need to be out no longer than that. They need to cut that down to at least a half an hour, so something will have some blood left in it."

And then when we were in Honduras we were riding down there with some idiot driving a hundred miles an hour. And we came along and those soldiers started to run towards the truck shooting. It looked like they were running toward us, and opening fire with automatic and semiautomatic weapons. Of course, that was an experience, but that didn't really scare me too bad, you know. Everyone else was on the floor and I was peeping up to see who they were really shooting at. And they were running right on down the road, guns blazing.

Some of the places we were in were very strange, especially when we couldn't speak the language. I remember driving in Madagascar and just wondering where in the hell I was! There were animals all over, goats, chickens, and these big cows, water buffaloes. We drove by a bus stop and there were people waiting for the bus along with these water buffalo. I could not relate to that . . . water buffaloes at the bus stop! And a lot of places there was so much poverty everywhere, and I kind of had to get used to soldiers and police carrying machine guns at the airports and even at our concerts.

It wasn't no vacation, but I'm ready to go back again whenever they call us up and ask us. But at the same time it was always great to come back home. I think that was especially true when we came back from Africa, because we had been away for so long. We had been in Europe and then went directly to Africa. I don't think I was ever so ready to get home. In fact, after we hit New York, I couldn't even wait for the flight down to D.C. I just jumped on a train as soon as I got through customs.

You have to learn to pace yourself, because any place you go they expect a show and then they want to take you out for a good time after it's over. At first, we would go wherever they wanted because our visit was like a big thing, so people would have parties for us. But you know, you can only take so much. So we had to learn to say no and we would try to get off by ourselves, go out to eat and go back to the hotel and play poker, and that kind of relaxed us after the concerts and whatnot.

Since then, Phil and I have been to the Soviet Union and China and we have a trip to Australia coming up. So I guess you could say we've been all over the world playing. I'll still go anywhere to play the blues and to teach people about Piedmont blues. But I think it takes a certain kind of person to handle the aggravation of being on the road so much. It's definitely a strain. I mean, we've been on the road so long that I keep a bag packed all the time. When I come home, I just take out all the dirty clothes and put in some other clothes and set my bag by the door.

People don't really realize how much work goes into being a musician. They just see you on stage and naturally they think that playing music is just so easy for you. And usually it is, onstage. But they don't know how far you've driven to get there or how far you have to drive after you leave or that you have to play some more gigs the next day.

There were times I wondered if it was worth all the hassle, all the driving, staying up all night at airports. Then there were times I wished we could play more or get paid more for what we were doing, especially around our home area. But I guess that's true for a lot of musicians. You feel that the hometown boys don't really get rewarded. And to a certain degree that's been true. We had to go out on the road to be recognized for what we were able to do. But it's hard to get that recognition in your hometown.

And then when you get your chance you got to get out there and you got to give one hundred percent all the time. You got to come up with new stuff all the time. And then you got to be a real human being. You got to be really good. You can't go out there jiving and trying to

Bowling Green Blues Trio

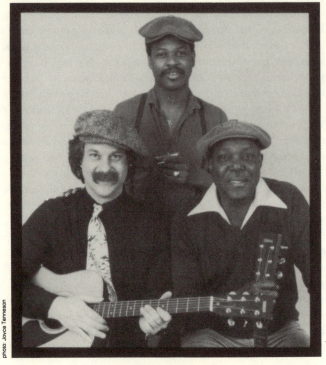

photo: Joyce Tenneson

JOHN CEPHAS, guitar
PHIL WIGGINS, harmonica
BARRY LEE PEARSON, guitar

NOCHE DE BLUES EN EL CBA

14 de septiembre de 1984 - Horas 20:30
La Paz - Bolivia
A Cultural Presentation of the United States of America

Publicity brochure for the Bowling Green Blues Trio,
Bolivia, 1984. *Photo by Joyce Tenneson.*

fool nobody. You can't be envious. You can't be jealous of nobody. You
just got to go out there and do your thing and just hope that what you
do that the people will like it.

So a musician's life is harder than it might seem to be. You have to
keep at it and not get discouraged. It's hard to get your foot in the door,
to get exposure. That's true for all traditional musicians, just trying to
get your foot in the door. You have to take the time to talk to people,
even if you don't feel like it. You have to talk to the press, do interviews
for magazines, radio, or television. You can't snub any of them because
you don't always know who they are. But really, I've very enthusiastic
about interviews, especially where people will get exposed to the conversations that we have and maybe get a better insight into the blues and
the blues musicians themselves. And I'm always eager to tell people
what it's all about, how I learned and what the blues is all about. That
creates more interest in the blues because a lot of people don't really
know. So much of our history has been suppressed or just hasn't been
paid attention to.

And another thing, playing music takes you away from your family
until you hardly know your children. You know, I have six children all
right down in Virginia where I live. Four by one marriage and two by
another. I have two sons, Carlyle and Christopher, then Yolanda and
Laverne Cephas. And by another marriage there's Donna and Kathleen.

I've been married three times in my life and I think the fact that I've
been a blues musician has contributed to the downfall of all my mar-
riages. I haven't found a woman yet that could accept the fact that I
wanted to go play music whenever I feel like it. I want to go play music,
and, of course, I've always invited them to come.

But this is something I'm gonna do. I'm gonna play music. And I
guess women don't want to play second fiddle to no guitar. Like playing
the music takes me away from home a lot and I'd be gone all the weekends and not devoting enough time to home, you know. Women get
tired of that. And musicians always seem to have a reputation that people put on them. If you're a musician, you don't have to do one thing,
but you will be credited with everything that's no good. Somebody is always trying to discredit you. They say, "He's got plenty of women. He's
knocking off all the women." But that's not true. I mean, I've had different girls, but not no whole bunch at one time. Well, not in the same
neighborhood, anyway.

But once you're in the limelight, brother, people, when they start to
talking, you don't even . . . when they start talking about you and you
hear it, you have to look around to find out, wonder who are they talking about. It's just amazing. Because people, they'll lie on you, tell un-
truths and attribute you with miracles until they think you walk on

water. That's because people are envious and jealous of you. And any wrongdoing, if you're in there anywhere, they say, "Oh yeah, he did it." And I think other musicians will tell you the same thing.[18]

Preaching the Blues

My recording career started back when I worked with Chief Ellis. We did an album for Pete Lowry's Trix label and also made a forty-five single. Dick Spottswood recorded me for the Library of Congress and I also made a record for the Blue Ridge Institute at Ferrum College for Kip Lornell back in 1977. I did some recording for Trix again, but it never came out. I don't know what the problem was there. The other albums Phil and I recorded. The first two were on a German label put out by Horst Lippmann. The first one was *Living Country Blues: Bowling Green John Cephas and Harmonica Phil Wiggins from Virginia, U.S.A.* That was followed by a second album, *Sweet Bitter Blues*, which was taken from a song we do written by Otis Williams, who teaches out at the University of Maryland. Both of those were on the L and R label, Lippmann and Rau, who also recorded Archie Edwards.

But our best album to date was recorded at my home down in Virginia by Joe Wilson, Larry McBride, and Pete Reiniger. Now that was a great session. When we recorded the songs for this album the conditions just seemed to be right. I felt really good. Phil felt really good. The sound, the technicians, the producer, everybody was just right on key. And all the numbers we recorded just took one take and it all came out perfect.

It first came out as a tape called *Let It Roll* for Larry McBride's Marimac Recordings, out of New Jersey. Then after a while a good part of it was picked up by Bruce Kaplan for Flying Fish Records out of Chicago. That was our *Dog Days of August* album, which got a lot of attention and went on to win the Blues Foundation's W. C. Handy Award for the Best Traditional Album of the Year.

The Handy award, that was quite a surprise. I really hadn't expected it, though I knew that we were nominated. We've been nominated several times for an award. But the foundation called up to the record company in Chicago and told them, indeed, that we had won the award and they'd like us to come down. So Bruce Kaplan got on the phone and called Phil up and told him, said that we had actually won the award and they wanted us to come down and receive it.

So Flying Fish, our record company, they got the money together and they arranged for a plane ticket for us to go down. The Blues Foundation people picked us up at the airport and just gave us a wonderful

"Blues Entertainers of the Year." Winners of the 1986 W. C. Handy Award. Left to right: Phil Wiggins, Joe Saverin, and John Cephas. Memphis, 1987. Photo by Otis Williams.

reception, hotel rooms for our entourage and everything. So we were there at the ceremony in our rented tuxedos, gratified that we had won such a prestigious award, and we were just having a good time backstage. But they had another surprise for us when we heard our names announced as the winners of Entertainers of the Year Award! I tell you, I was really dumbfounded. It was so emotional that when I went out to receive the trophy I just didn't think I could cut it. Man, there were tears in my eyes. It was so unexpected. I thought of all the years I had spent playing music and then to get this award, which is like the Oscar of the blues field. You expect, you know, the big names to walk off with the top awards, but you really don't expect it to go to traditional musicians.

But there's a lot of other traditional musicians out there and I would like to see them get some breaks, too. But that's the industry itself. I think they're responsible for who goes where. So let's hope that things are changing and the traditional artists won't have to take a backseat to rock and roll and all of that because a lot of those rock guys learned from the traditional musicians.

But that record really helped put us on the map, so now more people out there know about us. So we'll keep working on it so we can be heard by more people so they can be exposed to our music. And wherever we go, they want us to come back. We made a lot of friends out there and the audiences really liked our music once they had a chance to hear it. So it's not just a success for us, it's also a success for the type of music that we do.

Like the Long Beach Blues Festival, that was a big thrill. I actually felt then that we had made it to the big time, working with top-flight musicians like Snooks Eaglin, B. B. King, Robert Cray. They really extended a reception to us. We had a big, air-conditioned trailer, food and drink, people waiting on us just about hand and foot. Yeah, that was really the big time, and believe me, we did so well out there that it was fantastic.

You know, the promoters and blues people knew about us but they never had a chance to hear us live and to see us play for people who weren't that familiar with our type of music. Most people know about rock and roll and Chicago blues, but not too many have heard Piedmont players unless it was Sonny Terry and Brownie McGhee. So, I guess it's up to us to expose them to our type of music. That's why I like to play festivals, because the crowds are larger and you can play for more people.

And then sometimes at festivals, or when we tour, we'll have workshops and students can ask us to show them things. They'll bring their guitars and sit down and play with you. We do that quite often and I enjoy teaching. You know, I teach every year out in Seattle and in Elkins, West Virginia. And we also do that along with a lot of our university gigs. That's one thing I love to do, to teach young people and maybe inspire them to learn about the blues.

It's funny how things come around. When I was younger it was mostly blacks who were playing the blues. Then when I first started teaching, it seemed it was more young white kids interested in learning the blues. But today that's changing. I know quite a few younger blacks playing country blues like Larry Wise, James Jackson, Rick Franklin, and Jim Green. And I got a student, Mike Roach, who's head of the D.C. Blues Society, now he's really learning the country blues.

And in the places we play—the Smithsonian Festival, the Chicago Blues Festival, the San Francisco Blues Festival, Long Beach—the audience is mixed, black and white, young and old. So today it looks like just about everybody is getting into the blues.

Phil and I have worked hard to make a name for ourselves, playing the best music we know how. But there's always people along the way that give you a helping hand when you need it. When I think back, there's so many that have helped me. I'm sure my grandfather had some influence on me and, of course, my mother and father both. If I do have a leadership quality, they instilled that in me. You know, my mother, she was always instilling in me to be an upright, upstanding, respectable person in this world and to live a Christian life. Which I think, I hope, that it's really paid off. Of course, my father, he was a Baptist minister, and I'm sure that his influence is evident in my life. And Chief Ellis, he really helped me when I had become disinterested and about given up playing. I have to thank him for getting me going again. And also my cousin David, who, once I was on my way, kind of took me under his wing.

Me and him spent many hours together and he gave me a lot of personal instruction on the guitar. He helped teach me how to play. And I'd like to make reference to Barry for his support and his comradeship, for the wonderful times that we had. We got a relationship kind of like brothers. Barry supported us with people like the USIA, then went on tour with us and, boy, I'm going to tell you the truth, that was perfect. But he supported us even when he didn't go with us by just basically being a friend. It's not just pertaining to music, but it's pertaining to friendship. I mean, we've been just like brothers. That's the way I feel. Now put that in there, damn it.

And then I'd like to thank Joe Wilson, who I think has probably done more for our musical endeavors than anybody. Because when I was playing with Big Chief Ellis, Joe took interest. And he got me on the National Folk Festival. He introduced me to a whole lot of people back when I was obscure and really unknown. He's helped me in so many things, like getting recordings out and doing biographies, and he's taken so much time, giving of himself, and kept us busy on the road. He's also just like a brother to me. And Dick Spottswood, he's a very good friend, and in the beginning, helped me get started. And Kip Lornell, too. And, of course, my partner Phil, who's been with me a dozen years.

But I think, more than ever, I thank my aunt Lillian, who taught me. She taught me, and down through the years she pushed me to keep on with the music because she loved the music herself. She was really my first exposure to the blues, to the guitar. And she never ceased in pushing me toward perfection with this guitar, and she's even that way today. You let me hit a bad note if you think different. Yeah, she knows

John Cephas and friends at home in Bowling Green, Virginia. *Photo by Nick Spitzer.*

every note on the guitar, so she knows if I hit a bad one. So I'd like to thank her.

I've never regretted being a blues musician. It's something I wanted to do. It's like a part of my life. I always wanted to be a good blues musician. And I enjoy playing. Even though I play for audiences I still think I enjoy the music more than they do.

And it's been very good for us, for Phil and I, what we've been doing. The audiences have been very receptive and very appreciative. Just as we have been appreciative of them. If it wasn't for them, we wouldn't be where we are today. So it's been a great experience.

I really never had the ambition to be a noted blues player. It all just kind of happened. I played because I enjoyed playing and it was fun. I didn't care whether or not I got gigs or whether I played for money or whether I played for drinks or for food or whatever. I just enjoyed doing it, not really realizing what value there was in trying to keep the tradition alive. I never thought of it in that way. It just never occurred to me when I was a teenager that the tradition would die out. I thought it would always be here and that there would be plenty of young people coming up behind me that would carry on the tradition.

But now, there's not that many musicians that can effectively play the Piedmont style. So I guess I'm one of the few that's doing it. So this is our effort, to keep this kind of blues alive. I can play upbeat stuff, I can sing it, but I would rather do this. To let the people know what the black man's culture is, what his heritage is.

I guess I've been lucky because I love the music I play. But I've never worked full time at making music. I've had carpentry as my main job. That was my job and then the music came next. But now that I've retired, I hope I can continue to play as long as my health holds up. It's just in my blood. I just can't conceive that I wouldn't be able to play any more music.

Notes to Chapter 4

1. The Foggy Bottom section of Washington, D.C., like Georgetown, was once primarily black. Today, it is the site of George Washington University and the Watergate.

2. For John's versions of "Railroad Bill" and "Careless Love," see John Cephas's repertoire, pp. 208, 213.

3. Conjure refers to the Afro-American magical system more commonly known as hoodoo. Working roots, root doctor, and conjure man connect with traditional beliefs and practices combining magical practices and knowledge of natural ingredients. In folk tradition the conjure man or root doctor was often a specialist who sold magical formulas in bags or packets referred to as "tricks" or "hands." As John points out, his grandfather knew natural healing but did not dabble in magic.

4. For a survey of traditional one-string guitars, diddley bows, and other homemade guitars, see David Evans, "Afro-American One-Stringed Instruments," *Western Folklore* 29 (October, 1970), pp. 229–245.

5. See both John's and Archie's versions of "Stack O'Lee" or "Staggerlee."

6. Actually, John can do dozens of rhythm and blues songs, ranging from "Bye Bye Baby" to "Flip, Flop and Fly" to "The Things I Used to Do."

7. The quartet tradition also has deep roots in Afro-American folk tradition in Virginia, dating back to the turn of the century and connected to what is commonly referred to as "barbershop harmony" groups. See Kip Lornell.

8. Edna Gallmon Cooke was a great gospel artist who exerted a great deal of influence in the Washington area. The daughter of a pastor, she was nicknamed "The Sweetheart of the Potomac" and had a long and successful recording career. See Tony Heilbut, *The Gospel Sound: Good News and Bad Times* (New York: Simon and Schuster, 1971).

9. See "Richmond Blues," p. 216.

10. John Cephas and John Woolfork recorded several songs together for Kip Lornell back in 1977. See Kip Lornell, *Virginia Traditions: Tidewater Blues* (Ferrum, Virginia: Blue Ridge Institute, 1982), p. 16. BRI 006.

11. It is interesting that John Cephas singles out South Carolina and Haiti as areas connected with conjure. Haiti, of course, is the home of the voodoo religion and is commonly associated with different magical practices. South Carolina, particularly Charleston, has also been connected to folk magic.

12. John is referring to a 1986 tour of California when John, Phil, and I traveled from San Francisco to Long Beach.

13. Years later, in the summer of 1988, I stopped and talked to several men working on the boat *Thelma-Dale II*. They all remembered John, but had no idea he was a musician.

14. Wilbur "Big Chief" Ellis was a fine piano player from Alabama. During the time he worked with John he ran a liquor store in Southeast Washington. Dick Spottswood knew his work and reputation, and encouraged him to perform again.

15. Mississippi-born piano player Walter Davis was part of the St. Louis and Chicago blues scene, recording nearly a hundred records over two decades. He died in the 1960s.

16. Frank Hovington can be heard on LR 42.042 as Guitar Frank and on *Frank Hovington: Lonesome Road Blues*, Rounder Records 2017, 1976.

17. John is referring to a National Council for the Traditional Arts production titled *Saturday Night and Sunday Morning: A National Black Heritage Tour of Blues, Gospel, Buckdancing and Storytelling* that toured October–November 1986. John had multiple roles, serving as moderator, gospel vocalist, and, of course, blues artist.

18. For further discussion of the musicians' concern with jealousy and potential violence, see Pearson, 1986, pp. 101–104.

5
John Cephas's Songs

John Cephas, like Archie Edwards, identifies himself as a Piedmont bluesman, yet throughout his life he has performed church songs, first singing spirituals with his family and later working with professional gospel quartets. His broad repertoire embraces also ballads, the torch songs favored by his aunt Lillian, rhythm and blues, and country songs, particularly those of guitar legend Merle Travis.

Unlike Archie Edwards, Cephas remains a voracious learner, constantly assimilating new songs and styles from reissue recordings, songbooks, or any other source he can lay his hands on. His repertoire stems from personal contact with other musicians, phonograph recordings, and original compositions by himself, his partner, Phil Wiggins, and his friend, Maryland poet Otis Williams.[1]

His dozen-year partnership with harmonica virtuoso Phil Wiggins has resulted in a tight, energetic, integrated duet, its total effect somehow greater than the sum of the individual parts. As John puts it, they have "learned to feel each other's pulse." Over the years they have developed an unmistakable sound which, despite its acoustic, downhome flavor, is far more progressive than revivalistic. Music critic and scholar Joseph Wilson, who produced their prize-winning "Dog Days of August" album, labeled their music "urban acoustic blues."[2] The label is apt. Not only are they both native Washingtonians, their music is a progressive, sophisticated blend of traditional instrumentation and modern gospel-edged vocals that works for today's audiences wherever they play.

Over the past half-dozen years I have worked closely with John and Phil, touring Africa, South America, Central America, and the Caribbean as a member of the Bowling Green Blues Trio, which disqualifies me as an impartial observer. On the other hand, my close participation, on- and offstage, has allowed me to witness countless examples of repertoire changes through improvisation, rearranging, or composition. Sometimes these alterations took place on stage. For example, shortly before performing for a packed sports arena in Bamako, Mali, John enigmatically announced, "Don't be surprised at anything I do." Coming on the heels of four weeks of relatively stable sets, his proclamation caused mild concern. To Phil's and my surprise, he ended a set with a house-rocking version of the rhythm and blues classic "Flip, Flop and Fly," which I had never heard him do before and only once at my request since. According to the USIA report of the event: "The audience was alive and very responsive. The vibes were immediately felt by the Trio who threw out their planned numbers and went with an entirely different repertoire. . . . When the Trio joined the traditional musicians and dancers on the floor, the house almost came down."[3]

This glowing report refers to a single instance of John's talent for feeling the audience's mood and altering a fixed set to suit the moment. In this case, however, the song wasn't on any set list and illustrates his motto, "I practice on stage," which became the group's motto and a proverb of sorts.

But Cephas's motto is only partly true because he continuously plays for his own pleasure or to any group of attentive listeners including, as I recall, the kitchen staff of the Hilton Hotel in Antananarrivo, Madagascar. He draws immense satisfaction from learning new styles, like his Skip James tunes or Furry Lewis material, and is liable to try them out on stage, sometimes catching his partner by surprise.

On another occasion in Madagascar, at an after-hours song swap at the ambassador's residence, he generated a fairly complete version of Burl Ives's hit "A Little Bitty Tear Let Me Down," which we didn't add to the song list. But in the Caribbean we did add the country classic "Today I Started Loving You Again."

Finally, I especially recall a three A.M. party in the hallway of an Ohio motel, where he held forth as band leader for an assortment of guitars, harmonicas, violins, and clarinet. That year, John and Phil were participants at the National Folk Festival, which also included Cajun artists Dewey Balfa and D. L. Menard. Obviously impressed by the sound of the Cajun artists, John broke into a tune that followed a standard Cajun progression and, spurred by the moment and enhanced by Jack Daniels, he came up with a credible Cajun-sounding song made up entirely of imitation French lyrics. If there was a word of French in the song or, for that matter, English, it passed me by. I hesitate to call the song parody because the intention was sincere and it did sound awfully good.

He also worries popular standards like "Danny Boy," "A Shanty in Old Shanty Town," and "When I Grow Too Old to Dream," investing them with unseemly emotional impact, teasing the edge of parody with complex chord progressions and vocal pyrotechnics. But this simply shows him to be a capable musician who has gathered and practiced a wide range of songs throughout a lifelong love affair with music. While these songs may not coincide with the bluesman role he actively projects, they surface offstage when he plays at playing music.

In contrast to Archie Edwards, John has relatively little to say about the songs he performs, preferring to let them speak for themselves. Although a very articulate man and a capable workshop leader who can expound on instrumental technique for hours on end, he rarely fills stage time with commentary. Rather, his energy goes into the songs and the feelings they inspire. There are exceptions, however, depending on time and place. "John Henry" or "Staggerlee" may be discussed as legends or original compositions framed by an anecdote that describes the story behind the song. Despite the notable discrepancy, I have included whatever comments John Cephas offered.

Regarding format, I have placed the earliest songs he learned first, followed by house-party standards; tributes to Blind Boy Fuller, Gary Davis, Skip James, other Piedmont and Delta blues; and, finally, recent compositions.

His Thoughts on His Music

Phil and I play in the Piedmont style, which is pretty much the style I learned when I was growing up. We stick with the acoustic sound, which is typical of the Piedmont blues players. In my past I played electric guitar in combos, but that really wasn't my bag. To me the acoustic sound is more meaningful. It has more to say, a better feeling, and it's not so repetitive and loud. We get a full melodic sound with just the two of us, harmonica and guitar, where in Chicago, you got electrified instruments with four to six or even more people.

But the Piedmont style has a fuller sound because it's a little more sophisticated thumb and finger picking. See, my style is a little different from most modern blues players because I play with my thumb and fingers with an alternating thumb and finger style. It's an alternating thumb bass, and then you play the leading parts with your fingers. I never use a flat pick, though I can play that style. I use a thumb pick and one, maybe two, finger picks, though actually I play with all my fingers, like when I'm doing rolls.

My cousin, David Talliaferro, showed me how to do that and I practiced, seems like forever, until I got it. But what it is is alternating thumb and finger picking which keeps a solid beat. I keep a constant

John Cephas at the Smithsonian Folk Festival, 1985.
Photo by Lisa Falk.

bass line going with my thumb and on the treble strings I pick out the melody or the words of the song I'm singing. And when you put them together, that's the Piedmont style. My fingers play what I'm singing. They say what I say, and at the same time I'm getting the guitar to give me that accompanying bass. And it's almost like the guitar is actually talking, mimicking whatever your feelings are or the words to the song. And it's in a kind of loping fashion, like a bouncing, jumping rhythm. That steady bass gives it that loping sound, which is why it was called the Williamsburg Lope.

But most of the older guys played like that. They didn't play with flat picks, they played with their fingers. That's the way the older guys from Virginia and North Carolina played, so that's the way I learned, from watching them and playing with them. That's the style that's characteristic of this area and most of the musicians from around here could play in that style. Guys like Willie Trice, Frank Hovington, Pernell Charity, the Foddrell Brothers, John Jackson, Archie Edwards, my cousin David, they all played in that similar style. Blind Boy Fuller, Reverend Gary Davis, which are my mentors, they played the same way.

But those three—my cousin David, Blind Boy Fuller, and Reverend Gary Davis—they had the most influence on me as far as where my style of playing comes from. Of course, I learned from other musicians and people like my aunt Lillian, and I listened to all kinds of records by guys like Buddy Moss and Blind Blake, and Mississippi John Hurt. But, really, I think I learned to pick by my cousin showing me and listening to Blind Boy Fuller and Reverend Gary Davis. I would listen to them all and I guess it was just trial and error, experimenting and learning from some of the other guys in the neighborhood who could play. I always did have a good ear, so that's how I learned the skill and then just practiced it. That got me started and that's the way I play today.

Actually, when I first started out, I never knew there were different styles of blues until I got to really think more about it and listen to other people playing. I used to listen to guys like Lightning Hopkins, Muddy Waters, Hubert Sumlin,[4] and other guys from different regions of the

CEPHAS & WIGGINS
For Bookings Contact: John Ullman
TRADITIONAL ARTS SERVICES
P.O. Box 7138, Berkeley, CA, 94707 (415) 526-9042

Phil Wiggins and John Cephas, publicity photo, 1988.
Photo by Irene Young.

United States, or I would notice guys play with flat picks and say, "Well, that's not my style."

To me there are two definite styles of the blues: the Piedmont style and the Mississippi Delta style. The Mississippi style is more harsh, more raw, and it uses more single-string runs. Now there were guys around here that played with the single-string progressions because they would hear records of Lightning Hopkins or other guys, like from Mississippi or Chicago. Some of them played that way and some with the alternating finger-picking style. And most of them could play both styles just like I can. But to me the Delta sound is a little more harsh and the Piedmont style is a more full sound and has that loping beat.

We do songs by Delta artists Robert Johnson, Furry Lewis, and Skip James. I like all kinds of music and if I like it, I try to learn it. I used to listen to Merle Travis a lot, and I learned quite a few of his songs and some of his technique, some of his style. And Chet Atkins, too. You should see how many of their records I got. I'll play everything from gospel to country and western. Phil and I try to give the audience some variety, different styles in our shows; ragtime, low-down blues, more up-tempo stuff. But basically, we stay close to the Piedmont sound because that's our roots, you know.

I'm just fascinated by the guitar and any other string instruments I can get my hands on. In fact, when we travel around the world, everywhere I go I bring back different instruments and now my house looks like some kind of museum. I even bought a pedal steel guitar once and tried to learn to play that. I studied for a while with a fellow that had played down in Nashville with Ernest Tubb and then moved to Virginia. Now that's a unique instrument. I think it's one of the hardest to play. I tried to learn to play trumpet, violin, and banjo when I was younger, but I never attempted anything as hard as that pedal steel. Now my instructor, Bud Carlton,[5] he could play it like the old country blues. He sure could. But I never really advanced too far with it.

But I used to play slide when I was younger and even later I did songs like "John Henry" with a knife. When I was a youngster we used to play with a bottleneck or a knife, turn a guitar down flat and play it like a lap steel. But then I laid off that for a while until I bought my steel National. Now I really enjoy playing that style and we usually do some of it in our shows.

The style of blues I play will stay the same. I don't think you can change it too much. With that type of playing you can rearrange a song, like I did with "John Henry" or "St. James Infirmary," but there's not a real change in style. It's either the old style or you move into rock and roll. But I think my type of music will always have its place. It may be that the older people who played that type of blues will fade away, but the music won't die as long as someone picks it up and learns it.

So as far as Phil and I, I don't think we will get into rock and roll or even electric music. We have a heartfelt interest in keeping our music alive. We think it's good music and should be heard more, so we're gonna try to do our best. We have a kind of unique style that comes from playing together a long time. If one was to hear us they would know right off that it's Phil and I. I think we have played so much together that I kind of feel his pulse and he feels my pulse. It's almost like we've melded together to present our music and I think it's unmistakable.

Blues is a thing you've got to feel it in order to play it right. You can't play it if you don't feel it. It's got to be like a part of you. See, blues is an expression of your mind, of your inner self. As far as the music goes, it's not all that different from gospel. Gospel has a lot of feeling in it, too. If you listen closely to blues and gospel music, you'll see the music is just about the same, the chords are the same, the progressions the same. Only the words are different. In gospel, you sing about your feelings about God, whereas in the blues you sing about your feelings about your girl done you wrong, your job, your hardships.

But I think a lot of people have the concept that the two are so different that you could disassociate yourself from one or not be related to the other. But all you got to do is sing a spiritual song and tell me if it doesn't sound exactly like the blues. You know, a lot of the blues were inspired by religious music and if you listen to the voicings and the progressions, they sound alike. There's not much difference between religious music and this traditional music I'm doing.

In religious music you sing about your relationship with God and about daily things that may be adverse to your life. You sing about spiritual things that give you a spiritual uplifting. You sing about something that inspired you in your life or whoever wrote the song. Something happened to him to cause him to write the song. In the blues you do the same thing. Something happened in life to cause a guy to write about his life with the blues. It's all life stories told in song. It's very profound, you know. It's actually telling a story, true-to-life stories from out of the black community. It might be something that happened a long time ago, or might be happening today, like when Phil writes a song about something he feels or something he sees. Somebody, somewhere down the line, has lived that story.

Now people want to tell you that there is a big difference because some of the people in the church don't hold to you singing about anything other than your relationship with God. But then, I don't think God

intended for it to be like that. He gave us music, he gave us the knowledge to express ourselves in song. He gave us these instruments, he gave
us everything. So where's the difference between expressing your relationship with him and singing about your relationship to something else
in your life?[7]

I think people sell themselves out when they say, "Don't sing these
songs." That's ignorance. Of course, their minds may be influenced by
what they think about the places where people sing the blues. There
may be ungodly things in places where you hear the blues, but, really,
you can play the blues anywhere.

It really depends on where you are playing and what's going on.
Like when I was coming up people would dance to the blues until the
whole house would be rocking. Or today they might dance or at festivals
they might be trying to learn something from it. When you play a concert people may be attentive and not so emotional, but they're still listening and enjoying it. It's a true art form and some people appreciate it in
that respect so they don't want to make a whole lot of noise and miss
something. The blues is part of our heritage that we have shared with
the rest of the world. But most any place you go, people respond to the
blues in some way.

The songs I do, I learned most of them in the community where I
was reared. There were quite a few folks who could play, a lot of cousins and other people. So a lot of the old songs like "John Henry" or
"Railroad Bill," I learned them from other people singing. It was easy to
learn them because you would sing along with them until pretty soon
you had the whole song.

Then we would listen to records. We had some of those old 78's
and this old Victrola with a horn on it. You wind it up and the sound
comes out of the horn. We would have records by Blind Lemon Jefferson, Tampa Red, Rosetta Tharpe, and, of course, Blind Boy Fuller and
Reverend Gary Davis. I guess I kind of have a good ear for music so it's
easy for me to learn from records. Really, I never get tired of learning
new songs or styles, like the Skip James songs. I was fascinated by his
sound, so I tried to learn it. It took me a while, but I caught on to it.
And Furry Lewis, and some of the Delta artists like Robert Johnson . . .
when I got my steel National guitar, I learned more of their songs. I
mean, I had always liked that stuff, but I concentrated more because
these songs worked well with the steel guitar.

As far as original material, we do that, too. We write our own
tunes and we have several songs that were given to us by a poet at the
University of Maryland, Otis Williams. He wrote "Sweet Bitter Blues,"
which was the title cut on our second album and he also gave us "Hoodoo Woman." He's a good friend and a great writer, so I imagine we

may do more of his songs. Actually, he's a poet, so we take his poetry and add the music.

With our own songs I would say Phil's the more talented songwriter, at least so far. He's written some good lyrics, "Roberta," "Electric Chair Blues," "Guitar Man," "Butt Naked Blues," and "Dog Days of August." But we collaborate to put the song together. I guess I'm pretty good with the music, so we make a good team. And I've put together quite a few instrumentals, "Bowling Green Rag," "Burn Your Bridges," "Blue Day Blues," "Louisiana Chase," "Piedmont Rag," and all kinds of others.

I've written some songs. In fact, I've got a briefcase full of songs, but usually I'm not satisfied with them. I don't think they're ready yet. You know, I did that "Highway 301," that's the main road that goes through Bowling Green, and I thought that would be big. But nothing happened, and I guess I got discouraged. Usually the stuff that I write, I get disenchanted with it after I do it. Then, when I go back and listen to it again, I think, "Oh, well, I don't think that sounds good enough." It might have been dynamite, but then I gave up on it.

Now I got a new song called, "Black Cat on the Line." I've had it for over a year and I would keep reading over it and say this doesn't make sense. Then I'd put it down and I wouldn't bother with it. Then, when the recording session starts coming up, I start looking through my briefcase and I say, "Damn, let me try to work this one out." And this time, I stuck with it, and I think I got a pretty good song.

Now, I'll play a song to suit my mood. If I'm in a certain mood then that's what I'll play. But when we do shows we have a list and try to mix it up, fast songs and slow songs, happy songs and sad songs, to show a range of different types of songs. But whatever I play, I feel it because these songs come out of life.

The blues are about things that affect your everyday life, not just sad things, but happy things, too. But it also has a deeper meaning. It's a way of expressing yourself, of expressing your feelings. I think it takes a certain kind of person to play the blues like we do and really feel it. And, like I said, you can't play it right if you don't feel it. It's got to be a part of you, an expression of your inner self. And the guitars or harmonicas or other instruments that they use are like an added voice, an extension of yourself to make the expression more deep.

Like when I hear Phil play that harmonica, he gets these riding and soulful sounds. He's really expressing himself and that's what the blues is about. I tell you, it's an expression of your inner feelings, hard times and good times. Sometimes you feel bad. I know I've heard Phil when he was playing that harp and he was in a bad mood and he almost started to make me cry. And, sometimes, when he was happy, he could get those riffs and it would get me jumping and feeling good. And I know some of those days when I came off the stage after I really got down on a certain song, Phil would tell me, "Man, you really felt that."

And I guess that's the way it affects most people that play the blues. And it can have the same effect on the audience. If you really get down, they will feel it, too. Or if you're playing something jumping, a dance tune, then they'll feel that and be clapping or dancing in the aisles. So I think that first you have to feel the music yourself, and when we play we are immersed completely in our music. We actually feel it, and this is what radiates from our music. The audience, they can feel it, too, and are captured by it.

Repertoire

John Henry

John Henry, it's legendary. Back in the old times, up in Ohio or West Virginia someplace, he was working for the railroad and this was a time when they first brought out those steel-driving machines. John Henry had a bet with the captain, that he could out-drive the steam drill, which was actually true. He did beat the steam drill.

But it's a lot in the song that's kind of mythical. You know people exaggerate about some things. But he was a living person that actually had an encounter with a machine. This is a traditional song that's sung in almost every black community, as I know from when I came along as a kid. It's been recorded many times. This is my arrangement and it's different from the traditional arrangements of "John Henry." I did this in a D-minor tuning and it turned out really nice.

1   John Henry was a little boy
     You could hold him in the palm of your hand
     By the time that boy was nine year old
     He was driving steel like a man, Lord, Lord
     He was driving steel like a man

2   John Henry was a little boy
     He was sitting on his mammy's knee
     He picked up a hammer, a little bit of steel
     Said "This hammer gonna be the death of me," Lord, Lord
     This hammer's gonna be the death of me

3   John Henry said to the captain
     "A man ain't nothing but a man

Phil Wiggins and John Cephas, 1988.
Photo by Robert Saunders.

But before I let this steam drill beat me down
I'll die with this hammer in my hand," Lord, Lord
I'll die with this hammer in my hand

4   John Henry said to the captain
"Captain, you ought to see me swing
I weigh forty-nine pounds from my hips on down
And I love to hear that cold steel ring," Lord, Lord
I love to hear that cold steel ring

5   John Henry went to the tunnel
The steam drill was by his side
He beat that steam drill three chests and down
He laid down his hammer and he died, Lord, Lord
He laid down his hammer and he died

6   John Henry drove steel in the tunnel
     Till his hammer caught on fire
     He look at that water boy and said
     "A cool drink of water before I die," Lord, Lord
     A cool drink of water before I die

7   The captain said to John Henry
     "This mountain's caving in"
     John Henry said to the captain
     "That's just my hammer sucking wind," Lord, Lord
     That's just my hammer sucking wind

8   John Henry had a little wife
     Her name was Polly Ann
     John got sick and he couldn't get well
     And Polly drove steel like a man, Lord, Lord
     Polly drove steel like a man

9   They took John Henry to the graveyard
     They buried him in the sand
     And every time a locomotive drive by
     They said "There lies a steel driving man," Lord, Lord
     There lies a steel driving man

John Cephas sings an unusually complete and cohesive version of "John Henry." He learned the song as a youngster and first recorded it in 1976 for Richard Spottswood and Mack McCormick, and the recordings are available at the Library of Congress. The next year he recorded two more versions for Kip Lornell. Most recently he recorded it for Joe Wilson and Larry McBride; it was issued first on cassette and then on the *Dog Days of August* album. Textually, the song remains relatively consistent, averaging about ten verses in length. In this version he sings nine verses, combining two verses in the fifth verse of the song.

Musically, the piece has undergone significant changes. Although he first learned it in slide style in open tuning, he recorded it in standard tuning, in the key of A, for Spottswood and Lornell. When we toured Africa in 1982 he did not perform the song, except in workshops, where he reverted to slide style. Then one night in a hotel room in Belize, experimenting with D-minor tuning derived from Skip James's records, he rearranged the song for D-minor tuning and plays it that way today.

For transcription and other versions see: W. K. McNeil, 150–153; Kip Lornell 1977, 11; Mack McCormick, 9. For his most recent version see FF 394, 1986.

Other versions are available on BRI 001 and LBC 9. See also the notes to Archie Edwards's version.

Staggerlee

He was a bad guy. But this is more mythical. The setting was down in New Orleans and these two guys were gambling, as the story goes, and one cheated the other one. And then the other one went and got his gun and came back and shot him.

I think this was more mythical, but maybe characteristic of things that actually did happen. It's been called both "Stack O'Lee," or "Staggerlee."

1   I was standing on the corner
I heard my bulldog bark
Barking at the two men
Who were gambling in the dark
And he's bad, bad, bad, bad, old Staggerlee

2   Staggerlee and Billy
Two men who gamble late
Old Staggerlee threw seven
Billy swore that he threw eight
And he's bad, bad, bad, bad, old Staggerlee

3   Staggerlee told Bill
I can't let you go with that
You have won all my money
And my brand new Stetson hat
And he's bad, bad, bad, bad, old Staggerlee

4   Staggerlee went uptown
Got his forty-four
Said I'm going down to that bar room
Pay that debt I owe
And he's bad, bad, bad, bad, old Staggerlee

5   Staggerlee went to the barroom
Walk across the barroom floor
Old Staggerlee told Billy,
"I came to pay the debt I owe"
And he's bad, bad, bad, bad, old Staggerlee

6   Billy told Staggerlee
"Please don't take my life"
I got three little children
And a very sickly wife
And he's bad, bad, bad, bad, old Staggerlee

7   Staggerlee shot Billy
He shot that boy so bad
Till the bullet came through Billy
And it broke the bartender's glass
And he's bad, bad, bad, bad, old Staggerlee

8   Billy's wife came to the barroom
"I can't believe my man is dead"
Old Staggerlee told her,
"Count the bullets in his head"
And he's bad, bad, bad, bad, old Staggerlee

9   If you ever go to New Orleans
Walk on the barroom floor
Or every step you take
Will be in Billy Lyon's blood
And he's bad, bad, bad, bad, old Staggerlee

More complete than Archie's, John's "Staggerlee" is closer to the Lloyd Price version but has different lyrics. W. K. McNeil noted that "most of the singers who include this ballad in their repertoire are of the opinion that it refers to an actual person, but who that original was, even whether he was black or white, is in dispute." It is interesting, then, that John characterizes the song as mythical, although he localizes it in New Orleans.

See: Archibald (aka) Leon T. Gross, "Stack-A-Lee," Imperial 5060, October 1950; Lloyd Price, "Stagger Lee," ABC 9972, December 1958. See also the notes in Archie Edwards's version and FF 394.

Railroad Bill

That's one of the first songs I learned to play on the guitar. My uncle taught me that song and I used to do it all the time. I would play it myself or sometimes with other guys singing. My grandfather, he used to be crazy about that song. Every time we would get together he would sing it. My aunt Lillian, she knew it, too. Better than I did.

But that's an old song, a good song for picking in that loping, Piedmont style. In fact, I play it more than I sing it. It used to be there were all kinds of verses, like about "Railroad Bill and Old McKinley Tut," but I don't remember them. I sing a few verses, get past the second verse, and forget the rest. But there were other songs like that, that you played more than you sang. They were for guitar players. Like "Railroad Bill" and "Nine Pound Hammer," "Casey Jones." I played that, but never sang it. But they were real popular.

"Railroad Bill," that was one song that Frank Hovington and I played alike. He and I played it almost lick for lick. If I had never heard him and I would have heard him on a record, I would have to listen to it twice to see if it wasn't me. It was that close.

1   Railroad Bill, coming over the hill
     Huffing and a puffing like an old automobile
     Anytime, Old Railroad Bill

2   Railroad Bill, coming from the West
     Coming to see the girl that he loved the best
     Anytime, anytime, Railroad Bill

3   Railroad Bill, he was all bad
     Stole everything that the farmers had
     Anytime, oh, Lord, anytime

4   Railroad Bill was a mighty mean sport
     Shot all the buttons off the brakeman's coat
     Anytime, Old Railroad Bill

5   Railroad Bill, he was standing on the hill
     Thinks he's working, but he's standing still
     Anytime, Old Railroad Bill

6   Rubber tire buggy, rubber tire hack
     Take him to the graveyard, never bring him back
     Anytime, anytime, Railroad Bill

7   Kill a chicken, save me the wing
     Think I'm working, I ain't doing a thing
     Anytime, Old Railroad Bill

8   Railroad Bill, out on the line
     One eye was bloodshot, and the other was blind
     Anytime, Old Railroad Bill

9   Railroad Bill, coming cross the hill
         Huffing and puffing, like an old automobile
         Anytime, Old Railroad Bill

10   Railroad Bill, done made a will
         Never work and he never will
         Anytime, Old Railroad Bill

This popular Afro-American ballad supposedly tells the story of one Morris Slater, an Alabama outlaw who lived and died in the nineteenth century. Unlike the previous two ballads, which clearly focus on dramatic narratives, John's version of "Railroad Bill" does not tell much of a story. Rather, it is an instrumental dance song first, and then a collection of humorous comments about a character significantly distanced from any legendary event or historical occurrence.

Folksong scholars sometimes call these songs "blues ballads." For example, Norm Cohen considers "Railroad Bill" to be "a good example of a blues ballad, a narrative folksong with a rather loose organization rather than the temporarily correct sequence of the broadside ballad." He further distinguishes between types of blues ballads:

> Some blues ballads seem to have acquired their present structure through years of oral transmission with attendant imperfect memory or deliberate redaction. . . . Other blues ballads seem to have sprung forth in their loosely organized forms with little or no evidence for coherent and complete antecedent narrative ballads. In other words, blues ballads are not invariably the result of destructive processes, but testify to the existence in this country of a type of folksong that is persistent among both blacks and whites.

Cephas's version leans toward the latter category, although in his case, forgetfulness also affects the song. Frankly, without a story line to trigger his memory and hold the song together, he had to strain to recall these verses. In fact, it is one of several songs he will play but does not actively perform on stage. Nevertheless, since it was an important song in his younger days and popular in the black community, I have included it.

John Cephas recorded two versions of the song for Kip Lornell in 1977 as a duet with his cousin, John Woolfork. It is apparent that the song was conceptualized primarily as an instrumental dance song and a vehicle for showing out as a guitarist. Although the traditional melody is stable, both guitarists take off on blues-inflected solos. Neither seems all that eager to sing and John finally says, "I'll sing two, then you sing two." But he winds up doing all the limited vocal lines, including the intriguing half line, "Railroad Bill and Old McKinley Tut," which appears to come from "Whitehouse Blues."

Instrumentally, Cephas's song is similar to Frank Hovington's rendition, but textually it is closer to a version recorded by Turner Foddrell in 1977, also for Kip Lornell. Cephas's third, fifth, sixth, and seventh verses are the same as those in Foddrell's highly repetitive version. Other Virginians, Silas Pendleton in 1947 and Bill Williams in the 1970s, recorded the piece, as did West Virginian Frank Hutchison in 1929. All these versions share traditional verses as well as an overall lack of concern for the story line, indicating that, at least in Virginia, "Railroad Bill" was more about dancing and guitar playing than storytelling.

See: Olive Woolley Burt, 200–202; Carl Carmer, 122–125; Norm Cohen, 122–131; G. Malcolm Laws 1964, 252; MacEdward Leach and Horace P. Beck, 279–280; Lawrence Levine, 410–412; Alan Lomax 1960, 557, 568–569; John and Alan Lomax 1934, 118–120; Paul Oliver 1971, 12–14, and Oliver, *Songsters*, 1984, 241–242; E. C. Perrow, 155; Art Rosenbaum, 194, 200; Carl Sandburg, 384; Dorothy Scarborough 1925, 251; Happy Traum, 14–15; John Work, 240.

John Cephas's 1977 recording has not been issued, but see Frank Hovington, "Railroad Bill," *Songs of Migration and Immigration: Folk Music in America*, vol. 6, Library of Congress LBC6, 1977; Turner Foddrell, "Railroad Bill," *Virginia Traditions: Non-Blues Secular Black Music*, Blue Ridge Institute, Ferrum, Virginia, BRI 001, 1978; Frank Hutchison, "Railroad Bill," reissued on Rounder 1007; and Bill Williams, *The Late Bill Williams: Blues Rags and Ballads*, Blue Goose 20B, 1974.

St. James Infirmary

"St. James Infirmary" is a traditional song. It's an Irish song. All I know is it's been there for years. But people in the black community used to play it when I was younger. I used to hear it all the time, like "Staggerlee" and "Frankie and Johnny."

1   I went down to Old Joe's Bar room
     On the corner by the square
     We had our drinks as usual
     And a goodly crowd was there

2   On my left stood Joe McKenny
     And his eyes were bloodshot red
     As he gazed at the crowd around him
     These are the words that he said

3   "I went down to St. James Infirmary
     Lord, I saw my baby there
     She was stretched out on that long white table
     So cool, so sweet, so fair

4   "Let her go, let her go, God bless her
     And wherever she may be
     You can search this wide world over
     But she'll never find a man like me"

5   I said, "Hey, Mister Bartender
     Pass another shot of the booze
     And if anyone asks you my story
     Tell them I've got the mean St. James Infirmary blues

6   "And when I die, I want you to bury me
     Boxback suit and a Stetson hat
     I want you to tell all the boys round the barroom
     That I died standing pat

7   "I may be shot down, down with a pistol
     I may be blowed away with a cannonball
     But that girl down in St. James Infirmary
     She was the cause of it all"

"St. James Infirmary" lives on as a folk and popular standard with an interesting, if at times confusing, history. Scholars generally concede that it initially derives from a British broadside ballad entitled "The Unfortunate Rake," which dealt with the unfortunate effects of a sexually transmitted disease and the victim's morbid speculation about his funeral requirements. In the United States, ballad scholar G. Malcolm Laws lists it as "St. James Hospital: The Young Girl Cut Down in Her Prime." British folklorist Cecil Sharp collected it in Appalachia during his 1916–1918 fieldwork. In its various transmutations it has been collected as "The Dying Cowboy," "Gambling Blues," "Dying Crapshooter's Blues," and, of course, "St. James Infirmary." Paul Oliver noted:

> Of all the ballads of British origin which gained some popularity among black singers, only one, the Irish ballad of "The Unfortunate Rake," gained some currency. Though it passed into the American ballad tradition as "The Dying Cowboy," it was sung in black communities as "St. James Infirmary," "The John Sealy Hospital," or "The Dying Gambler."

Jazz legends Louis Armstrong and Cab Calloway popularized the song in the late twenties and early thirties, when it became a jazz and popular-music standard. Since then blues artists—including Piedmont performer Josh White—and white country, folk, and popular performers have cut and recut the song, making it an American classic.

John's version is fairly typical, although when we first worked together in 1982 he didn't use the introductory stanzas. Today he employs a very dramatic presentation, drawing out the first two verses and investing the piece with tremendous emotional impact. His version may strike purists as overly derivative of show-business techniques, but when he is into the song it is remarkably powerful, often bringing tears to the audience's eyes and, on rarer occasions, to his own.

John's version shows up in Carl Sandburg's 1927 collection under the title "Those Gambler's Blues." Sandburg included two versions of the piece, noting, "This may be what polite society calls a gutter song. In a foreign language, in any lingo but that of the U.S.A., it would seem less vulgar, more bizarre." The majority of John's verses correspond to Sandburg's "A" version, with verses four and seven found in the "B" version.

See: G. Malcolm Laws 1957, 285–286; Paul Oliver, *Songsters*, 1984, 230; Carl Sandburg, 228–231; and Cecil Sharp, 164–165. Other connected recordings include Louis Armstrong and his Savoy Ballroom Five, "St. James Infirmary," Okeh 8657, December 1928; Cab Calloway, "St. James Infirmary," Brunswick 6105, December 23, 1930; Willie McTell, "Dying Crapshooter's Blues," Melodian 7323, recorded initially November 5, 1940; Josh White, *Josh White at Midnight*, Elektra EKL-102; and John Cephas LR 42.054.

Careless Love

I used to hear "Careless Love" back when I went around with my grandfather. It was real popular in the black community. It's an old song, and lots of people have recorded it: Blind Boy Fuller, even Gary Davis, but it goes way back.

1   Oh love, oh, love, oh, careless love
     Love, oh, love, careless love
     It's love, oh, love, oh, careless love
     Can you see what careless love has done

2   Never drive a stranger from your door
     Never drive a stranger from your door
     Never drive a stranger from your door
     Well, it may be your best friend you'll never know

3   You passed my door, but you didn't come in
      You passed my door but you didn't come in
      You passed my door and didn't come in
      Oh love, oh love, oh, careless love

4   Oh you passed my door and you passed my gate
      You passed my door and you passed my gate
      Oh you passed my door and you passed my gate
      But you cannot pass my thirty-eight

5   Lord, I'm down here in this valley on my knees
      I'm down here in this valley on my knees
      I'm down here in this valley, Lord, I'm on my knees
      Well, no true love can I see

6   Make you kill yourself and your best friend, too
      Make you kill yourself and your best friend, too
      Make you kill yourself and your best friend, too
      Oh love, oh love, oh, careless love

7   Oh love, oh love, oh, careless love
      Love, oh love, oh, careless love
      It's love, oh love, oh, careless love
      You see what careless love has done
      You see what careless love has done
      You see what careless love has done

"Careless Love," collected as "Kelly's Love" and published as "Love-less Love," has been a favorite among both black and white singers since the late nineteenth century. According to W. C. Handy, the blues tradition's first spokesperson, the song was rooted in a ballad of sorts that commemorated the death of the son of the governor of Kentucky and included the verses "You see what careless love has done / It killed the Governor's only son" and "Poor Archie didn't mean no harm." Deleting the narrative line, Handy published a related song as "Loveless Love." Dorothy Scarborough, quoting Handy's authority, added that "it had the mythical one hundred verses and was widely current in the South, especially in Kentucky." Handy had a certain interest in the song, having published a version of it, and he and several other writers of the time were anxious to make the blues legitimate by proving it to be a folk form.

In any event, this sixteen-bar song predates the blues and appears to have been adaptable to black song tradition regardless of its origin.

John's version should be considered a blues in feeling, if not strictly in form. As he notes, it was popular among Piedmont artists, and this rendition is close to the 1937 Blind Boy Fuller recording.

See: B. A. Botkin, 901; Harold Courlander 1963, 138; Stefan Grossman 1970, 54–58; W. C. Handy 1941, 153; Handy 1972, 55–57; Alan Lomax 1960, 585; John and Alan Lomax 1936, 218–220; Howard Odum and Guy Johnson 1925, 194; Harry Oster, 426–427; Vance Randolph, 306–308; Eric Sackheim, 358; Carl Sandburg, 21; Dorothy Scarborough 1923, 52. See also: Blind Boy Fuller, "Careless Love," ARC 8-02-66, September 8, 1937, reissued on *Blind Boy Fuller with Sonny Terry and Bull City Red*, Blues Classics 11; Bill Jackson, *Long Steel Rail: Blues by Maryland Songster Bill Jackson*, Testament Records T-201; and Cephas, FF 470.

Going Down That Road Feeling Bad

"Going Down That Road Feeling Bad," that's the song that I learned the technique of the Piedmont style of playing, that alternating thumb and finger picking. That is the song that I practiced in order to get that "lope." That's the song that did it for me. That's the Williamsburg Lope. I practiced that song so long until I almost wore out all the strings on the guitar.

1   Going down that road feeling bad
     Going down that road feeling bad
     Going down that road feeling bad
     Lord, I ain't gonna be treated this way

2   Lord, what I got gonna sure bring you back
     Lord, what I got gonna sure bring you back
     Lord, what I got gonna sure bring you back
     Lord, I ain't gonna be treated this way

3   Lord, they feed me on corn bread and beans
     Lord, they feed me on corn bread and beans
     Lord, they feed me on corn bread and beans
     Lord, I ain't gonna be treated this way

4   Lord, I'm down here in this valley on my knees
     Lord, I'm down here in this valley on my knees
     Lord, I'm down here in this valley on my knees
     Lord, I ain't gonna be treated this way

5   Lord, I'm going down that road feeling bad
       Lord, I'm going down that road feeling bad
       Lord, I'm going down that road feeling bad
       Lord, I ain't gonna be treated this way

"Going Down That Road Feeling Bad," also known as "I Ain't Gonna Be Treated This Way" and "Lonesome Road Blues," comes out of a shared black and white string-band tradition. It has a distinct melody and can be done as an instrumental piece. Kip Lornell recorded an instrumental version by Suffolk, Virginia, guitarist Corner Morris in 1979. Morris, whose repertoire includes older tunes, such as "Railroad Bill," as well as blues, claims he learned the song in the early 1920s. Lornell notes that songs like Morris's "Going Down the Road Feeling Good" "are part of both Afro-American and Anglo-American tradition and, along with 'Poor Boy Blues' and 'Red River Blues,' constitute some of the earliest folk blues themes."

In conversation, Richard K. Spottswood commented that folk-revival performers knew the song as "Going Down That Road Feeling Bad," while white country artists generally titled the piece "Lonesome Road Blues." A "Lonesome Road Blues" was recorded by Virginian Henry Whitter as early as November 1923. Woody Guthrie also helped popularize the song, and it was used in the film version of *The Grapes of Wrath*. Although Guthrie copyrighted his version, the song is much older. John and Alan Lomax simply credited it to "Negro singers."

Cephas first recorded the song in 1976 and invariably uses it in workshops to demonstrate the Piedmont guitar style. He learned to pick using this song; it also characterizes the alternating thumb bass style, where the treble strings play the vocal melody over the regular thumb bass rhythm.

See: John Greenway, 206–207; Alan Lomax 1967, 215–216; John and Alan Lomax 1947, 229, 242–243; Kip Lornell 1982, 12; Art Rosenbaum, 176.

For recorded examples see: *Woody Guthrie and Cisco Houston: Folksongs Volume I*, Stinson SLP 44; Corner Morris, "Going Down the Road Feeling Good," BRI 006; Henry Whitter, "Lonesome Road Blues," Okeh 40015, November 1923; and Cephas LR 42.031.

Richmond Blues

I'm from around the Richmond area and I think that just about every musician in the neighborhood has a "Richmond Blues," and I have my version. I learned it from my cousin David. He taught me how to play that song. It's basically about this guy that's down in Richmond and obviously he had some problems with his girlfriend, so he goes on telling all these things he's gonna do. But it's a real blues tune because it's got a lot of good verses, a lot of good words in it. My "Richmond Blues" is like, oh boy, Blind Boy Fuller's "Mistreater Blues." I don't think he ever recorded "Richmond Blues," but he recorded "Mistreater Blues," which had the same progressions but different words. But "Richmond Blues" didn't come from him. It came from somebody else. Like, the local musicians used to play it and all of them had different words to it. Just like the words that I do, I put a lot of these verses in there myself. And I learned a lot of them from David Talliaferro.

It was definitely a local song and it was very popular. A lot of people played it and a lot of people couldn't. But then, almost everybody had different words that they would sing to the song.

1   I was standing down in Richmond
    On the corner of Broad and Main
    Up walked two policemen
    Said, "Son, what is your right name?"

2   I told him my name
    Was stamped on my shirt
    I'm a womenfolk lover
    And I sure don't have to work

3   My gal she went away
    Didn't even write to me
    Got my mind all worried
    Like water in the deep blue sea

4   Then I'm going uptown
    I'm gonna talk with the chief of police
    Lord, the little gal's in trouble
    And I sure can't find no peace

5   I'm gonna buy me a bulldog
    I'm gonna shuffle two greyhounds
    I'm gonna use these dogs
    To run my good gal down

6   I'm gonna use these dogs
    Just to watch me when I sleep
    To keep these men
    From making an early creep

7 Lord, I wrote one line
  Then I laid my pencil down
  My heart struck sorrow
  And the tears come rolling down

8 Uh-huh, Uh-huh
  You know doggin' ain't right
  If you gonna dog me
  I'll run both day and night

9 Uh-huh, Uh-huh
  Uh-huh, oh shucks
  You know two men loving you
  And one of us got to go

10 Then I feel like snapping
  My little pistol in your face
  Let some lonesome graveyard
  Be your resting place

11 Graveyard, graveyard
  Is a low-down dirty place
  Lie flat on your back
  Throw mud all in your face

12 I drink muddy water
  I sleep in a hollow log
  I ain't gonna stay here, woman
  And be treated like a dog

13 That's why I'm standing down in Richmond
  On the corner of Broad and Main
  Up walked two policemen
  Said, "Son, what's your right name?"

Many blues songs took their title from a local city or town known to the singer and his audience as a means of personalizing and localizing familiar traditional verses. Although the earliest recorded version of a song with this title comes from a North Carolina artist, Julius Daniels, who recorded the piece in 1927, evidence suggests all or part of it may have been traditional before then. Another North Carolina performer, Blind Boy Fuller's cohort, Bull City Red, recorded a popular version some eight years after the Daniels record. John Cephas's version is un-

like either and, as he indicates, the song was traditional around the
Bowling Green and Richmond area when he first began to play in
public.

Cephas alludes to Fuller's "Mistreater Blues" as a source, but "Richmond Blues" draws on numerous verses that can fit into the eight-bar
format. It closely follows Blind Boy Fuller's "Bulldog Blues," but verses
are also found in Fuller's "Evil Hearted Woman," "Weeping Willow,"
"Why My Baby Don't Write to Me," and "Pistol Snapper Blues." As we
can see, Cephas's version draws on various verses associated with Fuller's repertoire, but then Fuller himself was equally adept at rearranging
other artist's songs and drew heavily on traditional verses in his own
compositions. Cephas, his cousin, and other local musicians continue
the creative process, rearranging traditional verses and making their
own individualized versions of this regional blues.

See: Blind Boy Fuller, "Bulldog Blues," Decca 7878, July 12, 1937, reissued
on *Blind Boy Fuller: 1936–1940*, Old Tramp OT 1202; Julius Daniels, "Richmond Blues," Victor 21065, October 24, 1927; Bull City Red, "Richmond Blues,"
ARC 5-12-57, July 25, 1935; and John Cephas, LR 42.031. Cephas recorded the
piece for Kip Lornell, Pete Lowry, and Richard Spottswood, but it is unreleased.

West Carey Street Blues

A bunch of guys used to do that. That's a traditional song, "West Carey
Street Blues." Now, it's traditional because so many guys used to do it
and I don't know who the author was or where I even got it from. But I
know that almost all the blues musicians had a "West Carey Street
Blues." Some had a real fast one, some had a real slow one. And I did it
both ways and it went over good, fast or slow. I got it from local musicians. Some guy around Richmond, Virginia, used to play it because it
says, "I was standing on West Carey Street one day." See, Carey Street is
in Richmond, Virginia. Some of them recorded it as Cairo Street. I don't
know where that is, Kansas City or St. Louis or one of those towns out
there. But Carey Street is in Richmond, Virginia, and that's the version I
sing. So, it's a local version.

1 Honey baby, I'm all out and down
   Honey baby, I'm all out and down
   Honey baby, I'm all out and down
   Running around just as hungry as a hound

2 I was standing on West Carey Street one day
   Standing on West Carey Street one day

Standing on West Carey Street one day
Lord, one dime was all I had

3   One dime was all I had
     One dime was all I had
     One dime was all that I had
     Everybody sees hard luck sometime

4   Honey babe, what can I do for you?
     Honey babe, what can I do for you?
     Honey babe, what can I do for you?
     For you to treat me, oh, so mean

5   Mama, don't you treat your daughter mean
     Mama, don't you treat your daughter mean
     Mama, don't you treat your daughter mean
     You're the meanest woman a woman most ever seen

6   You want your friends to be bad like Jesse James
     Want your friends to be bad like Jesse James
     Want your friends to be bad like Jesse James
     That's the only way you know how to get fame

7   Well, I bought the Morning News
     I bought the Morning News
     I bought the Morning News
     Lord, I bought a cigar, too

Like Archie Edwards's "One Thin Dime Blues," John's "West Carey Street Blues" no doubt derives initially from the Blind Lemon Jefferson record "One Dime Blues." However, John considers it a local song and learned it from local Bowling Green–Richmond, Virginia, musicians. Bruce Bastin also noted a Virginia connection: "Actually, it is closer to two other Virginia recordings: played slowly, Cephas's version is melodically closest to 'West Kinney Street Blues' by the enigmatic Skoodle-Dum-Doo and Sheffield, recorded for Regis in 1943, but it shares the last three stanzas with not only Lemon's version, but also James Lowry's 1953 version, 'Karo Street Blues' from Bedford, Virginia."

The James Lowry version was recorded by a local radio station and later issued on the BRI 003 *Western Piedmont Blues*, 1978. Note that Archie Edwards learned it from the Jefferson record but also claimed that Virginian Willie Gaines performed it as well. This evidence strongly suggests it was traditional, whether it entered oral tradition from Blind Lemons's 1927 recording or not.

See: Bruce Bastin, 318; Lornell 1978, 11; and the notes to Archie Edwards's version. John can be heard on LR 42.031.

Keep Your Hands Off My Baby

That's another one that people used to play at house parties, "Keep Your Hands Off My Baby." That was Big Bill Broonzy. They played that years back. That was one of the favorite ones at the parties. Yeah, "Keep Your Hands Off Her."

1   She's long and tall and she's built up straight
     She's long and tall and she's built up straight
     She's long and tall and she's built up straight
     Boy, she don't belong to you

2   Keep your hands off her, keep your big hands down
     Keep your hands off her, keep your big hands down
     Keep your hands off her, you hear what I say
     Boy, she don't belong to you

3   Well, when she sees me coming, she holds her arms up high
     Well, when she sees me coming, she holds her arms up high
     Well, when she sees me coming, she holds her arms up high
     Boy, she don't belong to you

4   She got great big legs, she got little bitty feet
     She got great big legs, she got little bitty feet
     She got great big legs, she got little bitty feet
     Boy, she don't belong to you

5   Keep your hands off her, keep your big hands down
     Keep your hands off her, keep your big hands down
     Keep your hands off her, you hear what I say
     Boy, she don't belong to you

Another popular dance song, "Keep Your Hands Off My Baby" is based on Big Bill Broonzy's 1935 recording "Keep Your Hands Off Her." Broonzy was born in Mississippi but moved to Chicago, where he became a prolific recording artist and a mainstay of the commercial blues scene. Later still, he became a major figure in the blues revival, much like Piedmont artists Josh White, Sonny Terry, and Brownie McGhee. During the thirties and forties his blues recordings sold well on the East Coast, and I have run across them several times at flea markets and yard sales. John recorded the song in 1976, but it was not issued. According to Richard Spottswood, songs using the "take your hands off it" or "finger out of it" motif go back least as far as the Memphis Jug Band's "Sugar Pudding," recorded in 1928.

See: Big Bill Broonzy, "Keep Your Hands Off Her," Bluebird B6188, 1935; John Tinsley, "Keep Your Hands Off Her, She Don't Bear Touching," Mutual M-213, 1952; and Memphis Jug Band, "Sugar Pudding," Victor 21740, September 11, 1928.

Nine Pound Hammer

"Nine Pound Hammer" used to be in the black community and I used to hear it when I was a young man. I can only remember a couple of verses which I learned from the Merle Travis record. I learned the verses from a Merle Travis record, but he probably learned it from the traditional song because it was popular in the black community and I heard it way back. But that's the same verses they used to sing because, see, it had such good picking in it. Why, a guy would sing two verses, then pick for four verses.

1   Well, nine pound hammer
It's a little too heavy
For my size, buddy
For my size

Roll on, buddy
Roll on, buddy
How in the world can I roll
When the wheels won't go

2   It's a long way to Harlan
It's a long way to Hazard
Just to get a little brew
Just to get a little brew

Roll on, buddy
Roll on, buddy

How can I roll
When the wheels won't go

3   This old hammer
    Killed John Henry
    It won't kill me
    It won't kill me

    Roll on, buddy
    Roll on, buddy
    How can I roll
    When the wheels won't go

4   When I die
    Make my tombstone
    Out of number nine coal
    Out of number nine coal

John performs this traditional song as an instrumental display piece, using limited vocals derived primarily from the influential Merle Travis recording of the song. After Blind Boy Fuller, Reverend Gary Davis, and, more recently, Skip James, I would consider Merle Travis to be a major influence on Cephas's guitar style. John also plays the Travis version of "I Am a Pilgrim," and his "Steel Guitar Rag" is closer to the Travis version than the Bob Wills version. As much as he admires Travis, he seldom performs Travis material in concert. In workshops, however, he enjoys showing off his ability to work in the Merle Travis style.

Travis drew this song, as well as "I Am a Pilgrim" and other songs, from traditional sources. As Archie Edwards noted, his father played a version of "Nine Pound Hammer," and it was clearly traditional in Virginia well before the Travis recording. Several fine discussions of the song are available, particularly Archie Green's study in *Only a Miner*. Norm Cohen also surveys the song's history in *Long Steel Rail*. Both Green and Cohen note the impact of the Travis recording on later renditions of the song.

See: Norm Cohen, 571–582; Archie Green, 329–369; Alan Lomax 1960, 276, 284–285; Howard Odum, 236; and Merle Travis, "Nine Pound Hammer," Capitol 48000, August 8, 1946, reissued on the *Best of Merle Travis*, Capitol SM 2662. John's version has recently been released on cassette tape: *Walking Blues: Bowling Green John Cephas and Harmonica Phil Wiggins*, Marimac 8004.

The Moon Is Rising

The words to "The Moon Is Rising" come from a Lightning Hopkins song. I heard it way back. It must have been on a single, because I don't have it on an album. But that's one of those low-down blues.

1   The moon is rising, Lord, I got bad things on my mind
     Lord, the moon is rising, Lord, I got bad things on my mind
     Lord, I want to kill my woman
     Lord, I just can't kill that woman for crying

2   Lord, I'm going uptown, Lord, I saw my woman up there
     Lord, I went up town, Lord, I saw my woman there
     Lord, she was there with that other man
     Make me think that she don't care

3   Please tell me, mama, what more can I do for you
     Please tell me, mama, what more can I do for you
     Lord, you got me running around the streets
     Yes, I'm as hungry as a hound

4   Yeah, just as true as the birds, Lord, they flock in the air
     Just as true as the birds, Lord, they flock in the air
     You know, life ain't worth living
     Lord, if you ain't with the one you love

5   The moon is rising, Lord, I got bad things on my mind
     Lord, the moon is rising, Lord, I got bad things on my mind
     Lord, I want to kill that woman
     But, I just can't kill that woman for crying

John recorded this moody, aggressive blues with his cousin, John Woolfork, for Kip Lornell in 1977. Using a traditional framing verse, "The moon is rising," the song pursues the theme of mistreatment and violent fantasy. It is based on a 78 RPM recording titled "Moonrise Blues," by Lightning Hopkins, and is one of the few blues by Texas artists in Cephas's repertoire.

See: Lightning Hopkins, "Moonrise Blues," Aladdin 3077, February 25, 1948.

I Ain't Got No Loving Baby Now

I used to listen to records of Blind Boy Fuller, how he used to hit those notes, and I just couldn't do what he was doing. But, finally, I got it, and when I had it, it was a great feeling. I finally learned the style he was playing. I patterned my style of playing on Blind Boy Fuller and Reverend Gary Davis, more so than any of the others. They had the most influence on me.

I never saw Blind Boy Fuller, but I learned lots of his songs and I met other guitar players who played his songs, too. I feel like we were friends in spirit, because he had so much influence on my style. I still learn from his records.

1   Lord, I went down to that freight depot
     That freight came rollin' by
     Lord, now I ain't got no loving baby, now
     I ain't got no loving baby now

2   Lord, when I went off in the far distant land
     I wasn't there long before I received a telegram
     Saying, man, won't you please come home
     I ain't got no loving baby now
     I ain't got no loving baby now

3   Lord, then I went home and I look on my bed
     That old friend of mine was dead
     Lord, now I ain't got no loving baby now
     Lord, I ain't got no loving baby now

4   Lord, I'm sorry, sorry, sorry to my heart
     That old friends of mine must part
     Lord, I ain't got no loving baby now
     Lord, I ain't got no loving baby now

5   Just as true as the birds flock in the sky above
     Life ain't worth living if you're not with the one you love
     Lord, I ain't got no loving baby now
     Lord, I ain't got no loving baby now

6   If I knowed you didn't love me and want me too
     Lord, I'd take morphine and die
     Lord, I ain't got no loving baby now
     Lord, I ain't got no loving baby now

John Cephas has been performing "I Ain't Got No Loving Baby Now" since I first met him in 1978. It comes from a Blind Boy Fuller song called "Lost Lover Blues." In typical fashion, Cephas takes his title from the most repetitious line in the text. Paul Oliver wrote of Fuller's song, "Such a recording as his 'Lost Lover Blues' is pure folk poetry, moving and sad, the blues of a great artist." It is obvious that Cephas also considers Fuller a great artist whose songs deserve to be kept alive.

See: Bruce Bastin, 318; Stefan Grossman et al. 1973, 158; Paul Oliver, *Blues*, 1984, 98; and Eric Sackheim, 348; Blind Boy Fuller, "Lost Lover Blues," Okeh 05750, June 19, 1940, reissued on Oldie Blues, OL 2809; and Cephas, LR 42.031.

Mamie

1   Early one morning, just about the break of day
    Early one morning, just about the break of day
    Along came a dirty man, tried to take my Mamie astray

2   Curbstone is my pillow, cold sheet is my bed
    Hey, hey, cold sheet is my bed
    I ain't got no little Mamie, for to hold my worried head

3   I woke up this morning, my bedclothes was wet with tears
    Lord, I woke up this morning, my bedclothes all wet with tears
    I'd give a thousand dollars just to find out where Mamie is

4   Oh, Mamie, oh Mamie, oh, Mamie, oh, Mamie
    Lord, I wonder where, wonder where my Mamie is
    I'd give a thousand dollars just to find out where my Mamie is

5   I thought that I heard that woman call my name
    Lord, I thought I heard, thought I heard that woman call my
        name
    She didn't call it loud, called it, oh, so nice and plain
    Call me, Mamie

John first recorded "Mamie" for Kip Lornell back in 1977. To my knowledge, he never performed it during the first half of the 1980s. In late 1985, however, he began to perform it again and today it is one of his favorite numbers. He learned it from a Blind Boy Fuller recording, but evidence suggests it was in circulation in the Piedmont during the

1920s. According to Bruce Bastin, Carolina bluesman Willie Trice claimed he heard it in 1926. Furthermore, it was field-recorded by a group of convicts in 1934, three years before the Fuller recording.

See: Bruce Bastin, 225–239; Blind Boy Fuller, "Mamie," ARC 7-05-56, February 10, 1937, reissued on Yazoo 1060. John's version has been released on *Walking Blues: Bowling Green John Cephas and Harmonica Phil Wiggins*, Marimac 8004.

So Sweet

1   Hey woman, hey now
     Don't you hear me calling you
     You're so sweet, you're so sweet
     My woman's so sweet

2   Woe, woman, come on home
     Oh, Lord, I'm so sorry I done you wrong
     You're so sweet, you're so sweet
     Because you're so sweet

3   Woe, if I could holler, just like a jack
     Lord, I would go up on the mountain to call my baby back
     She's so sweet, she's so sweet
     Lord, she's so sweet

4   Oh, woman, you know that I love you
     If you don't come home, what am I gonna do
     So sweet, you're so sweet
     'Cause you're so sweet

Besides the ballads "John Henry" and "Staggerlee," this common eight-bar blues is one of the few songs John and Archie both perform. Blind Boy Fuller popularized the song, but as John's and Archie's versions indicate, there is a good deal of textual variation. Like its melodic counterpart, "How Long Blues," it has become a traditional frame for whatever eight-bar verses the singer deems suitable. John recorded the song at my house in 1982.

See: notes to Archie Edwards's version, pp. 109–10.

County Jail Blues

1   I'll never forget that day
     They transferred me to the county jail
     I'll never forget that day
     They transferred me to the county jail
     I shot the woman I love
     I ain't got nobody to go my bail

2   I sent for my good friends
     Please spare the rod
     I sent for my good friends
     Please spare the rod
     My friends sent word
     Times was too awful doggone hard

3   I got friends with money
     Come on and go my bail
     I got friends with money
     Come on and go my bail
     My friends sent me word
     What, you got no business
     In the county jail

4   I felt all right
     Until the judge turned around and frowned
     I felt all right
     Until the judge turned around and frowned
     I feel sorry for you, buddy,
     You on your last go round

5   Mmmmm, ain't nobody to go my bail
     Woooeee, ain't nobody to go my bail
     I'm sitting in the county jail
     I ain't got nobody to go my bail

A recent addition to his repertoire, "County Jail Blues" illustrates Cephas's continued affection for his early hero, Blind Boy Fuller. Another very soulful piece, it is patterned on Fuller's "Big House Bound," Vocalion 04897, October 29, 1938, reissued on *Blues Classics II*, BC 11.

Corrine

1   Corrine, what make you treat me so
      Corrine, what make you treat me so
      Corrine, Corrine, what make you treat me so
      You done stopped me from knocking on your door

2   Little girl, what have I done to you
      Little girl, what have I done to you
      Little girl, little girl, what have I done to you
      For you to treat me the way you do

3   Lord, have mercy on poor me
      Lord, have mercy on poor me
      Lord, have mercy on poor me
      Nothing but trouble in this world I see

4   Lord, I am going, your crying ain't going to make me stay
      I am going, your crying ain't going to make me stay
      I am going, your crying ain't going to make me stay
      I'm going, and I'm leaving here today

5   Little girl, little girl, how can it be
      Little girl, little girl, how can it be
      Little girl, little girl, how can it be
      That you love someone else and you don't love me

6   I am down in this valley on my knees
      I am down in this valley on my knees
      I am down in this valley, I am on my knees
      No true love do I see

"Corrine" employs the same tune as "Careless Love." In fact, John's sixth verse is also found in his version of "Careless Love," as well as in "Going Down That Road Feeling Bad." Along with those songs, "Corrine" shows John's affection for the four-line blues format.

See: Blind Boy Fuller, "Corinne, What Makes You Treat Me So," Decca 7881, 1937, reissued on *Blind Boy Fuller: Truckin' My Blues Away*, Yazoo 1060. John Cephas also recorded this piece under the title "Lucille," Marimac 8004, and as "Corrine," FF 470.

Weeping Willow

1   Lord, that weeping willow and that morning dove
      Lord, that weeping willow and that morning dove
      I got a girl up the country
      Lord, you know I sure do love

2   Now, if you see my woman, tell her I should hurry home
      Now, if you see my woman, tell her I should hurry home
      I ain't had no loving
      Since my girl been gone

3   For it ain't no love, ain't no getting along
      For it ain't no love, ain't no getting along
      My gal treats me so mean and dirty sometimes
      I don't know right from wrong

4   Lord, I laid down last night, tried to take my rest
      Lord, I laid down last night, tried to take my rest
      You know my mind got to rambling
      Like wild geese from the West

5   That's why I'll buy me a bulldog, watch you whiles I sleep
      That's why I'll buy me a bulldog, watch you whiles I sleep
      Just to keep these men
      From making this early morning creep

6   If you see my woman, tell her I should hurry home
      If you see my woman, tell her I should hurry home
      I ain't had no loving
      Since my little girl been gone

7   Well, you gonna want my love, mama, some old lonesome day
      Well, you gonna want my love, mama, some old lonesome day
      And it will be too late
      I'll be gone too far away

See: Blind Boy Fuller, "Weeping Willow Blues," Decca 7881, July 14, 1937, reissued on *Blind Boy Fuller: Truckin' My Blues Away*, Yazoo 1060; and Cephas FF 470.

Louise

1   Will my baby, take me back again
     Will my baby, take me back again
     Nobody in this world, what they care for me

2   Lord, I woke up this morning, my bedclothes wet with tears
     Woke up this morning, bedclothes all wet with tears
     Nobody in this world, what they care for me

3   Lord, I was standing here, matchbox hold my clothes
     Lord, I was standing here, wondering, will a matchbox hold my
          clothes
     I ain't got so many matches, got so far to go

Although John associates "Louise" with Blind Boy Fuller, it can't be verified. Perhaps it's an example of what Archie Edwards called "quilting." Textually spare, the song has a strong emotional impact and musically is similar to the next song, "Worried Man Blues," utilizing runs off the key of A, common to both Fuller and Gary Davis. The third verse is traditional and associated with Blind Lemon Jefferson's "Matchbox Blues." Although Fuller recorded a "New Louise, Louise Blues," there are several blues that share the title "Louise Blues."

See: Blind Boy Fuller, "New Louise, Louise Blues," ARC 7-11-58, September 8, 1937; and Cephas LR 42.042.

Worried Man Blues

Reverend Gary Davis was my other mentor. I listened to him a lot and I saw him once before he died. I do quite a few of his songs and his records influenced my style. Him and Blind Boy Fuller. But you know, they played some of the same songs and played together on some records. They had similar styles and I think Gary Davis might have taught Blind Boy Fuller some guitar. Anyway, they were the two that I liked the best when I was growing up, and my playing still shows their influence today. Gary Davis, he could really play. He did "Worried Man Blues," which I play, but mostly he did religious songs and I do some of his religious material. "I Saw the Light" —I think Gary Davis and Blind Boy Fuller recorded that number.

1   If I could holler just like a mountain Jack
     If I could holler just like a mountain Jack
     I'd use my steam just to call my baby back

2   Well, there's one thing sure bothers me
     Well, there's one thing sure bothers me
     Girl pack her suitcase and walk off and left me

3   Lord, Lord, what a fix she left me in
     Lord, Lord, what a fix she left me in
     I ain't got no home and I ain't got no friend

4   Lord, I'm going away, worry on my mind
     Lord, I'm going away, worry on my mind
     I'll be sitting there, just wringing my hands and crying

5   My baby left me, left a wreath on my door
     My baby left me, left a wreath on my door
     It ain't 'cause I was dead, she ain't coming back no more

"Worried Man Blues" derives from Davis's number "I'm Throwing Up My Hands." Davis recorded this and another blues song, along with various religious numbers, during his initial recording session in July 1935. Stefan Grossman notes that this piece, played in the key of A, uses figures adopted by both Blind Boy Fuller and Brownie McGhee. John took his title from one of the verses in the song. Gary Davis called the song "Mountain Jack Blues," using a reference in the first verse, a trait which is common in folk tradition. Cephas has consistently performed this song as his second number ever since I have known him.

For a transcription of the Davis version see: Stefan Grossman 1974, 108. Surprisingly, this number is not on a record by Cephas. Although it was recorded for Trix in 1980, it was never issued. However, for Gary Davis's version see: *Reverend Gary Davis: 1935–1949*, Yazoo L-1023, reissued from ARC 35-10-16, July 1935.

Twelve Gates to the City

1   Oh, what a beautiful city
     Oh, what a beautiful city

Oh, what a beautiful city
There's twelve gates to the city, Hallelujah

2   If you see my mother tell her to wait for me
Won't you please tell my mother to meet me in Galilee
Twelve gates to the city, Hallelujah

3   Oh, what a beautiful city
Oh, what a beautiful city
Oh, what a beautiful city
There's twelve gates to the city, Hallelujah

4   Three gates in the North, three gates in the West
Three gates in the East, three gates in the South
Twelve gates to the city, Hallelujah

5   If you see my mother, won't you do this favor for me
Tell my dear old mother, to meet me in Galilee
Twelve gates to the city, Hallelujah

Gary Davis recorded "Twelve Gates to the City" in July 1935 (ARC 7-04-55). Over the years it became his trademark or signature number. It is also available on Yazoo-1023 and on many other Gary Davis albums. For a transcription of the Davis version, see: Milton Okun, 50–52; Blind Boy Fuller also recorded the song as Brother George, Vocalion 05465, March 7, 1940. Reissued on *Blind Boy Fuller Blue and Worried Man*, Travelin' Man TM 801.

I Saw the Light

We do "I Saw the Light" every now and then. That's a bad number, Reverend Gary Davis from the heart. That's the kind of stuff he does on the guitar.

1   One morning I was walking alone
I saw the light from heaven come down
I heard a little voice, but I saw no one
I saw the light from heaven come down
I saw the light, Lord, I saw the light, Lord
I saw the light, Lord
I saw the light from heaven come down

2   I am happy and the devil is mad
       I saw the light from heaven come down
       He missed one soul that he thought he had
       I saw the light from heaven come down
       I saw the light, Lord, I saw the light, Lord
       I saw the light, Lord
       I saw the light from heaven come down

3   One of these mornings and it won't be long
       I saw the light from heaven come down
       You gonna look for me and I'll be gone
       I saw the light from heaven come down
       I saw the light, Lord, I saw the light, Lord
       I saw the light, Lord
       I saw the light from heaven come down

4   Going to glory, gonna sing and shout
       I saw the light from heaven come down
       Ain't nobody there gonna turn me out
       I saw the light from heaven come down
       I saw the light, Lord, I saw the light, Lord
       I saw the light, Lord
       I saw the light from heaven come down

5   I'm gonna argue with the Father, chat with the Son
       I saw the light from heaven come down
       Tell him about the world I come from
       I saw the light from heaven come down
       I saw the light, Lord, I saw the light, Lord
       I saw the light, Lord
       I saw the light from heaven come down

Not to be confused with the Hank Williams song, John's version is patterned on Gary Davis's "I Saw the Light," ARC 6-05-65, 1935. Cephas first recorded it for Pete Lowry, Trix label in 1976, but it was unissued. He recorded it again in 1983 on LR 42.054, and most recently on FF 394.

Death Don't Have No Mercy

1   Death don't have no mercy in this land
       Death don't have no mercy in this land

Woe, you look around and your friend will be gone
Death have no mercy in this land

2   Death always, always in a hurry in this land
He come to your house, won't stay long
Oh, look around, one of your children will be gone
Death don't have no mercy in this land

3   Death don't take no vacation in this land
Death don't take no vacation in this land
Oh, look around, and your father will be gone
Death don't have no mercy in this land

4   Death don't have no mercy in this land
Death don't have no mercy in this land
Woe, look around, and your mother will be gone
Death don't have no mercy in this land

Numerous religious songs incorporate the personified image of
death as an implacable visitor for whom a true Christian must always
be ready. African-American spirituals "Oh Death," "Death Have Mercy,"
"Travellin' Shoes," "Soon One Morning," and "Run, Sinner, Run" all focus on a confrontation with death. Cephas's version, like the Gary Davis
version, focuses on the stark reality of death without the solace of Christian redemption.

Cephas sang this piece at my home but has not yet recorded it. For a fine
version by Gary Davis see: *Blind Gary Davis: Harlem Street Singer*, Prestige
Bluesville 1015, recorded 1960.

I Am a Pilgrim

1   I am a pilgrim and a stranger
Traveling through this barren land
I have a home in yonder city
And it's outside of man

2   I have a mother, sister, and brother
Who have gone on before
I have a home in yonder city
And it's outside of man

Like "Nine Pound Hammer," Merle Travis popularized "I Am a Pilgrim," making it a standard among country and folk revival musicians. However, also like "Nine Pound Hammer," the song was known in the black community and recorded by gospel quartets. Much of what Cephas said of "Nine Pound Hammer" applies here as well except, of course, it is not a house-party song. John approaches the song as an instrumental display piece and simply repeats the two verses included here. But he is anxious to learn more lyrics and has asked me to transcribe the black gospel version for him.

I am including this song with the Gary Davis material simply because of its religious content. Initially, I had not intended to include it at all because of its incomplete text, but Cephas performs it and included it on his first album. Also, it is important to note the impact of Travis on Cephas's music.

See: Merle Travis, "I Am a Pilgrim," *The Best of Merle Travis*, Capitol SM-2662 and *Folksongs from the Hills*, Capitol AD 50, 1949.

For an earlier version see: The Heavenly Gospel Singers, "I'm a Pilgrim and a Stranger," February 13, 1936, reissued on *A Capella Gospel Singing*, Folklyric Records 9045, 1986. The Heavenly Gospel Singers relocated from Detroit to Spartanburg, South Carolina, where, according to Ray Funk's liner notes, "they travelled extensively throughout the Carolinas and the coal mining country of West Virginia." An even earlier version is associated with the Virginia-based Silver Leaf Quartet. John Cephas, LR 42.031.

Tribute to Skip James: Sickbed Blues

I was fascinated by Skip James. I loved his sound and tried to learn how to do it. I guess the first song I learned was "Sickbed Blues." It's on one of our German albums, *Sweet Bitter Blues*. But on tour, I could really identify with the words, and I kept trying to get the sound. And then he does a lot of numbers in E-minor tuning so it was kind of hard for musicians that wanted to copy him. They couldn't figure out how he was getting such an eerie sound out of his guitar, but it was the tuning. It has a real sad sound.

I think right now, after Blind Boy Fuller and Reverend Gary Davis, he's about my favorite. We do quite a few numbers from his repertoire, "Cherry Ball," "Special Rider," and several others.

1   Lord, I was sitting on my sickbed
     Lord, I was sitting on my sickbed
     Lord, I was sitting on my sickbed
     Had a lot of friends, now they wish I was dead

2   You take stones, you can bruise my bones
      You take stones, you can bruise my bones
      You take stones, you can bruise my bones
      Know you gonna miss me, baby, when I'm dead and gone

3   Doctor walked in and he was looking sad
      Doctor walked in and he was looking sad
      Doctor walked in and he was looking sad
      Diagnosed my case, said it looked very bad

4   He walked away, he was mumbling low
      He walked away, he was mumbling low
      He walked away, he was mumbling low
      Said, you may get some better, but never be well no more

5   Oh, Lordy Lord, I ain't gonna cry no more
      Oh, Lordy Lord, I ain't gonna cry no more
      Oh, Lordy Lord, I ain't gonna cry no more
      Down this road every traveler must go

6   Been across the ocean, I been across the sea
      Been across the ocean, I been across the sea
      Been across the ocean, I been across the sea
      Couldn't find no woman to share my sympathy

7   Had a long, long trip and I'm just too weak to ride
      Had a long, long trip and I'm just too weak to ride
      Had a long, long trip and I'm just too weak to ride
      A thousand people standing at my bedside

8   You take stones, you can bruise my bones
      You take stones, you can bruise my bones
      You take stones, you can bruise my bones
      You know you gonna miss me, baby, when I'm dead and gone

John's affection for Skip James's music came to fruition in the 1980s. It may not seem to make sense for a Piedmont musician to become captivated by a Delta performer, but Skip James was a highly idiosyncratic guitar technician and stylist. As I mentioned earlier, Cephas is a voracious learner and he found Skip James's songs a challenge. He tends to play Skip James in open D-minor or open E-minor tuning.

Although Skip James came to Washington and performed with Archie Edwards, John never met him. He wrote "Sickbed Blues" while in

Washington General Hospital in Washington, D.C. Through James's recordings, John has studied his music and today is a fine interpreter of his unusual vocal and instrumental style. I have included four songs derived from Skip James, although Cephas does several others as well. Like "Going Down That Road Feeling Bad," "Careless Love," and "Corrine," "Sickbed Blues" also illustrates John's attraction to four-line songs.

See: Stefan Grossman et al. 1973, 68; Skip James, "Sickbed Blues," Melodion 7321, 1964; and Cephas LR 42.054.

Cherry Ball

1   I love Cherry Ball, better than I do myself
     I love Cherry Ball, better than I do myself
     If she won't love me, I won't love nobody else

2   Cherry Ball quit me, quit me in a nice good way
     Cherry Ball quit me, quit me in a nice good way
     I intend to get her back, I keep it every day

3   I left her standing, standing in the back door crying
     I left her standing, standing in the back door crying
     She know that I love her, her disposition I despise

4   Just like a spider, he keep climbing up the walls
     Just like a spider, he keep climbing up the walls
     Cherry Ball quit me, she quit me without a cause

5   You take the Southern, I'll take the Santa Fe
     You take the Southern, I'll take the Santa Fe
     I'm going to ride and ramble, till she comes home to me
          someday

See: Stefan Grossman et al. 1973, 61; Skip James, "Cherry Ball Blues," Paramount 13065, February 1931, reissued on *Skip James: 1931*, Yazoo L-1072; and John Cephas, Marimac 8001 and FF 394.

Special Rider

1   I ain't got no special rider here
     I ain't got no special rider here
     I ain't got nobody to feel my loving care

2   Well, I woke up this morning, looked at the special rising sun
     Well, I woke up this morning, looked at the special rising sun
     And I prayed to the good Lord, my special rider was gone

3   Well, I got off my pallet, and I laid down on my bed
     Well, I got off my pallet, and I laid down on my bed
     And I went to eat my breakfast, and the blues was all in my
         bread

4   I received a letter and what do you reckon it read?
     I received a letter and what do you reckon it read?
     It said, "Hurry, come home, man, your special rider is dead"

5   I said, "No, sweet man, ain't no special rider here"
     I said, "No, sweet man, ain't no special rider here"
     I ain't got nobody to feel my loving care

      See: Stefan Grossman et al. 1973, 81; Harry Oster, 234; Skip James, "Special Rider," Paramount 13098, February 1931, reissued *Skip James: 1931*, Yazoo L-1072; and John Cephas, Marimac 8001 and FF 394.

Cypress Grove

1   I'd rather be buried in some cypress grove
     I'd rather be buried in some cypress grove
     Than stay in New York City and be treated this way

2   I'd rather be buried in some cypress grove
     I'd rather be buried in some cypress grove
     Than to have a country woman, that I never could control

3   I'd rather be buried six feet in the clay
I'd rather be buried six feet in the clay
Than stay in New York City and be treated this way

4   When your knees start aching and your body getting cold
When your knees start aching and your body getting cold
You know you're getting ready for some cypress grove

5   Come on, don't want to go
Come on, don't want to go
I can't go back South, they gonna kill me sure

See: Stefan Grossman et al. 1973, 53; Eric Sackheim, 177; Skip James, "Cypress Grove Blues," Paramount 13088, February 1931, reissued on *Skip James: 1931*, Yazoo L-1072.

Reno Factory

I don't know where that came from, but it's kind of like an old logging camp song. I learned it from the Foddrell Brothers but I heard it somewhere years ago. Then, when I heard the Foddrells, it brought it back to mind. They put it on an anthology we recorded for the Blue Ridge Institute with Kip Lornell. I guess I always liked it, so I added it to my repertoire.

But as far as I know that's one of the old songs that originated down on the Virginia-Tennessee border at one of those logging camps. That's the area it came from. It's a traditional song from down there.

1   That Reno factory is burning down
And there ain't no water round
And there ain't no water round

2   Someday I'm going away
I'm gonna bring my baby back
Yes, I'm gonna bring my baby back

3   Oh, Lordy me, oh, Lordy my
And, oh Lord, what have I done
Oh Lord, what have I done

4   Some old stranger come last night
And he took my gal and he gone
Yes, he took my gal and he gone

5   The last time I saw my gal
        She was standing in that freight train door
        She was standing in that freight train door

6   She waved her hands back at me
        Lord, it made me want, want to go
        Lord, it made me want, want to go

7   Reno Factory's burning down
        Lord, it ain't no water round
        And it ain't no water round

8   Someday I'm going away
        Lord, I'm gonna bring my baby back
        Lord, I'm gonna bring my baby back
        Lord, I'm gonna bring my baby back

John learned "Reno Factory Blues" from Marvin Foddrell, another fine Virginia musician. A somewhat enigmatic piece, it echoes Peg Leg Howell's "Rolling Mill Blues," which marginally connects it to the "In the Pines," "The Longest Train," and "Reuben's Train" song family. Archie Edwards flat out states, "My father used to play that song, called it 'Ruby.' " However, it doesn't quite fit the mold. Bruce Bastin, no doubt relying on Kip Lornell's fieldwork, noted that it only had recorded parallels in Virginia. Lornell pointed out that the song was similar to a blues in its emotional impact, but that Marvin Foddrell did not think of it as a blues but rather "an old country song." According to Lornell, Marvin Foddrell learned the song from his father, Posey Foddrell. Whether it originated in black or white folk tradition, Foddrell's and Cephas's version should be considered a pre-blues song with a strong blues feeling.

See: Bruce Bastin, 318; Kip Lornell 1977, 9; Marvin Foddrell, "Reno Factory," BRI 001, 1977; G. B. Grayson and Henry Whitter, "Train 45," Victor 21189, October 18, 1927; and John Cephas FF 394.

Crow Jane

It's very few musicians I picked up songs from. I kind of tend to want to pick songs from more older guys. Not guys that I've actually played with myself. But there are a few. I know I got some from Carl Martin. I got one real good song, "Crow Jane." That was one I picked up from him and that was years ago on a festival with Martin, Bogan, and Armstrong.

1   Crow Jane, Crow Jane
      Don't you hold your head high
      Someday, baby, you know you got to die
      You know you got to die

2   Now I am going to buy me a pistol
      Just about four feet tall
      Shoot Crow Jane just to see her fall
      She got to fall

3   That's the reason I told Crow Jane
      Not to hold her head so high
      Someday baby, you know you got to die
      You got to lay down and die

4   When I dug her grave with that silver spade
      Ain't no one going to take my Crow Jane's place
      You can't take her place
      You can't take her place

5   You know I let her down with a golden chain
      And with every link I would call my Crow Jane's name
      Call her name
      I call her name

6   You know I didn't miss my water till my well ran dry
      Didn't miss Crow Jane till the day she died
      Day she died
      The day she died

7   You know I dug her grave eight feet in the ground
      Didn't feel sorrow till they let her down
      Let her down
      They let her down

8   Crow Jane, Crow Jane
      Don't hold your head so high
      Someday, baby, you know you got to die
      You got to lay down and die

"Crow Jane" has been in and out of John's repertoire since he learned it from fellow Virginian Carl Martin, shortly before Martin's death. A common eight-bar blues, it is sometimes used to designate a broader tune family embracing other eight-bar songs, including "Red River Blues." Recorded by Julius Daniels of North Carolina in 1927, the song is one of the most common traditional Piedmont blues. Although Paul Oliver and other scholars connect the song with the Carolinas, Cephas's version may also draw on Mississippian Skip James's later version.

See: Bruce Bastin, 302; Stefan Grossman et al. 1973, 64; Paul Oliver, *Blues*, 1984, 283; and Jeff Titon 1977, 169.

See also: Julius Daniels, "Crow Jane," Victor 21065, October 24, 1927; Bo Weavil Jackson, "Pistol Blues," Paramount 12389, September 1926; and Carl Martin, "Crow Jane," Bluebird B 6139, July 27, 1935, reissued on *East Coast Blues 1926–1935*, Yazoo L-1013; and John Cephas, Marimac 8004.

Rising River Blues

I learned that song later on in life. A guy named George Carter wrote it. But that song, to me it's about a guy who has been drunk all the time and he's brooding about no success with women.

1   Rising river, water all around my door
      Rising river, water all around my door
      River running like I've never seen before

2   I got the blues in the alley, they won't allow me on the street
      I got the blues in the alley, they won't allow me on the street
      Lord, I've been mistreated by every gal I meet

3   I say, run here, mama, let me speak my mind
      I say, run here, mama, let me speak my mind
      To cure these rising river blues, it takes a long, long time

One of Cephas's deepest blues, "Rising River Blues" textually derives from a recording made by George Carter. Musically, however, John's treatment of the song bears no resemblance to the Carter original. Probably the lyrics came from a printed source and Cephas created the intensely emotional musical arrangement.

For a transcription of the Carter version see: Stefan Grossman et al. 1973, 50; George Carter, "Rising River Blues," Paramount 12750, February 1929, reissued on *The Georgia Blues 1927–1933*, Yazoo L-1012; and John Cephas, LR 42.031.

Police Dog Blues

I used to hear a lot of songs by Blind Blake when I was a youngster and years ago I played other songs by him. A lot of those ragtime pieces they used to play came from him. And there was a run we called "the Florida flip," that was from him. We played that years ago. Back years ago you used to hear his stuff, especially all the ragtime songs. And my grandfather, he liked that style. Now I only do a couple of his tunes.

1   All my life I have been a traveling man
     All my life I have been a traveling man
     Staying alone and doing the best I can

2   I shipped my trunk down to Tennessee
     Shipped my trunk down to Tennessee
     Hard to tell about a man like me

3   I met a girl I couldn't get her off my mind
     I met a girl I couldn't get her off my mind
     She passed me by, she didn't like my time

4   I ain't going to bother round her house at night
     I ain't gonna bother round her house at night
     She got a police dog waiting for a fight

5   His name is Rambler, and when he gets a chance
     His name is Rambler, and when he gets a chance
     He makes his mark on everybody's pants

6   I guess I'm gonna travel, I guess I'll let it be
     I guess I'm gonna travel, I guess I'll let it be
     Before she sics that police dog on me

See: Stefan Grossman 1970, 115–123; and Stefan Grossman et al. 1973, 126; Blind Blake, "Police Dog Blues," Paramount 12904, August 17, 1929, reissued on *The Georgia Blues 1927–1933*, Yazoo L-1012; and John Cephas FF 470.

Walking Blues

"Walking Blues," that's Robert Johnson. It's a Delta song that's also done up in Chicago. Robert Johnson played it with a slide, but I do it in stan-

dard tuning, in the key of A. It's got a good beat to it, and Phil and I
really like to play it. I really admire Robert Johnson. He was a great
songwriter.

1   Hey, I woke up this morning, feel all around for my shoes
    Yeah, tell me, pretty mama, I got them old walking blues
    Yeah, I woke up this morning, I was feeling all around for my
        shoes
    Yeah, I reckon I got them, I got them, I got them walking blues

2   Lord, I woke up this morning, feeling all around my bed
    Went to get me a bit to eat, you know, and the blues was in my
        bread
    Lord, I woke up this morning, the blues was in my bed
    Woe, went to get me a bit to eat now, the blues was all in my
        bread

3   Oh, you know some people say the blues ain't so bad
    Worst old feeling that I most ever had
    Well, some people say that the blues, say the blues ain't so bad
    Oh, the worst old feeling that I most ever had

4   Lord, I woke up this morning, I had the blues three different ways
    One said, "Go," know that the other two said, "Stay"
    Yes, I woke up this morning, I had the blues three different
        ways
    Oh, the one said, "Go," you know, the other two said, "Stay"

5   Lord, I'm leaving here, baby, if I have to ride the blinds
    Lord, I'm so disgusted, mama, I'm so damn dissatisfied
    Lord, I'm leaving here, baby, if I have to ride the blinds
    Lord, I'm so disgusted, mama, I'm so damn dissatisfied

6   Lord, them minutes seem like hours, hours seem like days
    I'm so disgusted, mama, why don't these old blues go away
    Well, the minutes seem like hours, hours seem like days
    Lord, I'm so disgusted, mama, why don't these, why don't these
        blues go away

7   Lord, I'm leaving here, baby, if I have to ride the blinds
    Lord, I'm so disgusted, mama, I'm so dissatisfied
    Lord, I'm leaving here mama, if I have to ride the blinds
    Lord, I'm so disgusted, I'm so dissatisfied

Musically, Cephas's version of "Walking Blues" combines the drive of the Robert Johnson version with musical figures associated with another Robert Johnson song, "Kindhearted Woman." "Walking Blues" has become a standard of Chicago blues and has been recorded by Muddy Waters, Johnny Shines, and many other artists.

See: Samuel Charters, 52–53; Stefan Grossman et al. 1973, 129; Eric Sackheim, 216; Robert Johnson, "Walking Blues," Vocalion 03601, November 27, 1936, reissued on Columbia LP 62456; and John Cephas, Marimac 8004.

Brownsville Blues

I always liked Furry Lewis, but he played mostly in slide. I learned that style when I was young, but later in life I didn't do much of it because it didn't really suit the type of guitar I had. Then when I bought my National, I started playing slide again and listening to Furry Lewis. My version is patterned after the way he plays it.

1   Well, I'm going down to Brownsville
    I am going to take that right-hand road
    Well, I'm going down to Brownsville
    I am going to take that right-hand road
    Now, I ain't gonna stop walking, till I reach my baby's door

2   Now the women I love
    Got long, curly hair
    Now the women I love
    Got long, curly hair
    Now her mother and her father won't allow me there

3   I am going to write me a letter
    I am going to mail it in the air
    I am going to write me a letter
    I am going to mail it in the air
    Now if any man can stay there, he can stay most anywhere

4   Now my first name is John
    I ain't going to tell my second name
    Now my first name is John
    I ain't going to tell my second name
    Now, the way she treats me, it's a low-down dirty shame

5   Now I knew you didn't love me
When you laid down on my bed
Now I knew you didn't love me
When you laid down on my bed
I could smell white lightning, swimming all round your head

6   I am going down, down, down
I am going down, down, down
I am going down, down, down
I am going down, down, down
I am just about crazy, about to lose my mind

John became interested in Furry Lewis's music when he began to practice slide guitar again and purchased his steel National. He plays "Brownsville Blues" in slide fashion, in open-D tuning. Although Sleepy John Estes recorded an unrelated "Brownsville Blues," John's version stems from a Furry Lewis rendition of Estes' recording "The Girl I Love She Got Long Curly Hair," currently available on *Sleepy John Estes 1929–1940*, RBF8.

Furry Lewis, "I'm Going to Brownsville," Folkways FS 3823, February 18, 1959, and "I'm Going Back to Brownsville," Bluesville BULP 1036, October 3, 1959, and John Cephas, FF 470.

Sitting on Top of the World

1   One summer day she went away
She's gone and left me, she's gone to stay
But now she's gone, but I don't worry
Because I'm sitting on top of the world

2   I work all the summer, work all the fall
I had my Christmas in my overalls
But now she's gone, but I don't worry
Because I'm sitting on top of the world

3   I'm going down to the station, I'm going to meet a train
I'm going to leave this town, work done got too hard
But now she's gone, but I don't worry
Because I'm sitting on top of the world

4   One summer day she went away
She's gone and left me, she's gone to stay

But now she's gone, but I don't worry
Because I'm sitting on top of the world

John recorded "Sitting on Top of the World" at my home in October 1982. He was playing an electric guitar and performed the song in an urban blues style with single-string guitar runs. His version, like Archie Edwards's, was slow and soulful.

See: notes to Archie's version.

Sweet Bitter Blues

Phil and I, we have a friend, Otis Williams, who teaches at the University of Maryland. We play for his classes now and then, and he's kind of like a griot. He's a blues poet, and we've taken several of his poems and put them to music. "Sweet Bitter Blues" is a poem he wrote. We really liked it, so we put it on our second album along with another one of his poems, "Hoodoo Woman." We would take his words and work on the music and everything just seemed to fit. He's quite a performer himself, and a really good friend.

1   Well, it's sweet bitter blues
     Walk all around my bed
     Well, it's sweet bitter blues
     Walk all around my bed
     Sometimes I wonder, am I alive or dead

2   Lord, I work so hard
     Trucking steel like a slave
     Lord, I work so hard
     Trucking steel like a slave
     Hard work and trouble, take me to my grave

3   You know, bad times follow
     Everywhere I go
     You know, bad times follow
     Everywhere I go
     Bad time and trouble, only life I know

4   Lord, I went to the river, see what I could see
     The river say, "Hey, John," come on and be with me
     Sweet bitter blues, walk all around my bed
     Sometimes I wonder, am I alive or dead

5   Lord, I ain't no mean man, I don't fuss or fight
      I want to shoot my baby, Lord, she just won't do right
      Lord, sweet bitter blues, walk all around my bed
      Sometimes I wonder, am I alive or dead

6   Tell me, woman
      How blue can you be
      Tell me, woman
      How blue can you be
      No way in the world, you can be as blue as me

7   Lord, I'm blue as indigo
      My baby, she just left town
      Lord, I'm blue as indigo
      My baby, she just left town
      Left with the preacher man, oh glory, they cannot be found

8   Well, I'm going down Louisiana, down behind the sun
      Get me a mojo hand, then I'll have some fun
      Oh, sweet bitter blues, walk all around my bed
      Sometimes I wonder, am I alive or dead

9   Well, it's sweet bitter blues
      Walk all around my bed
      Well, it's sweet bitter blues
      Walk all around my bed
      Sometimes I wonder, am I alive or dead

Otis Williams is a friend and my colleague at the University of Maryland in College Park, a suburb of Washington, D.C. A poet and a scholar, he teaches and preaches about the Afro-American musical tradition. Over the years he has given several of his poems to John and Phil, who have shaped them into excellent blues songs.

Otis Williams is a true blues poet in that his poetry works as song, reflecting the traditional language and values of the blues. Born in Grenada, Mississippi, he has met many blues artists, including Mississippi John Hurt and Magic Sam. Today he also administers the Nyumburu Cultural Center at the University of Maryland, and frequently invites John, Phil, and Archie to perform for his classes or special events.

See: Otis Williams, "Blues in B-Flat," *The Blues Is Darker than Blue*, 4–5; and John Cephas LR 42.054.

Hoodoo Woman

1   Hoodoo woman, hoodoo woman, well, I don't know what you
        doing
    Hoodoo woman, hoodoo woman, well, I don't know what you
        doing
    You got me ripping, you got me running
    You got me coming when I should be going

2   Hoodoo woman, hoodoo woman, yes, you're messing up my mind
    Hoodoo woman, hoodoo woman, yes, you're messing up my mind
    You got me slipping, you got me sliding
    Laughing and I should be crying

3   Well, I'm going to get myself together, get me a mojo, too
    Fix me a magic potion, cast a spell on you
    Hoodoo woman, hoodoo woman, well, I don't know what you
        doing
    You got me ripping, you got me running
    Laughing when I should be crying

4   Hoodoo woman, hoodoo woman, well you done put a spell on me
    Hoodoo woman, hoodoo woman, well you done put a spell on me
    Got me sneaking, you got me peeping
    Looking, but I still can't see

5   Hoodoo woman, hoodoo woman, well, I'm gonna do the best I
        can
    Hoodoo woman, hoodoo woman, well, I'm gonna do the best I
        can
    If you be sweet to me, baby
    You know I declare I'm gonna be your man

6   Well, I'm going to get myself together, get me a mojo, too
    Fix me a magic potion, cast a spell on you
    Hoodoo woman, hoodoo woman, well, I don't know what you
        doing
    You got me ripping, you got me running
    Laughing when I should be crying

   Otis Williams also wrote "Hoodoo Woman," a poem that refers to
African-American magic as it is typically used in the blues idiom. Var-

ious aspects of black folklore are touched on in blues songs, but usually within the parameters of a man-woman relationship. While the tension between lovers may mask other types of social commentary, the problems that commonly affect man-woman relationships provide the usual format for most blues. References to magic generally reflect sexual tension and translate to power over the opposite sex. "Hoodoo Woman" speaks directly to this tradition.

See: Otis Williams, unpublished manuscripts, *Otis Williams' Songbook Number One*, LR 42.054.

Dog Days of August

When it's really hot and it's raining and the sun is shining, they say the Devil is beating his wife. That's part of the dog days of August. Those hot, humid days.

1   It's the dog days of August, Devil is beating his wife
     It's the dog days of August, Devil is beating his wife
     I got a wrong-doing woman
     I got trouble in my life

2   Lord, the dog days of August, see the steam rising from the street
     Lord, the dog days of August, see the steam rising from the street
     I keep singing these lonesome blues
     To the shuffle of my feet

3   I got sweat dripping from my forehead, I got tears streaming from
          my eyes
     It's the dog days of August and all I can do is cry
     Yeah, the dog days of August, the Devil is beating his wife
     I got a wrong-doing woman, I got trouble in my life

4   It's the dog days of August, Devil is beating his wife
     It's the dog days of August, Devil is beating his wife
     I got a wrong-doing woman
     I got trouble in my life

Many of John and Phil's recent additions to their repertoire come from their own creative imaginations. Harmonica wizard Phil Wiggins has proved to be the most consistent source of new material. His compositions include "Dog Days of August," "Guitar Man," "Roberta," "Electric

Chair Blues," and "Butt Naked Blues." John is vocalist on "Dog Days of August" and "Guitar Man." Recently, we all did a radio show in Santa Barbara, California, and, as we had expected, one of the first questions in the interview was, What are the dog days of August? People in Washington, D.C., however, know about the brutal "dog days." This song lends its title to John and Phil's award-winning album on Flying Fish, FF 394.

Guitar Man

1   Done got tired of fussing, done got tired of fighting
     Done got tired of you accusing me when I come home late at
         night
     Woe, I'm a guitar man, Lord, that's what I am
     One of these lonesome days I hope you'll understand

2   Baby, I'm not no liar, no, I'm not no cheater
     I been out here making music, I'm not running in the streets
     Woe, I'm a guitar man, Lord, that's what I am
     One of these lonesome days, I hope you'll understand

3   You don't have to worry, you don't have to cry
     I'm going to bring it home to you baby, keep you satisfied
     Woe, I'm a guitar man, Woe, Lord, that's what I am
     One of these lonesome days, I hope you'll understand

"Guitar Man" is one of Phil's most successful compositions and a mainstay of John and Phil's stage act. Recently, it was chosen as the title cut of their new album, FF 470.

Highway 301

"Highway 301," that was one of my own concoctions, and I recorded it on L and R. That was one of my own things. But I thought it would make a big hit. I thought it would do something for the record. But after it didn't I thought, "To heck with it! Maybe the song ain't all that good." So I stopped singing it.

1   Well, I'm gonna leave here walking
     I'm going down that Highway 301
     Well, I'm gonna leave here walking

I'm going down that Highway 301
I'm gonna find my sweet woman, we going out and have some
   fun

2   I said, "Ooowee, baby
I'm gonna make everything all right"
I said, "Ooowee, baby
I'm gonna make everything all right"
If I don't be home on Sunday, I'll be home tomorrow night

3   You know that Highway 301
You know, it runs right by my door
You know that Highway 301
You know, it runs right by my door
It runs from way up in Boston, it runs down to Mexico

4   I received your letter
By long-distance telegram
I received your letter
By long-distance telegram
And if I don't be on the train Sunday
I'll be on that old Greyhound

Highway 301 runs through the center of Bowling Green, Virginia.
Many blues artists localize the highway theme and, using traditional
verses, compose a song about their own town. John's version is very
slow and more in the Delta style, reminiscent of "Highway 51," a Delta
standard. David Evans notes the song comes from Charlie Pickett's
"Down the Highway."

For a discussion of the highway theme in the blues see Paul Oliver 1970,
21–22; Charlie Pickett, "Down The Highway," Decca 7707, August 3, 1937; and
John Cephas LR 42.054.

Black Cat on the Line

I wrote another song, that's the most recent song I've done. It's called
"Black Cat on the Line." It's six verses of it. I've written a lot of songs,
but this is the only one I've come up with that I was satisfied with, and
I think it's gonna go. Now all I have to do is get it copyrighted and
perform it. And the words are real meaningful. It's true-to-life situations.
I worked this one out and this is what I came up with.

1   Oh baby, how can I keep on loving you
Oh baby, how can I keep on loving you

When you keep on doing the things you do
Oh baby, there's a black cat on the line
Oh baby, there's a black cat on the line
You know I am not no fool
You keep telling me I am out of my mind

2   I came home from work
Kind of late the other night
I wanted a little loving
But you tried to start a fight
Oh baby, there's a black cat on the line
Oh baby, there's a black cat on the line
You know I am not no fool
You keep telling me I am out of my mind

3   I came home another night
I wanted you to fix me something to eat
You looked at me and said
"Fix it yourself," 'cause you was too beat
Oh baby, there's a black cat on the line
Oh baby, there's a black cat on the line
You know I am not no fool
You keep telling me I am out of my mind

4   I came home another night
I said we're going to a show
You said you ain't got nothing to wear
And you ain't going out that door
Oh baby, there's a black cat on the line
Oh baby, there's a black cat on the line
You know I am not no fool
You keep telling me I am out of my mind

5.   I been knowing you a long time
I think I know you pretty well
That cat you are seeing must smoke
Because you got a brand new smell
Oh baby, there's a black cat on the line
Oh baby, there's a black cat on the line
You know I am not no fool
You keep telling me I am out of my mind

6   Listen to me, woman
       You better listen well
       You better be gone with that black cat
       Or I am going to send you both to hell
       Oh baby, there's a black cat on the line
       Oh baby, there's a black cat on the line
       You know I am not no fool
       You keep telling me I am out of my mind

John's most recent composition, "Black Cat on the Line" is very much in the mainstream of the blues tradition, blending the themes of mistreatment and revenge. John and Phil recently recorded the piece as the lead song on their *Guitar Man* album. A fine song, it shows the blues artist's gift for connecting traditional images and values with innovative contemporary poetry. Other songs use the phrase "black cat on the line," which also connects to another phrase, "dead cat on the line," which appears in recorded sermons such as Reverend J. M. Gates's "Dead Cat on the Line."

See: Reverend J. M. Gates, "Dead Cat on the Line," Okeh 8684, March 18, 1929; and Cephas FF 470.

Notes to Chapter 5

1. Otis Williams writes poetry and teaches at the University of Maryland in the Afro-American Studies Department.

2. See Joe Wilson's notes to the *Dog Days of August* album, FF 394, 1986.

3. Culled from the officer of cultural affairs's report from Bamako, Mali, to the Arts America Program, United States Information Agency, 1982.

4. The late Lightning Hopkins is considered a major Texas bluesman while Muddy Waters and Hubert Sumlin represent the Delta to Chicago tradition.

5. Bud Carlton is considered a fine country and western steel guitar session man and has recorded extensively.

6. John Cephas first acquired his National guitar, an instrument similar to Archie Edwards's "steel-pan" Gretsch, in 1987.

7. John's commentary is paralleled by many other artists, especially piano player and guitarist Henry Townsend, in Pearson 1986, p. 153.

6
Conclusion

Archie Edwards and John Cephas have each made significant contributions to American music: as artists, as historians of their regional tradition, and as teachers actively working to pass along the techniques of an art form they have worked with all their lives. As representative artists, they also shed light on the role of the artist in American society. More important, they help us understand why some people choose to keep traditional art forms alive and, in their case, in the public eye. Because of their efforts, we can gain a clearer understanding of the Piedmont blues in particular and American folk music in general.

Today, both men are retired, although Archie Edwards continues to run his barbershop and John Cephas still commutes between Washington, D.C., and Bowling Green, where he tinkers with his tractor and pursues the lighter chores suitable to a gentleman farmer. Up until their retirement, each worked at a variety of jobs before settling into positions with different branches of the District of Columbia Government Service: Archie as a special policeman and John as a carpenter for the D.C. National Guard. It is fair to say that throughout their working lives playing music was a part-time activity, a vehicle for self-expression, and a means to supplement their income. Now, however, they have more time to devote to performing music and to promoting their regional tradition.

Having considered each artist's life and art separately, we can now draw several conclusions about what they have taught us. First, however, at the risk of redundancy, let me summarize what I perceive as the primary stages of their musical lives.

Initially inspired by his father and a handful of family friends, Archie Edwards began to be exposed to the Piedmont blues in his home. At an early age, he turned to phonograph recordings by both black and white country artists to expand his repertoire and further develop his instrumental skills. While still a youngster under the guidance of his older brother Willie, he ventured out on the house-party circuit, gaining valuable performance experience and picking up pointers from other community musicians.

By the age of sixteen he sought work at a local sawmill, where he continued to learn songs and gain experience both on the job and during the evening jam sessions which included co-workers from distant parts of the state. These contexts—home, community, house parties, and work camps—served as his music school, where he tested and sharpened his skills. Although he acknowledges the influence of his father, Boyd Maddox, and John Cosby, both Archie and his brother Robert progressed beyond the musicians of their father's generation by learning "professional music" off of the recordings of Mississippi John Hurt, Texan Blind Lemon Jefferson, and local favorite Blind Boy Fuller. Archie's expertise and ability to cover the professionals allowed him to hold his own with the musicians he met at house parties and other informal gatherings. This series of events constitutes the first phase of his musical life. Having established himself as a musician in Franklin County, he left home, for the most part putting his music aside.

Over the next twenty years he performed infrequently, working various jobs, serving in the army, and supporting a family. Then, in the 1960s, sparked by the blues revival and his momentous meeting with John Hurt, he began to reestablish himself as a musician. It is hard to overestimate the impact of John Hurt on his life, but if the conditions which led to the rediscovery of John Hurt, and his relocation in Washington, D.C., had not also existed there may not have been sufficient interest in Archie's music to bring him back into public performance. A renewed interest in traditional music, however, set the stage for his fateful encounter with his idol, John Hurt. Hurt not only encouraged Archie and accompanied him to his first major performance, he validated Archie's commitment to country blues and consistently provided direction and advice. This second phase of his musical career, however brief, finished his musical education.

When John Hurt died, Archie briefly retired from public life, but returned with renewed determination, soon becoming a major figure in the D.C. area's blues community. By the time I met him in 1976, his nonmusical work requirements were easing, allowing him free time to perform on a more regular basis.

John Cephas's musical education also began at home, with his mother providing the inspiration and initial vocal training. Another woman, his aunt Lillian, introduced him to the sound of blues and the guitar, giving him his first few pointers on the guitar and instilling in him the idea that he, too, could learn to play. The third key figure in his early life was his grandfather, John Wesley Dudley, who, more than anyone, served as a role model, teaching him about country life, house parties, corn whiskey, and good-time music. These three family members, each within their own sphere of influence, were his initial guides.

As a youngster, Cephas's musical world included family singing sessions, often presided over by his grandfather, and church performance with his brother Ernest. At the same time, he began performing in school productions, eavesdropping on the adult music of the house-party circuit, and secretly practicing on his father's guitar. Throughout his youth his eclectic musical experiences embraced city and country traditions, ranging from doo-wop and quartet experience to playing the guitar in open tuning with a slide. As he came of age, his determination won him his father's guitar and the implicit right to play whatever music he chose.

As a young man, Cephas's music continued to reflect the pull between city and country, church music and the blues. His developing interest in gospel singing culminated in his joining a professional group, the Capitol Harmonizers. Touring with this group provided valuable vocal experience and his first exposure to professional life on the road. On the down-home blues side his cousin, David Talliaferro, stands out as his primary teacher and companion on the house-party circuit, where John began to participate as an adult. Under David's instruction and through listening to phonograph recordings, he sharpened his instrumental skills and broadened his song repertoire. At the time, however, he claims he was unable to combine his gospel vocal training and blues guitar training. Eventually, he became disenchanted with both gospel touring and the house-party circuit and, following his military service and a series of dead-end jobs, he hit a low point in his life, giving up music completely.

The next stage of his musical life began with his chance encounter with Alabama pianist Wilbur "Big Chief" Ellis and continues to the present day. Chief lured John Cephas out of retirement and expanded his horizons, introducing him to the folk-revival audience. In 1976, Phil Wiggins joined up with John, Chief, and James Bellamy, forming the Barrelhouse Rockers. Over the past dozen years, since Chief Ellis's death, Phil has been the last key figure to shape John's music, contributing his sound and musical ideas as co-composer, fellow traveler, and friend.

Comparing Archie's and John's separate stories, one is immediately struck by the importance of home and family and the impact of family activities on their musical education. Music, whatever the form, literally brought their families together. While Archie started off hearing secular

music and blues and John first heard religious songs, their first memories fuse music, family, and home. Both were inspired by their parents
and shared their musical interests with their brothers. Archie had Robert and John had Ernest as his first musical partner. Archie and his
brothers chipped in to buy their own guitar; John inherited his from his
father. Even the recordings from which they learned were family prop-
erty. In Archie's case, brother Willie borrowed the records, then he and
Robert stole the music from them. Archie's father and brother, John's
grandfather, aunt, and cousin all contributed to their blues education.

Both men also discuss their experiences with the church, although
it had greater impact on Cephas's life and music. Archie Edwards's
membership in the church came later in life, when he was a teenager,
and stands in sharp contrast to Cephas's experience. Whereas John's
father and mother were active members who raised him in the church,
Archie's parents were not deeply involved when he chose to join. John's
father was a preacher; Archie's dad rapped the banjo and hollered,
"Shout, children, shout, because you ain't going to heaven no how."
Eventually, Archie led his father into the church, inverting the tradition
of the prodigal son. Over the course of his life, however, he saw no in-
consistency between attending church and playing the blues.

John Cephas's parents initially discouraged him from learning the
type of music Edwards's family took for granted. His grandfather and
aunt, however, encouraged him to learn blues, and, in retrospect, it is
apparent that his family's opposition to the blues was more token resis-
tance designed to keep the youngsters away from their parent's guitar
and from adult activities. As John Cephas grew older and demonstrated
his determination and musical talent, his music was accepted and even
encouraged at home. In contrast to Archie's experience, John's musical
life has been characterized by the pull between playing blues or performing religious music, and only later in life was he able to resolve
completely this musical tension.

It is important to note, however, that neither musician had any real
difficulty moving back and forth between the church and blues community and that they were equally welcome in church or where people
were playing blues and dancing. Today, both men profess to be Chris-
tians and consider the notion that Christian living and playing the blues
don't mix as decidedly old-fashioned. The difference between the two
men is that Archie Edwards remains a regular church member whereas
Cephas, like his grandfather, studies his religion on his own. Moreover,
because of his experiences on both sides of the fence, he feels qualified
to talk about traditional church-blues tension, and has concluded that
the church's anti-blues bias is propaganda without any real moral basis.

As a musician and a thoughtful Christian, he has weighed the distinction between the church music he performs and the blues, and he sees them as parallel and complementary.

While family, home, and church stand out as major topics in Archie's and John's stories, the country house party emerges as the dominant institution of their early musical lives. Weekend parties, country breakdowns, and selling parties are described in great detail with obvious nostalgia. Their experiences at these secular events span roughly thirty years, ranging from rural Franklin County to Richmond and Washington, D.C. In the company of brother Willie, and later brother Robert, Archie made his debut as a musician at local parties as a youngster. John was introduced to house parties by his grandfather and later participated with his cousin David. Until they began to work the festival and club circuit in the 1970s, the two men played their country blues almost exclusively in the house-party setting. These segregated, self-contained, weekend parties flourished as the primary arena for musical expression, where they learned from other musicians and perfected their musical skills.

House parties added a special richness to country life, providing a welcome relief from the hard work week and a healthy competitive showcase for musicians and dancers. House parties, selling parties, and seasonal communal work parties were positive responses to the rigors of segregation and, in many cases, they also served an economic function by combining the need for recreation with an informal, community-based system of helping the less fortunate. Although the church and the house party competed, to a degree, for the hearts, minds, and dollars of rural Virginians, it is apparent that the institutions were compatible. John's statement about partying all weekend and then sitting in church on Sunday corroborates blues scholar Jeff Titon's position that the transition between the two major institutions was less difficult than church propaganda implies.[1]

Recently, music historian Nelson Georges compared the decline of rhythm and blues to the disappearance of the segregated black baseball leagues, both victims of integration.[2] In parallel fashion, the house-party tradition lost its centrality as patterns of segregation changed and other types of recreation became available. John Cephas's eulogy for the country house parties eloquently captures this sense of loss and gain.

The house-party tradition never completely vanished. For example, John ran into Chief Ellis at a Washington, D.C., house party, and, more recently, I have been to several at John Cephas's and John Jackson's homes. Even through the 1960s and 1970s, Piedmont blues was maintained in settings like Archie's barbershop jam sessions, but such informal affairs have left little historical record beyond personal memories.

Up to the 1960s we see a few other references to the places where music was performed. Perhaps the most intriguing is Archie's description of working at the sawmill and log camp; there workers accompanied their daily activities with hollers and blues fragments, and at night they entertained themselves by playing blues and other songs. Musicians from other parts of the country also discuss the musical activities associated with work camps, log camps, levee camps, and coal camps.[3] In a similar fashion, music was part of the work day as well as a component of evening leisure time. Finally, both men make passing references to more formal musical settings in restaurants and juke houses in Rocky Mount, Bowling Green, and Lewes, Delaware. But they are also quick to point out that in comparison to house parties, these performances were unusual occurrences.

After the 1960s the two men's musical contexts altered dramatically, shifting from a home-grown, community-based setting to concerts and festivals patronized by a new and generally nontraditional audience. Prior to this shift to the folk-revival audience, both men saw their music decline in popularity in the black community and each, for his own reasons, put his music on hold. After weathering a bleak period, both musicians met an older, better known, traditional bluesman, who brought them out of retirement and eased their transition to the folk revival. These older, wiser veterans dispelled any doubts they had about their personal skills or the value of their art form and coached them in the rules of what had become a new game. Responding to their teachers, both rediscovered their musical voices and have gone on to become teachers in their own rights.

Of the two musicians, Archie had the more difficult time. Charged with John Hurt's instructions to carry on his music, Archie worried about how the public would react to an unknown artist invoking the name and spirit of a blues legend. As time passed, however, he became more at ease, carrying on John Hurt's musical legacy as he once carried on his father's music. Today, confident in his own skills, he never fails to call John Hurt's name.

In regard to Archie's and John's music, we see two very different versions of the Piedmont blues tradition. Although they share a few songs in common, each has his own musical approach and repertoire, reflecting different personalities, musical experiences, and personal preferences. Onstage, Archie Edwards works alone. He is a somewhat idiosyncratic performer, and his style coincides with his individualism and self-sufficiency. John Cephas, on the other hand, works with a partner and has always appeared to enjoy the interplay of working with other musicians: throughout his life, music has been a social activity involving other performers and he is at ease as a role player sharing the spotlight.

The vocal styles of the two musicians are also strikingly different, illustrating diversity within a supposedly homogeneous region. Here again their different personalities and musical experiences come into play. Archie's vocal approach derives more directly from his father's blues and string-band tradition. Moreover, he had little in the way of vocal coaching and his church experience began later in life. Although he sings spirituals, he performs them as he does his other songs, without demonstrative emotion. It is fair to say that Archie's vocal style shows little church influence. A man of words, he pays attention to the sensibility of his text, employing a restrained, carefully enunciated vocal. I think he considers the overtly emotional techniques of gospel song inappropriate to his type of music and personality. And his hero and friend, John Hurt, sang in the same relaxed manner.

In contrast, John's voice shows a heavy church influence, reflecting his early vocal training and his later hands-on gospel experience. His skill as an actor and flair for theatrical productions also affects his vocal styling, as does the emotionalism of the torch songs and rhythm and blues songs he has learned. Although he claims to work instinctively, as do most other soul-blues vocalists, he uses his voice as an instrument, paying careful attention to phrasing and tone color. A technician vocally and instrumentally, John can afford to trust his instincts because they are rooted in knowledge and practical experience.

When one compares the two musicians' work as songwriters, Archie holds the edge, but John has the greater gift for bringing words to life by investing them with deep feeling. While Cephas is also careful about projecting a song's story line, he can, in a pinch, cover a textual error by boosting the lyric's emotional quotient. A folk proverb that pertains to the separation of the blues and church claims, "You can't serve two," yet John Cephas has successfully merged the various techniques of his eclectic musical education, so that today he is a blues artist who can play with Piedmont complexity and sing with gospel-tinged intensity.

The songs Archie and John choose to perform partly reflect the difference in their ages and their contacts with other musicians, but mostly they represent a personal preference. Although their repertoires include similar types of songs—ballads, non-blues seculars, white country songs, religious songs, and down-home blues—and although they both show an appreciation for Blind Boy Fuller, they perform by and large different songs. Archie favored John Hurt, while John was partial to Gary Davis, Merle Travis, and Skip James. Archie's active repertoire is smaller, only a few more songs than are included in this book: Jimmie Rodgers's "T for Texas," John Hurt's version of "Keep A-Knocking but You Can't Come In," "Salty Dog," "I'll Be Glad When You're Dead, You Rascal You," "Little Lean Woman," "Do Lord Remember Me," and instrumentals such as "The West Virginia Rag" and his own "Saturday Night Hop."

John Cephas has a more eclectic repertoire that is double what is included here. At one time or another he has performed popular standards such as "Danny Boy," "When I Grow Too Old to Dream," "A Shanty in Old Shanty Town," "Home Sweet Home," and "Why Should I Care"; religious pieces including "I'll Fly Away," "Great Change Since I've Been Born," "I Will Do My Last Singing in This Land Somewhere," "Mother's Prayer," "Nobody's Fault but Mine"; rhythm and blues hits such as "C.C. Rider," "Flip Flop and Fly," "Drown in My Own Tears," "Bye Bye Baby," "The Things I Used to Do," "Eyesight to the Blind," "Going to the River," "You Made Me Lose My Happy Home," "Baby, I'm in Love with You"; blues classics including "Key to the Highway," "Worried Life Blues," "Good Morning Little Schoolgirl," "Big Boss Man," "Running and Hiding," "Little Red Rooster"; down-home blues such as "Black Rat Swing," "Devil Got My Woman," "Illinois Blues," "Chump Man Blues," "I Crave My Pig-Meat," "Memphis Blues"; country songs like "Eight More Miles to Louisville," "Today I Started Loving You Again"; folk revival numbers like "Freight Train," and dozens of other songs and instrumentals. Depending on what is on John's mind or who he has been listening to, songs come and go. Nevertheless, he too has kept a relatively stable core repertoire, and those are the songs in this book.

Archie and John also mention other titles, including the ballads "John Hardy," "Casey Jones," and "Whitehouse Blues," or "McKinley Blues," all of which were performed by both black and white singers. These songs, along with the ballads they actively perform, demonstrate the genre's popularity among rural blacks in Virginia and are drawn from a common pool of songs shared by all rural Virginians. They also list pre-blues reels and banjo songs, also common in both black and white traditions, including "Reuben's Train," "Georgie Buck," "Cumberland Gap," "The Preacher Got Drunk and Laid His Bible Down," "The Fox Chase," and "Little Liza Jane." John refers to other religious songs as well: "Amazing Grace," "Didn't It Rain Children," "Daniel Was a Good Man," "Help Me Dear Saviour I Pray," "I Love the Lord," and several popular tunes of the day: "That's When Your Heartaches Begin," "There's Darkness on the Delta," and "Please Don't Talk About Me When I'm Gone." Taken as a whole, these songs cross racial boundaries and, in some cases, bridge folk- and popular-song traditions.

Their songs span the range of blues stylings, especially the common twelve- and eight-bar formats. We also see ballads using the couplet and refrain form and, perhaps most interesting, an unexpectedly high number of four-line songs: "Going Down That Road Feeling Bad," "Careless

Love," "Corrine," and "Monday Morning Blues," for example. These pieces also indicate a bridge between blues and earlier forms.

Significantly, in Archie's and John's discussions of musical instruments, including the guitar, harmonica, piano, banjo, and fiddle, as well as the more unusual accordion, washtub bass, and one-string guitar, it is the guitar in its multiple manifestations—homemade, mail-order, acoustic, steel, and electric—that stands out as the clear instrument of choice. The two also offer technical information about open tuning, how to construct a bottleneck slide, and how to mend a broken string by tying it back together.

The two men also show the close relationship between their music and dance, including group activities such as square dancing and "swinging the four hands," couple dancing, both fast and slow, and solo display dancing, such as buckdancing. Dance in all of its forms, as competitive self-expression or as a method of getting to know the opposite sex, stands out as an integral part of the house-party tradition which supported the Piedmont blues. Blues in the Piedmont and elsewhere is clearly music for dancing.

We also encounter folk beliefs, which, in some cases, pertain to music, such as references to the blues and secular music as the "devil's music," or to certain instruments said to be sinful. More in line with traditional stereotypes about musicians and their character, both Archie and John allude to the beliefs that musicians are a threat to wives and girlfriends. John Cephas also brings up several allusions to African-American folk magic or conjure and working roots. His personal experience narrative, connected with his being considered a "fast dude," ties hoodoo magic to the equally malevolent practice of poisoning. Archie Edwards, for his part, makes a passing comment about a local musician, Buck Jackson, whose reputation as a magic worker has been attested to by other Franklin County residents.

Other types of folklore can also be found in the musicians' narratives: folk medicine, customs associated with agricultural work such as tobacco planting and food production, and social events such as corn shuckings or hog-butchering parties. Both men also note the prevalence of moonshining, a venerable institution that continues today. Corn liquor and home-brew were part of country life, a staple at house parties, and an important way to supplement farm income, if not an occupation in its own right.

In the area of occupational lore, Archie provides a vivid account of sawmill work and John briefly touches on his waterman experience. Obviously, both could tell us more about the traditions of their nonmusical work: cab driving, carpentry, police work, the D.C. National Guard, but instead they concentrate on the lore of blues musicians with the assumption that that's what their readers or listeners are interested in.

Their stories and comments about their music include various forms of spoken tradition: proverbs, rhymes, anecdotes, personal experience stories, legends, and other combinations of oral history and folklore. All told, their accounts are laced with the folklore of their region and art form, including musician's terms like "Sebastopol," or "Williamsburg Lope," "juke joint," and "country breakdown." These terms flavor their narratives and give us a document that combines historical information and entertainment, as in Archie's description of the army camp alligator or in the following passage:

> Mississippi John Hurt said, "Always keep your hat on." "You know," he says, "back in those days there was quite a lot of jealous guys in the audience and sometimes you have to run." "But," he said, "If you got your hat on your head, and have to run, you know you left the house with it. So if you lose it, try to remember the way you went so when you come back, you'll either find it on the ground, or on some bush where it was snatched off and it's still holding it for you." So this is why we musicians keep our hats on our heads.

Drawn from what amounts to a genre of "Mississippi John Hurt says" folk wisdom, Archie's playful rap weaves together elements of the tall tale, folk belief, and straight advice as he answers an expected question as to why he wears a hat when he performs.

It is also notable that, with several exceptions—Archie's description of segregation in the army and John's passing comments on poverty and segregation in rural Virginia—neither dwells on racial discrimination or the effects of segregation on their lives. Their reluctance to focus on protest themes, a trait common among Mississippi blues artists, does not mean they never encountered discrimination. Obviously they did, since they lived through segregation and eventual social change. Both, for example, went through periods where they had difficulty finding jobs suited to their skills and self-esteem. However, as Archie clearly states, he intended to improve his situation; and, in fact, both men did just that, using whatever means they could—family contacts, their military experience, and D.C. government connections—to better their position.

Like many Americans of a similar age and background, both men were taught to be firm believers in self-sufficiency. In retrospect, they appear to focus more on their own efforts and accomplishments rather than on the conditions that made their lives harder and their victories sweeter. In this sense, their stories are not cast in terms of pain and struggle, but rather as accounts of good, meaningful lives. Sharing a relatively conservative and religious outlook, they look back on a world that is in many ways preferable to today's materialism, violence, and unpredictability. Prominent in their visions of the past are family and neighborhoods and communities where people knew each other and helped each other as best they could within a set of rules and boundaries they understood, but may have not approved of or accepted. Their stories are tempered by their personal sense of having made it in a hard world, and the phrase "good times when times were bad" captures their nostalgia for certain aspects of the way things used to be.

It is telling that Archie and John reserve their strongest complaint for the way they perceive that their art form, the Piedmont blues, has been misused. Yet even in this case, their determination to stick with traditional music has been vindicated. As John puts it:

> Phil and I, we're committed to traditional music in the hope that we can keep it alive and interest some of the younger people in it. The type of music we play is the grass roots of most American music and we have a heartfelt interest to do everything we can to try to preserve it. White people have their country music, but the blues we play is the black man's country music. It was born in the black community, out in the country at house parties and country breakdowns where people would get together and dance all night long. But today, anybody can learn the blues. If you're a musician, color doesn't make any difference. You can learn to play blues if you're black, white, gray, grizzly, or green. For me, it's part of my heritage. It's in my blood. This is the black folks' folk music, but it's also all our music. It's an American tradition.

Archie Edwards and John Cephas are both articulate and thoughtful tradition-bearers. Yet several of my colleagues have questioned exactly how traditional they are, citing their festival experience and friendship with folklorists as somehow diminishing the purity of their art. Actually, their relative success, in comparison to lesser-known blues artists, is more a function of their talent, determination, geographical location, and willingness to travel, especially since their retirement from nonmusical occupations, than of any compromising of their traditional art forms. They carry on what they have always considered damn good music. Along the way they have learned that the style they work with is less known and less commercial than other types of the blues.

With or without the input of folklorists, Archie and John saw and continue to see themselves as standard-bearers for a regional acoustic tradition within a field dominated by electric blues bands. They also understand that other traditional artists share their goal of reaching a broader audience and that they confront the same sorts of obstacles. The two may be more conscious of their role as caretakers of a tradition because of their association with folklorists, but they more essentially value their version of the blues because of personal preference and because it is the music they chose to learn and play while growing up in Virginia. Quite reasonably, they assume that a general audience will also appreciate their music once people are given the opportunity to hear it, and so far this assumption has proved correct.

Thanks to Archie's and John's perseverance and willingness to share what they have learned, others can know substantially more about Virginia and Washington, D.C., blues, and, hopefully, that knowledge can be applied to understanding folk music in general. They have shown, for example, that relying on phonograph recordings to reflect musical activity can prove misleading: until Archie and John came along, Union Hall and Bowling Green musicians made lots of music, but simply did not make any records. At the same time, it is important to note how dependent Archie and John were on recordings as tools for learning and as sources for new songs. While both men learned songs from other people and composed new material, the majority of their songs can be traced back to recordings they heard at some point in their lives.

It also becomes apparent that musical categories based on genre, race, and region can similarly hinder our understanding of musical activity if we apply them too strictly. In the context of real lives, the categories we use to organize and describe the world tend to break apart. Instead we see a more fluid world where distinctions between generations, genres, races, and regions blur. Archie Edwards's and John Cephas's music carries the stamp of many other musicians: Roy Edwards, John Hurt, John Wesley Dudley, Cephas's aunt Lillian, and David Talliaferro. Archie's father and John's grandfather bridged the string-band and blues traditions. Archie's and John's memories portray a time when instrumental dance music was popular at country dances, when the bottleneck slide style was still common in Virginia, and when musicians like Robert Edwards and others played the guitar but didn't sing, a characteristic shared by North Carolina guitarists.[4] These features of Virginia folk music illustrate the slow and easy transition to the vocally centered blues.

Furthermore, Archie's and John's blues coexisted with and drew on all kinds of music: reels, ballads, and popular songs. Aunt Lillian, for example, played blues but also mastered the complex chord progressions of the popular songs of her day, and she passed her knowledge on to John. Archie Edwards's music shows the influence of rock and roll legend Chuck Berry. John's blues draw heavily on the gospel-inflected rhythm and blues of the 1950s and 1960s, and his vocal styling was influenced by hard gospel and the earlier Virginia quartet tradition.

Both men also list white country artists among their influences, including Jimmie Rodgers, Uncle Dave Macon, Frank Hutchison, and Merle Travis. In their own time these musicians admired and absorbed the music of the black community, showing an ongoing, interactive pattern of cross-racial influence. Archie's and John's music crosses regional as well as racial boundaries. It may be Piedmont blues, but it is influenced by Mississippians John Hurt and Skip James, and Texans Blind Lemon Jefferson and Lightning Hopkins. In the end we are left with good music that they drew from whatever sources were available, filtered through their individual preferences, and eventually, if they liked it, performed in their own unique style.

Even institutions that have been stringently separated, such as the house party and the church, seem much closer in Union Hall and Bowling Green. Time passes and Saturday night becomes Sunday morning, and over time the music of both rituals has altered. The house party sound track slowly shifted from string-band dance music to the blues. The straight church music Archie and John recall gave way to gospel and newer forms of religious expression. Then, as the house-party tradition withered, the Piedmont blues began to lose its traditional sustaining audience.

Today Bowling Green is losing its rural flavor as the interstate, with its homogenized sampling of fast-food restaurants, and shopping malls extend from Washington, D.C., deeper and deeper into Virginia. At the same time, blues, in its electric manifestations, has been embraced by the mainstream and can be heard nightly in television commercials pitching beer and blue jeans. Traditions die when they don't work anymore and in most cases deserve to be left to die with dignity. But the music Archie and John have remained true to still works, its emotional power is undiminished. While Piedmont blues may help America, particularly black Americans, connect with a valuable past, it is not simply a reminder of the past. As Harmonica Phil Wiggins, a representative of the next blues generation, notes, "It's still happening today. It's got a good beat and you can still dance to it."

Back at the barbershop Archie was telling me how he almost missed his flight home from Germany. Luckily, he made it, because the next flight out, Pan Am 103, exploded over Scotland, killing all on board. Introspectively, he concluded that he must have a little further to go down the road with his music. Sitting in his barber's chair, holding his steel-pan guitar on his lap, he gestured toward the familiar photographs lining the barbershop wall:

> We're sitting here today with two old professors looking at us, Mississippi John Hurt, over there, and Mance Lipscomb, right there. I have brought some great musicians to this barbershop. So I says, I tell John Hurt, I want to look at him but I don't want him to say a doggone word. Because if he says anything, it's going to mess up business! But don't forget to mention that in my book. Don't leave out my buddy John. I definitely want John Hurt there.

We laughed together, and he took a sip of Jack Daniels and 7-Up and continued:

> You know, my little grandson Antonio, he's singing now. He sings "Stack O'Lee" and "Spoonful." I learned them from John Hurt, now he's learned them from me. He takes my tape recorder and he knows how to turn it on. He listens to all the other musicians, like John Cephas or Blind Lemon, but when he gets to me he says, "This is you, Granddaddy, this is you." He'll sing, "Stack O'Lee, Stack O'Lee, please don't take my life." And he tells me, "I'm gonna play your blues. I'm gonna sing your blues, Granddaddy." So I tell him, "This is what I want you to do, Grandson, sing and play Granddaddy's blues."

Notes to Chapter 6

1. See Jeff Todd Titon, *Early Downhome Blues: A Musical and Cultural Analysis* (Urbana: University of Illinois Press, 1977), pp. 19–23.

2. Nelson Georges, *The Death of Rhythm and Blues* (New York: Pantheon Books, 1988), pp. 57–58.

3. For example, Sunnyland Slim told me of his experience in a country work camp where Little Brother Montgomery was playing, and, more recently, Howard Armstrong described performing in coal camps. Pearson, *"Sounds So Good to Me,"* p. 90.

4. Howard Odum's fieldwork prior to 1911 led him to categorize three kinds of black musicians: musicianers, who played but did not sing; songsters, who sang but might not play: and musical physicians, who sang, played, and traveled—the latter best describes our two subjects. Howard Odum and Guy Johnson, *The Negro and His Songs* (Chapel Hill: University of North Carolina Press, 1925), pp. 156–157.

Key to Repertoire References

Abrahams (1963)   Abrahams, Roger. *Deep Down in the Jungle*. New York: Aldine Press, 1963.

Abrahams (1970)   Abrahams, Roger. *Positively Black*. Englewood Cliffs, New Jersey: Prentice Hall, 1970.

Bastin   Bastin, Bruce. *Red River Blues: The Blues Tradition in the Southwest*. Urbana: University of Illinois Press, 1986.

Botkin   Botkin, B. A. *A Treasury of American Folklore*. New York: Crown Publishers, 1944.

Brown   Brown, Sterling. "Negro Folk Expression: Spirituals, Seculars, Ballads and Work Songs." *Phylon* 14 (First Quarter, 1953), 45–61.

Buckley   Buckley, Bruce R. "Uncle Ira Cephas—A Negro Folk Singer in Ohio." *Midwest Folklore* 3 (spring 1953), 5–18.

Buehler   Buehler, Richard E. "Stacker Lee: A Partial Investigation into the Historicity of a Negro Murder Ballad." *Keystone Quarterly* 12 (1967), 187–191.

Burt   Burt, Olive Woolley. *American Murder Ballads and Their Stories*. New York: Oxford University Press, 1958.

Carmer   Carmer, Carl. *Stars Fell on Alabama*. New York: The Literary Guild, 1934.

Chappell   Chappell, Louis W. *John Henry: A Folk-Lore Study*. Jena: Frommarsche Verlag, 1933.

Charters   Charters, Samuel. *Robert Johnson*. New York: Oak Publications, 1973.

Cohen   Cohen, Norm. *Long Steel Rail: The Railroad in American Folksong*. Urbana: University of Illinois Press, 1981.

Courlander (1963)   Courlander, Harold. *Negro Folksong U.S.A.* New York: Columbia University Press, 1963.

Courlander (1976)   Courlander, Harold. *A Treasury of Afro-American Folklore*. New York: Crown Publishers, 1976.

Dorson (1954)   Dorson, Richard M. "Negro Tales." *Western Folklore* 13, no. 3 (July 1954), 160–162.

Dorson (1959)	Dorson, Richard M. *American Folklore.* Chicago: University of Chicago Press, 1959.
Evans	Evans, David. *Big Road Blues: Tradition and Creativity in the Folk Blues.* Berkeley: University of California Press, 1982.
Ferris	Ferris, William. *Blues from the Delta.* New York: Anchor Press, 1978.
Funk	Funk, Ray. *A Capella Gospel Singing.* Folklyric Records 9405.
Garwood	Garwood, Donald. *Masters of the Instrumental Blues Guitar.* New York: Oak Publications, 1968.
Godrich	Godrich, John, and Robert M. W. Dixon. *Blues and Gospel Records 1902–1943.* Chigwell, England: Storyville Publications and Company Limited, 1982.
Green	Green, Archie. *Only a Miner: Studies in Recorded Coal Mining Songs.* Urbana: University of Illinois Press, 1972.
Greenway	Greenway, John. *American Folksongs in Protest.* Philadelphia: University of Pennsylvania Press, 1953.
Grissom	Grissom, Mary Allen. *The Negro Sings a New Heaven.* 1930, rpt. New York: Dover, 1969.
Grossman (1970)	Grossman, Stefan. *Ragtime Blues Guitarists.* New York: Oak Publications, 1970.
Grossman (1974)	Grossman, Stefan. *Rev. Gary Davis/Blues Guitar.* New York: Oak Publications, 1974.
Grossman et al. (1973)	Grossman, Stefan, Hal Grossman, and Stephen Calt. *Country Blues Songbook.* New York: Oak Publications, 1973.
Handy (1941)	Handy, W. C. *Father of the Blues.* New York: MacMillan, 1941.
Handy (1972)	Handy, W. C., and Abbe Niles. *Blues: An Anthology.* New York: Collier Books, 1972.
Hurston	Hurston, Zora Neale. *Mules and Men.* New York: Perennial Library, 1935.
Jackson	Jackson, Bruce. "Stagolee Stories: A Bad Man Goes Gentle." *Southern Folklore Quarterly* 29, no. 2 (June 1965), 188–194.
Johnson	Johnson, Guy. *John Henry: Tracking Down a Negro Legend.* Chapel Hill: University of North Carolina Press, 1929.
Laws (1957)	Laws, G. Malcolm, Jr. *American Balladry from British Broadsides.* Philadelphia: The American Folklore Society, 1957.
Laws (1964)	Laws, G. Malcolm, Jr. *Native American Balladry.* Philadelphia: The American Folklore Society, 1964.
Leach	Leach, MacEdward, and Horace P. Beck. "Songs from Rappahannock County, Virginia." *Journal of American Folklore* 63 (July–September, 1950), 257–284.
Levine	Levine, Lawrence W. *Black Culture and Black Consciousness: Afro-American Folk Thought from Slavery to Freedom.* New York: Oxford University Press, 1977.
Lomax, A. (1960)	Lomax, Alan. *The Folk Songs of North America.* Garden City, New York: Doubleday, 1960.
Lomax, A. (1967)	Lomax, Alan. *Hardhitting Songs for Hard Hit People.* New York: Oak Publications, 1967.
Lomax and Lomax (1934)	Lomax, John and Alan. *American Ballads and Folksongs.* New York: MacMillan, 1934.

Lomax and Lomax (1936)	Lomax, John and Alan. *Negro Folk Songs as Sung by Lead-belly*. New York: MacMillan, 1936.
Lomax and Lomax (1947)	Lomax, John and Alan. *Best Loved American Songs*. New York: Grosset and Dunlap, 1947.
Lornell (1977)	Lornell, Kip. *Virginia Traditions: Non-Blues Secular Black Music*. Ferrum, Virginia: Blue Ridge Institute, 1977.
Lornell (1978)	Lornell, Kip. *Virginia Traditions: Western Piedmont Blues*. Ferrum, Virginia: Blue Ridge Institute, 1978.
Lornell (1982)	Lornell, Kip. *Virginia Traditions: Tidewater Blues*. Ferrum, Virginia: Blue Ridge Institute, 1982.
McCormick	McCormick, Mack. *Folk Music in America: Songs of Death and Tragedy*. Washington, D.C.: Library of Congress, 1978.
McCulloh	McCulloh, Judith. "In the Pines: The Melodic-Textual Identity of an American Lyric Folksong Cluster." Ph.D. diss. Indiana University, 1970.
McNeil	McNeil, W. K. *Southern Folk Ballads: Volume One*. Little Rock: August House, 1987.
Morris	Morris, Alton. *Folksongs of Florida*. Gainesville: University of Florida Press, 1950.
Odum and Johnson (1925)	Odum, Howard, and Guy Johnson. *The Negro and His Songs*. Chapel Hill: University of North Carolina Press, 1925.
Odum and Johnson (1926)	Odum, Howard, and Guy Johnson. *Negro Workaday Songs*. Chapel Hill: University of North Carolina Press, 1926.
Okun	Okun, Milton. *Something to Sing About*. New York: MacMillan, 1968.
Oliver (1969)	Oliver, Paul. *The Story of the Blues*. New York: Chilton Book Company, 1969.
Oliver (1970)	Oliver, Paul. *Aspects of the Blues Tradition*. New York: Oak Publications, 1970.
Oliver (1971)	Oliver, Paul. "Railroad Bill." *Jazz and Blues* 1 (May 1971), 12–14.
Oliver (1984)	Oliver, Paul. *Blues Off the Record: Thirty Years of Blues Commentary*. New York: Da Capo, 1984.
Oliver, Songsters (1984)	Oliver, Paul. *Songsters and Saints: Vocal Traditions on Race Records*. Cambridge: Cambridge University Press, 1984.
Oster	Oster, Harry. *Living Country Blues*. New York: Minerva Press, 1975.
Palmer	Palmer, Robert. *Deep Blues*. New York: Viking Press, 1981.
Pearson	Pearson, Barry Lee. *"Sounds So Good to Me": The Bluesman's Story*. Philadelphia: University of Pennsylvania Press, 1984.
Perrow	Perrow, E. C. "Songs and Rhymes from the South." *Journal of American Folklore* 25 (1912), 137–155.
Raim	Raim, Walter. *The Josh White Song Book*. Chicago: Quadrangle Books, 1963.
Randolph	Randolph, Vance. *Ozark Folksongs*. 4 vols. Columbia: The State Historical Society of Missouri, 1948.
Rosenbaum	Rosenbaum, Art. *Folk Visions and Voices: Traditional Music and Song in North Georgia*. Athens: University of Georgia Press, 1983.

Russell	Russell, Tony. *Blacks, Whites and the Blues*. New York: Stein and Day, 1970.
Sackheim	Sackheim, Eric. *The Blues Line: A Collection of Blues Lyrics*. New York: Schirmer Books, 1969.
Sandburg	Sandburg, Carl. *The American Songbook*. New York: Harcourt Brace, 1927.
Scarborough (1923)	Scarborough, Dorothy. "The Blues as Folksong." *Coffee in the Gourd*. Austin: Texas Folklore Society, 1923.
Scarborough (1925)	Scarborough, Dorothy. *On the Trail of Negro Folk-Songs*. 1925, rpt. Hatboro, Pennsylvania: Folklore Associates, 1963.
Sharp	Sharp, Cecil, and Maud Karpeles. *English Folk-Songs from the Southern Appalachians*. London: Oxford University Press, 1932.
Titon (1977)	Titon, Jeff. *Early Downhome Blues: A Musical and Cultural Analysis*. Urbana: University of Illinois, 1977.
Titon (1981)	Titon, Jeff. *Downhome Blues Lyrics: An Anthology from the Post-World War II Era*. Boston: Twayne Publishers, 1981.
Traum	Traum, Happy. *Finger Picking Styles for Guitar*. New York: Oak Publications, 1969.
White	White, Newman Ivey. *American Negro Folksongs*. Cambridge: Harvard University Press, 1928.
Work	Work, John W. *American Negro Songs and Spirituals*. New York: Bonanza Books, 1940.
Williams, B.	Williams, Brett. *John Henry: A Bio-Bibliography*. Westport, Connecticut: Greenwood Press, 1983.
Williams, O.	Williams, Otis. *The Blues Is*. Baltimore: JOW Productions, 1982.

Discography

Archie Edwards

1977

Sounds Reasonable Incorporated, 45 RPM Single
  "The Road Is Rough and Rocky" DR 5328-1
  "Circle Line Boat" NR 5328

1981

The Introduction of Living Country Blues U.S.A., L & R Records, LR 42.030, West Germany
  "Bearcat Mama Blues"

1982

The Road Is Rough and Rocky: Living Country Blues Volume 6, L & R Records, LR 42.036, West Germany
  "That Won't Do"
  "My Old Schoolmates"
  "I Called My Baby Long Distance"
  "Pittsburgh Blues"
  "Baby, Please Give Me a Break"
  "Duffel Bag Blues"
  "Lovin' Spoonful"
  "The Road Is Rough and Rocky"
  "Jinky Lou"
  "Stack O'Lee"
  "T for Texas"
  "Do Lord"

1983

East Coast Blues with Guitar Slim, John Cephas, Archie Edwards, A.O. Living Country Blues Volume 12, L & R Records, LR 42.042, West Germany
  "Three Times Seven"
  "Everybody Blues"

"East Virginia John Henry"
"Sitting on Top of the World"

John Cephas

1976

Big Chief Ellis, Trix 3316
John accompanies Chief on:
"Fare You Well Mistreater"
"Sweet Home Chicago"
"Blues for Moot"

1977

Virginia Traditions: Non-Blues Secular Black Music, Blue Ridge Institute, Ferrum, Virginia, BRI 001
"John Henry"

1978

Songs of Death and Tragedy: Folk Music in America, Library of Congress, Washington, D.C., LBC 9
"John Henry"

1981

Bowling Green John Cephas and Harmonica Phil Wiggins from Virginia, U.S.A., Living Country Blues Volume I, L & R Records, LR 42.031, West Germany
"Black Rat Swing"
"Eyesight to the Blind"
"Guitar and Harmonica Rag"
"Rising River"
"I Am a Pilgrim"
"Chicken, You Can't Roos Too High for Me" (instrumental)
"I Ain't Got No Lovin' Baby Now"
"West Carey Street Blues"
"Richmond Blues"
"Pony Blues" (Phil Wiggins, vocal)
"Going Down That Road Feeling Bad"

1982

Virginia Traditions: Tidewater Blues, Blue Ridge Institute, Ferrum, Virginia, BRI 006
With John Woolfork:
"Black Rat Swing"
"Richmond Blues"
American Folk Blues Festival 82, LR 50.001, West Germany
"Bye Bye Baby"

1983

Bowling Green John Cephas and Harmonica Phil Wiggins: Sweet Bitter Blues, L & R Records, LR 42.054, West Germany
"Sweet Bitter Blues"
"St. James Infirmary"
"I Saw the Light"

"Tribute to Skip James (Sickbed Blues)"
"Piedmont Rag" (instrumental)
"Dog Days of August"
"Roberta—A Thousand Miles from Home" (Phil Wiggins, vocal)
"Highway 301"
"Hoodoo Woman"
"Louisiana Chase" (instrumental)

East Coast Blues with Guitar Slim, John Cephas, Archie Edwards, A.O. Living Country Blues Volume 12, L & R Records, LR 42.042, West Germany
"Reno Factory"
"Louise"

1985

Let It Roll: Bowling Green John Cephas and Harmonica Phil Wiggins, Cassette, Marimac Recordings, 8001
"Let It Roll"
"Dog Days of August"
"John Henry"
"Reno Factory"
"Roberta" (Phil Wiggins, vocal)
"Burn Your Bridges" (instrumental)
"Hard Time Killing Floor Blues"
"Special Rider"
"Cherry Ball"
"Electric Chair Blues" (Phil Wiggins, vocal)
"I Will Do My Last Singing in This Land"

1986

Bowling Green John Cephas and Harmonica Phil Wiggins: Dog Days of August, Flying Fish, FF 394
"Reno Factory"
"Cherry Ball"
"Dog Days of August"
"Staggerlee"
"Hard Time Killing Floor Blues"
"John Henry"
"I Saw the Light"
"Roberta" (Phil Wiggins, vocal)
National Downhome Blues Festival Volume Two, Southland SLP-22
"Burning Bridges" (instrumental)
"Staggolee"

1988

Walking Blues: Bowling Green John Cephas and Harmonica Phil Wiggins, Marimac 8004
"Mamie"
"Memphis Blues"
"Baby, I'm Crazy About You" (Phil Wiggins, vocal)
"Lucille"
"Illinois Blues"
"Nine Pound Hammer"

"Walking Blues"
"Crow Jane"
"Little Red Rooster"
"Pigmeat"
"Butt Naked Blues" (Phil Wiggins, vocal)
"I Won't Be Down No More"

1989

Guitar Man, Flying Fish, FF 470
"Black Cat on the Line"
"Richmond Blues"
"Weeping Willow"
"Guitar Man"
"Police Dog Blues"
"Corrine"
"Careless Love"
"Brownsville Blues"

Unissued Recordings

1976

March 29, Trix session for Pete Lowry
"Black Rat Swing"
"Eyesight to the Blind"
"Going Down the Road Feeling Bad"
"Richmond Blues"
"You're Still My Baby"
"Keep Your Hands Off My Baby"
"I Saw the Light"
"When I Grow Too Old to Dream"
"Careless Love"
"Why Should I Care"
"Key to the Highway"
"Going to the River"
"Drown in My Own Tears"
"C.C. Rider"
"Naylor Rag" (instrumental)
"Eight More Miles to Louisville"
"John Henry"
"End of My Journey"
June 1, Trix session
"Careless Love"
"Richmond Blues"
"Black Rat Swing"
"Polack Town" (?)
June 1, Library of Congress AFS 18.469–18.470 LWO 9055
"John Henry" (three versions recorded by Richard Spottswood)
June 9, Library of Congress AFS 18.723–18.724 LWO 9102; recorded by Richard
Spottswood, Joe Wilson, and Mike Rivers
"John Henry"
"Careless Love"

"Black Rat Swing"
"Key to the Highway"
"I Saw the Light"
"Talk About Your Woman" ("Eyesight to the Blind")
"Richmond Blues"
"Keep Your Hands Off My Baby"

1977

John Cephas with John Woolfork in Bowling Green, Virginia; recorded by Kip
Lornell, September 17, 1977
"The Moon Is Rising"
"Careless Love"
"Eight More Miles to Louisville"
"Home Sweet Home"
"Caroline County Rock" (instrumental)
"Taliaferro Buck" (instrumental)
"Black Rat Swing"
"Key to the Highway"
"Going to the River"
"Steel Guitar Rag" (instrumental)
"The Things I Used to Do"
"Mamie"
"Railroad Bill"
"Still My Baby"
"Keep Your Hands Off Her"
"I Saw the Light"
"Richmond Blues"
"Lulu's Back in Town" (John Woolfork, vocals)
"Eyesight to the Blind"
"John Henry" (John Woolfork, vocals)

1980

Trix session with Phil Wiggins; recorded by Pete Lowry
"Reno Factory"
"Blue Day Blues" (instrumental)
"Lost Lover Blues"
"Key to the Highway"
"Going Down That Road Feeling Bad"
"Richmond Blues"
"Burning Your Bridges" (instrumental)
"I Saw the Light"
"Black Rat Swing"
"Eyesight to the Blind"
"Good Morning Little School Girl"
"Careless Love"
"Worried Man Blues"
"Steel Guitar Rag"
"John Henry"
"One Dime Blues"

1982

American Blues Trio, Voice of America, promotional cassette with Phil Wiggins
and Barry Lee Pearson, September 1982
  "St. James Infirmary"
  "I Ain't Got No Lovin' Baby Now"
  "Black Rat Swing"
  "Richmond Blues"
  "Careless Love"
  "Blue Dog Blues" (instrumental)
  "Worried Man"
  "Reno Factory"
  "Bye Bye Baby"
  "Running and Hiding, Let It Roll"
  "Sweet Home Chicago" (Barry Pearson, vocal)
  "Last Fair Deal" (Phil Wiggins, vocal)
  "Rambling Blues" (Barry Pearson, vocal)
  "I Saw the Light"

1987

D.C. Blues Society Benefit Concert, Marimac, December 1987
  "St. James Infirmary"
  "Dog Days of August"

Related Discography

Blind Blake: Ragtime Guitar's Foremost Fingerpicker. Yazoo Records, Yazoo
  L-1068.
Barbecue Bob: Chocolate to the Bone. Mamlish Records, Mamlish S-3808.
Big Bill Broonzy: Do That Guitar Rag 1928–1935. Yazoo Records, Yazoo L-1035.
East Coast Blues 1926–1935. Yazoo Records, Yazoo L-1013.
Sleepy John Estes 1929–1940. RBF Records, RBF8.
Blind Boy Fuller 1936–1940. Old Tramp, OT-1202.
Blind Boy Fuller 1935–1940: Blue and Worried Man. Travelin' Man, TM 801,
  1983.
Blind Boy Fuller 1909–1941: Death Valley. Oldie Blues, OL 2809.
Blind Boy Fuller: Truckin' My Blues Away. Yazoo Records, Yazoo 1060.
Blind Boy Fuller with Sonny Terry and Bull City Red. Blues Classics, no. 11.
The Georgia Blues 1927–1933. Yazoo Records, Yazoo L-1012.
Guitar Wizards 1926–1935. Yazoo Records, Yazoo 1016.
Frank Hovington: Lonesome Road Blues. Rounder Records 2017.
Mississippi John Hurt: His First Recordings. Biograph Records, BLP C4.
Mississippi John Hurt: 1928 Sessions. Yazoo Records, Yazoo 1065.
Long Steel Rail: Blues by Maryland Songster Bill Jackson. Testament Records,
  T-201.
Jim Jackson: Kansas City Blues. Agram Blues, AB 2004.
John Jackson: Step It Up and Go. Rounder Records, 2019.
Skip James: King of the Delta Blues Singers. Biograph Records, BLP 12029.
Skip James: The Complete 1931 Session. Yazoo Records, Yazoo 1072.

A Tribute to Skip James. Biograph Records, BLP 1209, Vol. 1.

Blind Lemon Jefferson 1926–1929: Master of the Blues. Biograph Records, BLP 12015, Vol. 2.

Furry Lewis: Blues Masters Vol. 5. Blue Horizon, BM 4605.

Furry Lewis in His Prime: 1927–1928. Yazoo Records, Yazoo 1050.

Mama Let Me Lay It On You 1926–1936. Yazoo Records, Yazoo L-1040.

Brownie McGhee and Sonny Terry: Blues All Around My Head. Prestige Bluesville 1020.

Memphis Minnie. Blues Classics, BC 1.

Mississippi Sheiks and Beale Street Sheiks 1927–1932: Sitting On Top of the World. Biograph Records, BLP 12041, 1972.

The Complete Recordings of William Moore, Tarter and Gay, Bayless Rose, Willie Walker in Chronological Order: Ragtime Blues Guitar 1928–30. Match Box Bluesmaster Series, MSE 204.

Buddy Moss: Georgia Blues 1930–1935. Travelin' Man, TM 800.

Buddy Moss: Red River Blues 1933–1941. Travelin' Man, TM 802.

Buddy Moss: Rediscovery. Biograph Records, BLP 12019, Vol. 1.

O J L's Georgia: The Black Country Music of Georgia, 1927–1936. Origin, OJL-25.

Sonny Terry: Whoopin the Blues. Charly R & B, CRB 1120, 1986.

Ramblin' Thomas 1928. Biograph Records, BLP 12004.

John E. Tinsley: Blues Roots Revived. Outlet Recordings, STLP-1012.

Virginia Traditions: Non-Blues Secular Black Music. BRI 001, 1978.

Virginia Traditions: Southwest Virginia Blues. BRI 008, 1988.

Virginia Traditions: Tidewater Blues. BRI 006, 1982.

Virginia Traditions: Western Piedmont Blues. BRI 003, 1980.

Bill Williams: The Late Bill Williams Blues, Rags and Ballads. Blue Goose 2013.

Song Lists

Archie Edwards's Repertoire

Baby Let Me Lay It on You; Baby That Won't Do; Baby, Won't You Please Give Me a Break; Bearcat Mama Blues; Candy Man; Cherry Red River Blues; Chinch Bug Blues; Christmas Blues; The Circle Line Boat; Down Today But I Won't Be Down Always; Duffel Bag Blues; Eagle-Eye Mama Blues; East Virginia John Henry; Everybody Blues; Frankie and Johnny; Going Up the Country; Greyhound Bus Blues; How Long Blues; I Called My Baby Long Distance; I Expect I Better Go; I Had a Little Girl, She Was Sweet as She Could Be; I'm Gonna Send You Back to Your Mother Payday; Jinky Lou; Kansas City Rock; The Longest Train I Ever Saw Ran on the Red River Line; Lovin' Spoonful; Meet Me in the Bottom; Monday Morning Blues; My Little Girl Left Me; My Old Schoolmates; New Step It Up and Go; One Thin Dime Blues; Pittsburgh Blues; Poor Boy a Long Way from Home; The Road Is Rough and Rocky; Screaming and Crying Blues; Sitting on Top of the World; Some People Call Me Crazy; Stack O'Lee; Take Me Back Baby; Three Times Seven; The Train That Carried My Girl from Town; Undertaker Blues; You're So Sweet, My Woman's So Sweet.

John Cephas's Repertoire

Black Cat on the Line; Brownsville Blues; Careless Love; Cherry Ball; Corrine; County Jail Blues; Crow Jane; Cypress Grove; Death Don't Have No Mercy; Dog Days of August; Going Down That Road Feeling Bad; Guitar Man; Highway 301; Hoodoo Woman; I Ain't Got No Loving Baby Now; I Am a Pilgrim; I Saw the Light; John Henry; Keep Your Hands Off My Baby; Louise; Mamie; The Moon Is Rising; Nine Pound Hammer; Police Dog Blues; Railroad Bill; Reno

Factory; Richmond Blues; Rising River Blues; Sitting on Top of the World; So Sweet; Special Rider; St. James Infirmary; Staggerlee; Sweet Bitter Blues; Tribute to Skip James: Sickbed Blues; Twelve Gates to the City; Walking Blues; Weeping Willow; West Carey Street Blues; Worried Man Blues.

Bibliography

Abrahams, Roger, and George Foss. *Anglo-American Folksong Style*. Englewood Cliffs, New Jersey: Prentice Hall, 1968.

Bastin, Bruce. *Crying for the Carolines*. London: Studio Vista, 1971.

————— "From the Medicine Show to the Stage: Some Influences upon the Development of a Blues Tradition in the Southeastern United States." *American Music 2*, no. 1 (spring 1984), 27–42.

Bernhardt, Clyde. *I Remember: Eighty Years of Black Entertainment, Big Bands and the Blues*. Philadelphia: University of Pennsylvania Press, 1986.

Brown, Sterling A. "The Blues." *Phylon 13*, no. 4 (1952), 286–292.

Burton, Thomas. *Tom Ashley, Sam McGhee, Bukka White: Tennessee Traditional Singers*. Knoxville: University of Tennessee Press, 1981.

Cantwell, Robert. *Bluegrass Breakdown: The Making of the Old Southern Sound*. Urbana: University of Illinois Press, 1984.

Charters, Samuel. *The Bluesmen: The Story and the Music of the Men Who Made the Blues*. New York: Oak, 1967.

————— *Sweet as Showers of Rain: The Bluesmen Volume 2*. New York: Oak, 1977.

Clifford, Tom. "Traditional Bluesmen Hit the Bigtime." *Tempo: Prince George's Journal* (January 29, 1988), B1, 6.

Conway, Cecilia, and Tommy Thompson. "Talking Banjo." *Southern Exposure 2*, no. 1, n.d., 63–66.

Davis, Arthur Kyle, Jr. *Folksongs of Virginia: A Descriptive Index and Classification*. Durham: Duke University Press, 1949.

Evans, David. "Afro-American One Stringed Instruments." *Western Folklore 29* (October 1970), 229–245.

Fleder, Rob, and Stephen Calt. "Bill Williams: Nobody Had to Ask Me to Play." *Sing Out 21*, no. 1 (1971), 12–13.

Georges, Nelson. *The Death of Rhythm and Blues*. New York: Pantheon Books, 1988.

Groom, Bob. *The Blues Revival*. London: Studio Vista, 1971.

Guralnick, Peter. "Skip James." *Living Blues 2*, no. 5 (summer 1971), 10–15.

Harrington, Richard. "Bowling Green Bowled Over." *The Washington Post* (December 2, 1987), B7.

Heilbut, Tony. *The Gospel Sound: Good News and Bad Times*. New York: Simon and Schuster, 1971.

Hines, James Robert. *Musical Activity in Norfolk, Virginia 1680–1973*. Doctoral thesis. Chapel Hill: University of North Carolina, 1974.

Hinson, Glenn. *Virginia Work Songs*. BRI 007. Ferrum, Virginia: Blue Ridge Institute, 1982.

Joyce, Mike. "The Barbering Bluesman: Archie Edwards a Long Time Coming to the Forefront." *The Washington Post* (May 22, 1987), B3.

——— "Bringing the Blues on Home." *The Washington Post* (November 1985).

——— "John Jackson Interview: Part I." *Cadence 7*, no. 3 (March 1981).

——— "John Jackson Interview: Part II." *Cadence 7*, no. 4.

Kent, Don. "On the Trail of Luke Jordan." *Blues Unlimited 66* (October 1969), 4–5.

Leadbitter, Mike. *Nothing But the Blues*. New York: Oak, 1971.

Leadbitter, Mike, and Neil Slaven. *Blues Records January 1943 to December 1966*. New York: Oak, 1968.

Lightfoot, William. A Regional Style: The Legacy of Arnold Shultz. Manuscript sent to author, 1988 (unpublished).

Lornell, Kip. "Down in Virginia: Sam Jones and Pernell Charity." *Living Blues 13* (summer 1973), 25.

——— "Living Blues Interview: J. B. Long." *Living Blues 29* (September–October 1976), 13–23.

——— "North Carolina Pre-Blues Banjo and Fiddle." *Living Blues 18* (autumn 1974), 25–27.

——— "Tarter and Gay." *Living Blues 27* (May–June 1976), 18.

——— *Virginia's Blues, Country and Gospel Records 1902–1943: An Annotated Discography*. Lexington: University Press of Kentucky, 1989.

Lowry, Peter B. "Atlanta Black Sound: A Survey of Black Music from Atlanta During the Twentieth Century." *The Atlanta Historical Society Bulletin 11*, no. 2 (summer 1977).

——— Blues of the South East: A Historical Survey. Unpublished manuscript, 1981.

——— Consider the Wall: Concretization in a Musical Style. Unpublished manuscript, 1984.

——— "Hard Times, Bad Luck and Trouble: A Fallacy About Blues." Paper delivered to the American Folklore Society, October 29, 1983.

Meade, Mary. "John Jackson." *Sing Out 21*, no. 3 (1972), 7–9.

Moore, Dave. *"Brownskin Gal": The Story of Barbecue Bob*. TerAar, The Netherlands: Agram Blues, 1976.

Nichols, Ashton. "John Cephas . . . A Blues Singing Man." *The Free Lance Star & Town and Country Magazine* (August 14, 1976), 3–5.

Obrecht, Jas. "John Cephas: Classic Delta and Piedmont Country Blues." *Guitar Player 21*, no. 3 (March 1987), 68–71.

Olsson, Bengt. "The Grand Old Opry's De Ford Bailey." *Living Blues 21* (May–June 1975), 13–15.

Palmer, Robert. "A Night of Piedmont Blues." *New York Times* (March 11, 1983).

Pearson, Barry Lee. "Archie Edwards' Barbershop Blues." *Living Blues 63* (January–February 1985), 22–28.

——— "Bowling Green John Cephas and Harmonica Phil Wiggins: D.C. Country Blues." *Living Blues 63* (January–February 1985), 14–21.

——— "Good Times When Times Were Bad: Recollections of Rural Houseparties in Virginia." *Folklore and Folklife in Virginia 3* (1984), 45–56.

——— *Guitar Man: Bowling Green John Cephas and Harmonica Phil Wiggins.* Flying Fish, FF 470, 1989.

——— "The Piedmont Blues: Bringing Good Sounds to Hard Times." *A National Black Heritage Tour.* Washington, D.C.: National Council for the Traditional Arts, 1986, 3–8.

——— "Washington, D.C. Blues." *Living Blues 63* (January–February 1985), 7–10.

Pearson, Barry Lee, David Goren, and Susan Day. "Big Chief Ellis." *Living Blues 63* (January–February 1985), 28–39.

Pearson, Barry Lee, and Cheryl Brauner. "John Jackson's East Coast Blues." *Living Blues 63* (January–February 1985), 10–13.

Perdue, Charles L., Jr. "I Swear to God It's the Truth If I Ever Told It." *Keystone Folklore Quarterly 14*, no. 1 (spring 1969).

——— *John Jackson: Blues and Country Dance Tunes from Virginia.* Berkeley: Arhoolie Records F1025, 1966.

——— *John Jackson: More Blues and Country Dance Tunes from Virginia.* Berkeley: Arhoolie Records F1035, 1968.

Phillips, Bill. "Piedmont Country Blues." *Southern Exposure 2*, no. 1, n.d., 56–62.

Pollack, Bill. "John Jackson's Good Time Blues." *Living Blues 37* (March–April 1978), 36–37.

Reagon, Bernice. "The Lady Street Singer." *Southern Exposure 2*, no. 1., n.d.

Rickford, John R., and Angela E. Rickford. "Cut-Eye and Suck-Teeth: African Words and Gestures in a New World Guise." *Journal of American Folklore 89*, no. 353 (July–September 1976), 294–309.

Roberts, John W. *From Trickster to Badman: The Black Folk Hero in Slavery and Freedom.* Philadelphia: University of Pennsylvania Press, 1989.

Rosenberg, Bruce A. *The Folksongs of Virginia: A Checklist of the W.P.A. Holdings, Alderman Library, University of Virginia.* Charlottesville: University of Virginia Press, 1969.

Taft, Michael. *Blues Lyric Poetry: A Concordance.* New York: Garland, 1984.

Tilling, Robert. "Carl Martin: A Brief Appreciation." *Blues Magazine 2* (December 1976), 16–18.

Titon, Jeff. *From Blues to Pop: The Autobiography of Leonard "Baby Doo" Caston.* JEMF Special Series 4. Los Angeles: John Edwards Memorial Foundation, 1974.

Welding, Pete. "Carl Martin, 1906–1979." *Living Blues 43* (summer 1979), 28–29, 40.

——— *Long Steel Rail: Blues by Maryland Songster Bill Jackson.* Testament Records T-201, Chicago, 1962 (?).

——— "Stringin' the Blues: The Art of Folk Blues Guitar." *Downbeat 32*, no. 19 (July 1, 1965), 22–24, 56.

Weston, Frank, and Sylvia Pitcher. "John Tinsley." *Blues Unlimited 142* (summer 1982), 26–29.

Wilgus, D. C., and Eleanor R. Long. "The Blues Ballad and the Genesis of Style in Traditional Narrative Song." *Narrative Folksong: New Directions*, ed. Carol Edwards and Kathleen E. B. Manley. Boulder, Colorado: Westview Press, 1985, 437–482.

Index